Praise for *The Big Re*

"*The Big Rewind* has something real and scuffed and quite winning at its core."

—Dwight Garner, *The New York Times*

"Nathan Rabin chronicles his search for salvation in pop culture through trying episodes like familial abandonment and institutionalization. With his uncanny grasp of cultural zeitgeist, Rabin could unseat Chuck Klosterman as the slacker generation's vital critical voice."

—*Heeb* magazine

"[*The Big Rewind* is] written with [Rabin's] trademark humor, quirkiness, and self-deprecation. It's an homage to pop culture."

—*USA Today*

"Rabin's sense of humor is substantially darker . . . than anyone's. . . . What's more unusual is the tone, which has been sandblasted of self-pity and emerged as a kind of brutal truth-telling that leads Rabin to get at least half of the big laughs at his own expense, because you can be both the hero and the doofus in your own life, and that's a very valuable lesson indeed. The writing is enormously vibrant and forceful—if this were music, there would be a lot of drums, in the best way."

—Linda Holmes, Monkey See blog on npr.org

"Nathan Rabin enriches *The Big Rewind* with pop culture asides and enjoyable digressions on the nature of criticism. . . . Highly literate Gen-Xers with sophomoric senses of humor will get the most out of Rabin's memoir, though his story of surmounting hardship is one Charles Dickens would recognize."

—*The Cleveland Plain Dealer*

"As a storyteller, Rabin thrives on adversity; it provides him with the perfect backdrop for his sardonic, Shecky Greene asides."

—*The Boston Globe*

"Thanks to his acerbic voice and dark humor, the author transforms his miserable childhood and prolonged battles with depression into an improbably entertaining, even uplifting tale. . . . Alternately engaging, maddening, hilarious, and excessive."

—*Kirkus Reviews*

"Underneath all of the quirky structure, mewling apathy, and caustic wit, Rabin tells a sweet tale of finding one's place in life. Give this to fans of *The Catcher in the Rye* and *Reservoir Dogs*."

—*Booklist* (starred review)

"Nathan Rabin's life reads like a fanboy's collision with Dostoyevsky. This hilarious, sad, truthful memoir is compulsively readable—a page-turning soap opera about a child abandoned by his mother, loved by his wise, thrice-divorced, painfully crippled, often unemployed father, shuttled through foster homes and asylums, and yet with an invincible sense of humor that led him to contribute briefly to the original *Onion* in Madison, then leave over 'creative differences,' then rejoin the paper as a film critic for its *A.V. Club* for the last decade, and star on an AMC program named *Movie Club with John Ridley* with an optimistic dreamer as his producer and fellow critics who ranged from a darkly Marxist intellectual to a skinny blonde who used the word 'Shakespeare' as a condemnation, while surviving a romantic relationship with 'O,' a sado-masochistic intellectual grad student whose hyperactive sex life only occasionally involved him. He chronicles his adventures with a cross between utter shamelessness and painful honesty, and he is very funny."

—Roger Ebert

"Nathan's memoir is your memoir is my memoir. You will experience moments of sour disagreement, followed by, 'Oh wow, me too!' A book that reads like a conversation. Terrific."

—Patton Oswalt

"I'm not as interested in anything as much as Nathan Rabin is interested in everything."

—Chuck Klosterman

"Rabin writes like the secret love child of Woody Allen and Lester Bangs: honest, erudite, neurotically manic, and very funny."

—Neal Pollack

"*The Big Rewind* is heartbreaking and hilarious. Based on the incidents in this book, it's amazing Nathan Rabin is still alive, much less one of the sharpest pop culture critics around. I just hope he's learned his lesson about dating loonball polyamorists."

—Rich Dahm, co-executive producer of *The Colbert Report*

The
Big Rewind

A Memoir Brought to You by Pop Culture

NATHAN RABIN

SCRIBNER

New York London Toronto Sydney

SCRIBNER

A Division of Simon & Schuster, Inc.
1230 Avenue of the Americas
New York, NY 10020

First Scribner trade paperback edition July 2010

SCRIBNER and design are registered trademarks of The Gale Group, Inc.,
used under license by Simon & Schuster, Inc.,
the publisher of this work.

For information about special discounts for bulk purchases,
please contact Simon & Schuster Special Sales at
1-866-506-1949 or business@simonandschuster.com.

The Simon & Schuster Speakers Bureau can bring authors to your live event. For
more information or to book an event contact the Simon & Schuster Speakers
Bureau at 1-866-248-3049 or visit our website at www.simonspeakers.com.

Designed by Kyoko Watanabe
Text set in Sabon

Manufactured in the United States of America

2 4 6 8 10 9 7 5 3 1

Library of Congress Control Number: 2008034049

ISBN 978-1-4165-5620-6
ISBN 978-1-4165-5621-3 (pbk)
ISBN 978-1-4391-6576-8 (ebook)

For Dad, Anna, and all the brothers and sisters who've had enough of the Man

"I've had one motto I've always lived by: Dignity. Always dignity."

—Gene Kelly, *Singing in the Rain*

"What else is there to do but laugh an' joke . . . how else can you bear up under the unbearable?"

—Jim Thompson, *Pop. 1280*

THIS MACHINE GENTLY SCOLDS FASCISTS

Contents

Introduction

I've wasted far too much time fantasizing about my funeral. It would begin with the Magnetic Fields' *The Charm of the Highway Strip* and Quasimoto's *The Unseen* both being played in their entirety, followed by screenings of *Pee-wee's Big Adventure, Rushmore, Jules et Jim,* and *Grey Gardens.* An appropriately solemn, grief-stricken Sir Too $hort would stop by to perform "Gettin' It" backed by a full gospel choir, the ceremony concluding with a dramatic reading of Jim Thompson's *Pop. 1280,* with the ghost of Warren Oates in the lead role. Hey, it's my fantasy. Fuck verisimilitude. All in all, this wildly excessive tribute to me, me, me would take up the better part of two days. Not even death's sweet release can keep me from being self-indulgent and wasting everyone's time.

It'd be a veritable deathapalooza, a far-out posthumous happening that would sum up my dark life through the entertainment I loved. But this book is not about my funeral. It's about my life and the way music, books, films, television, and, to a much lesser extent, haikus, bumper stickers, and *Love Is . . .* comic strips shaped and molded me, along with countless other members of my generation, a lost tribe of latchkey kids raised on hip-hop and Quentin Tarantino, a demographic for whom pop culture references constitute an invaluable common cultural currency. It's a fun book about how popular culture helped me survive my lifelong battle with depression, that treacherous foe

Winston Churchill referred to as "the Black Dog" and that I, for reasons I no longer remember, call "Vice Admiral Phinneas Cummerbund."

As a child and teenager, pop culture was a life-affirming form of escape. As an adult, pop culture is my life. I live, think, eat, sleep, and dream pop culture. For I have the world's single greatest job. For over a decade I've had the honor of serving as the head writer for *The Onion A.V. Club*. As a film critic/hip-hop writer it has been my distinct pleasure to interview Sir Mix-A-Lot and Bernardo Bertolucci, RZA and Anna Karina. Actually I'm not as much of a professional anomaly as you might imagine: *New Yorker* film critic David Denby was briefly a member of the Wu-Tang Clan under the name Syanide Assassin, and Gene Shalit famously had "Thug Life" tatted on his stomach in the aftermath of 2Pac's death.

My career has taken me to some curious places. I once accidentally asked Angelina Jolie if she wanted to live inside of a chimpanzee. Seth Green once bounded into a room and, without saying a word, sat in my lap. Topher Grace vomited profusely mere inches away from me after I retrieved his lucky hat. I've asked Steve Albini to share the secrets of his boudoir for an elaborate one-off parody of men's magazines called *The A.V. Club for Men*. Focus group respondents for my poorly rated, mildly disreputable basic-cable movie-review panel show (*Movie Club with John Ridley*) speculated that all the male critics on the show were "gay" and that the show as a whole was "too gay."

The Big Rewind tells my shaky life story through the sturdy prism of popular culture. Each of this memoir's twenty-two chapters begins with a book, song, album, film, or television show that helped define the corresponding period of my development or provided a framework for me to better understand myself and the world around me.

It's my heartwarming tale of triumph over adversity™ in book form. Incidentally, I've not only trademarked the phrase "heartwarming tale of triumph over adversity™"; I've also trademarked the concept of triumphing over adversity in a heartwarming fashion. So if any of you youngsters are even thinking about overcoming formidable obstacles, you'd better think twice unless you want to pay me big-ass royalties.

In a blatant wash of generational pandering, every sentence in this book contains a *Mr. Show* and a *Simpsons* reference. That might seem unpossible, but I think this shameless gimmick will embiggen the book's commercial and literary value in a most cromulent fashion. And oh, the profanity! Every curse word and profane phrase known to man, from "Cunt-fucking Christ on a Crucicracker" to "Thassa lotta salami, Mr. McGillicuddy!" resides within the following tome. If you've ever screamed it in a moment of rage, possibly after whacking your thumb with a hammer, you'll find it in these pages.

The Big Rewind also provides an unprecedented look into the glamorous life of a film critic, a giddy existence that revolves around living in one's own filth and dressing like a hobo. Hey, if it's good enough for Boxcar Pete and Sam the Tramp, then it's good enough for me.

This is a darkly comic book about the intersection of my life and the dizzying, maddening, wonderful world of entertainment. But it's also about a motherless child's search for family, a quest that took me from a mental hospital to a foster family whose patience and generosity knew only strict and unyielding boundaries, to a group home for emotionally disturbed adolescents, to the scuzziest, most drugged-out co-op in Madison, to *The Onion* and a deranged pirate ship of a television show that began as the answer to my childhood fantasies but ended a comic nightmare, and finally to popular culture, where I found my lasting family in the art and junk that has sustained me through the years.

Like an ideal family, our personal pantheon will never let us down. Ella Fitzgerald's version of "Bewitched, Bothered and Bewildered" will never abandon you. Belle and Sebastian's *If You're Feeling Sinister* will never run off with your best friend.

John Kennedy Toole's *A Confederacy of Dunces* will never tell you that it finds the prospect of having sex with you less appealing than watching back-to-back reruns of *The Golden Girls*.

My unwitting collaborators in the strange journey we're about to embark on together include an Orthodox Jewish reggae superstar, a New Wave gay cowboy, the world's most famous reclusive author, a suicidally depressed rapper, Preston Sturges, F. Scott Fitzgerald, a cinematic visionary who traded the false god of cinema for the even falserer god of Marxism, impoverished relatives of Jackie Onassis, the black community, and best of all, real, live sideshow freaks! Yes, real, live sideshow freaks!

In the following pages I hope to attain a Cronenbergian state of spiritual and physical communion with the pop culture that means the most to me. I will explain the meaning, value, context, and significance of my personal pantheon and in return my personal pantheon will hopefully help explain me.

Lastly, I would like to apologize to my family, friends, and to society as a whole for the role my penis plays in this book. I understand that no one wants to read about my sex life, but as diligently as I tried to leave him out of it, the Kid stayed in the picture.

Experience Male Genital Mutilation in a Celebratory Environment

"King Without a Crown"
My Summer Among the Hasidim

When a formerly Reconstructionist, Pennsylvania-born Phish fan born Matthew Paul Miller changed his name to Matisyahu and became the world's first Hasidic reggae superstar, much of the buzz surrounding his unlikely career centered on the incongruity of a guy who looked like an extra from *Yentl* excelling at a form of music perfected by pot-smoking black men from tropical island nations. The first time I saw Matisyahu, he was performing at a glitzy, star-studded Seder in a hopelessly muddled documentary about anti-Semitism called *The Protocols of Zion*. Though the film quickly disappeared from my psyche, I was transfixed by the image of a conservatively dressed Orthodox Jew performing with an orgasmic sense of rapture. Matisyahu seemed possessed by a strange and powerful spirit, touched by a divine sense of purpose.

Matisyahu's popularity exploded out of the ghetto of religious music and spread like wildfire among jam-band aficionados who grooved hard on the infectious optimism of his music and his spellbinding live performances even if they had little use for organized religion, especially of the orthodox variety. For me Matisyahu's left-field ascent to pop culture prominence represented a strange return to one of the more peculiar detours of my childhood. The connection was driven home with pile-driver force when I first heard him joyously demand, "I want Moshiach now!" on his crossover hit "King Without a Crown."

I was instantly transported back eighteen years. Suddenly I was an eleven-year-old sitting at an outdoor table alongside two dozen Hasidic boys in black dress pants and white button-down shirts, their long sideburns twisted into payot cork-screws, yarmulkes affixed to their kinky heads with a hair clip. We screamed, "We want Moshiach now! We want Moshiach now!" with delirious abandon.

"Louder! Louder!" our teenage counselors yelled at us. "So Hashem can hear you!" They were trying to whip us into a frenzy of devotion. It was working. It felt a little ridiculous: if G-d is everywhere, as Judaism teaches, why do we have to yell? But it was also strangely infectious. I was the most secular Jew in the world but in that moment I wanted to believe. I wanted to have faith, to get swept up in the same wave of religious fervor as everyone around me.

When I was eleven years old my stepmother enrolled my heathen ass in Gan Israel, an Orthodox summer day camp run by the Lubavitchers, the Jewiest Jews in all of the known Jew-niverse. Why? Perhaps because she'd been feeling guilty about our secular lives. Or maybe because she'd finagled a deal to trade her professional services as a graphic designer for a full scholarship for me.

My summer among the Hasidim marked the strangest inter-lude in my complicated relationship with Judaism. On one level, Judaism is central to my being. It affects every facet of my life: relationships, politics, my sense of humor, the way I perceive the world and my place in it, my pervasive sense of being an out-sider, even my diet. Yet before I received an Orthodox conver-sion before my dad's second marriage, I was a gentile in the eyes of the Orthodox community.

I learned late in life that my biological mother was not born Jewish but converted to appease my father. Now, I don't want to suggest that my mother's conversion was somehow half-hearted or arbitrary, but I suspect that she secured her conversion through one of those companies that advertise their wares in the back of comic books with hyperbolic pitches that read:

Become One of the "Chosen" People!
Convert to Judaism!

Why work like a "schmuck" when you can get in on the world-famous "International Jewish Conspiracy"? Simply complete the patented "Acme Conversion Correspondence Course" and you'll be swimming around in a pool of "gelt" in no time! Just get a load of the benefits awaiting you, you soon-to-be Jew!

- Make tons of new enemies instantly!
- Discover the joys of persecution!
- Experience Male Genital Mutilation in a Celebratory Environment!
- Follow archaic, seemingly nonsensical dietary laws and restrictions!
- Learn a backward moon-man language called "Hebrew" filled with crazy squiggles and a made-up alphabet!
- Enjoy a nosh and talk about the weather!
- Become a man or woman in a fancy schmancy ceremony! Read a portion of scripture and earn cold, hard cash$$$$$$$$$$$.
- Retire eventually to Miami Beach and impress strangers with stories about your son the doctor, and your other son the lawyer, and, as if Hashem had not blessed you enough, your other son the Rabbi!

She sent in the requisite two dollars and three Ovaltine labels, received the kit in the mail two to four weeks later, and was officially ordained a certified Member of the Tribe.

Despite an inauspicious beginning, Judaism represented the core of my upbringing. I went to the Milwaukee Jewish Day School from first to fourth grade. I spent much of my adolescence in a group home run by the Jewish Children's Bureau. I attended college on the Cohen Scholarship. Yet even after my Orthodox conversion I was still a religious nowhere man in the eyes of the ultrafaithful: my mother was a gentile, bullshit conversion or not, and I missed out on all the ceremonies designed to make children feel like welcome members of the Jewish community. I never received a bris (no male genital mutilation in a celebratory environment for me!) and my nuclear family fell apart before I could experience a Bar Mitzvah officially commemorating my ascent from boy to man, which may be why I remain a boyish man to this day.

Nevertheless at eleven I was thrown into a den of Hasidim and forced to fend for myself. Every morning we'd study Hebrew and the Torah. Then we'd break for lunch and spend the afternoons playing sports or going on field trips. I looked forward to field trips, both because they represented a much-needed break from praying and because a group of payot-sporting, yarmulke-clad little boys in black pants and white dress shirts is a surreal sight gag everywhere it goes.

You haven't lived unless you've seen a ten-year-old Hasid attack the Whack-a-Mole at a rundown theme park with the furious intensity he'd otherwise reserve for praying for the Moshiach's return, or seen little mini-Lubavitchers plunge down a water slide at a crumbling water park. The Lord works in mysterious ways.

One misbegotten weekend, our counselors took us camping overnight at a local campground without remembering to bring along minor provisions like tents or sleeping bags. Why bother with such earthly matters when Hashem will provide for his chosen people no matter what? We slept under the stars as mosquitoes feasted on our succulent young flesh. When I arrived home my body was riddled with so many bright red mosquito bites that my arms and legs looked like relief maps of the Himalayas.

Another example of the Hasidim's surreal disconnect from common sense occurred when our counselors eagerly described a contest designed to test our commitment to our beloved day camp and/or gullibility. The counselors would call a handful of campers that night at home and if they answered the phone by screaming "Gan Yisroel is the best camp!" they'd be rewarded with a Raspberry Joy bar. Imagine, an entire forty-cent candy bar just for sacrificing our dignity! It seemed too good to be true.

But when I told my stepmom about my plans to spend the night hovering over the phone in nervous anticipation of receiving that fateful call, she was apoplectic. What if her clients called? What would they make of some helium-voiced youngster madly professing the superiority of something called "Gan Yisroel" to all other camps in lieu of a more conventional, less insane greeting? I was forbidden from expressing my enthusiasm for Gan Yisroel or any other camp over the phone for the entire evening. The phone never rang. I never answered. It was the worst thing that ever happened to anybody in America.

I grew up in the Reform tradition and went to a synagogue where our rabbi was famous for having set the Guinness World Record for jumping rope the longest. I am so not making that up. Then again, Rabbi Hillel famously reigned as the king of the one-armed push-up, and a steroid-crazed Rabbi Menahem Schneerson could juggle three midgets for hours at a time, so maybe rabbis and sideshow freaks have more in common than most people realize.

Even as a kid I sensed that there was something hopelessly compromised about Reform Judaism. By contrast the Lubavitchers seemed infinitely more in touch with the infinite and the unknowable. They oozed authenticity and conviction. They radiated a profound sense of religious joy.

Growing up synagogue was little more than a grudging obligation, but religion meant more to the little Hasidim around me lost in their own intense spiritual reveries. The Lubavitchers' segregation of the sexes and subjugation of women was problematic to say the least. But there was also much about the Lubavitchers that I found appealing. Those qualities are the same ones that draw secular Jews and gentiles to Matisyahu's music.

Like the Deadheads enamored of Matisyahu, I was drawn to the optimism of the Hasidic message, to its sense of boundless possibilities. There's something intoxicating about the idea that the Messiah is more than just an impossible aspiration. The Hasidim at Gan Yisroel genuinely believed that the emergence of the Messiah was within their grasp, that it was a world-changing development they could help bring about. I envied the moral certainty of people who woke up every morning with the fierce conviction that they were living in complete accordance with the will of a benevolent, loving, and all-powerful G-d. I think that's what attracts the ungodly to Matisyahu.

I wanted desperately to believe that all of the world's answers were contained in the core scriptures of Judaism. I longed for the comfort of supreme faith, that empowering sense that a heavenly being guides your every step. But I also appreciate that Judaism is a faith of questioning and struggle, of rigorous contemplation and perpetual debate.

Nowhere is the inquisitive nature of Judaism represented more purely than in the Passover Seder, an institution where even the most secular of Jews commemorate Charlton Heston freeing the Jews from the evil wrath of Yul Brynner by reading torturously translated accounts of the Exodus from Egypt from paper prayer books called Haggadahs printed in the midsixties by the good folks over at Maxwell House.

These ubiquitous Maxwell House Haggadahs have to qualify as one of the most brilliant branding promotions of all time. For the price of a bunch of cheaply printed pamphlets, Maxwell House won a permanent place in the hearts of the Jews, who famously run the media, international banking, and show business. I'm surprised Maxwell House didn't try to further weasel their way into the hearts of the Chosen Ones by subtly slipping in product placement. It's a no-brainer. After all, nothing makes unleavened bread go down smoother than a rich, delicious cup of Maxwell House™ Instant Coffee, right? For Jews on the run from Pharaoh-type dudes, it's good to the last drop™.

At every Seder the youngest person at the table must read "The Four Questions." Questions include:

1. Why is this night different from every other night?
2. Why do we eat slouching instead of sitting straight up?
3. Why do we eat bitter herbs?
4. What is the deal with airline food? Seriously, who are the ad wizards who dreamed this up?

That last question helps explain why Jews have a higher percentage of great comedians than any other religion, race, or nationality (suck it, Germans!). These questions and many more are answered in the ensuing text, but even after the four questions receive four answers, there's plenty of questioning and answering left, not to mention nit-picking, ponderous prose, and mind-numbing rituals.

Yet I love Passover Seders all the same. I treasure the sense of tradition that comes with performing the exact same rituals my ancestors performed millennia ago and, assuming global warming doesn't kill us all within the next hundred years, my descendants will be performing millennia from now. That is, of course, if my children and children's children can somehow resist the shiksa's eternal siren song and assimilation's relentless pull. Mmmm, shiksas. The Passover Seder has filled me with a sense of consistency, continuity, and stability at times when my life sorely lacked all three. There's something reassuring about knowing that Judaism will always be there for me even if I'm not always there for Judaism.

For me Judaism is as much cultural as religious. It has less to do with the Talmud and the ancient cadences of cantors than with Woody Allen turning *Manhattan* into a swooning love letter to a new promised land set to the soaring, all-American strains of Gershwin's "Rhapsody in Blue." It's Kafka's paranoia and Philip Roth proving that you can become synonymous with masturbation jokes and still be considered the world's greatest living writer, and the way Sigmund Freud used his own anxieties and urges as a Rosetta Stone for understanding the mysteries of the human psyche. It's a young punk like Rick Rubin hearing a new kind of tribal sound and starting a hip-hop empire in his NYU dorm room with a skinny black kid named Russell Simmons. It's Malcolm McLaren turning chaos into cash and Groucho Marx wryly observing that he wouldn't want to belong to any club that would have someone like him as a member.

It's Stanley Kubrick and Peter Sellers turning the promise of mutually assured destruction into the most resonant sick joke this side of *A Modest Proposal* in *Dr. Strangelove*. It's Sasha Baron Cohen's Borat fanning the flames of anti-Semitism by getting a club full of redneck shit-kickers in the Deep South to drunkenly croon "Throw the Jew Down the Well" yet walking away unharmed. It's Andy and Charlie Kaufman's postmodernism and Bob Dylan's homespun rasp and shape-shifting mutability and the Beastie Boys connecting the dots between funk, hardcore punk, and hip-hop.

It's J. D. Salinger's and Lenny Bruce's outsider angst and Karl Marx's impossible dream. It's Jon Stewart making sense of an insane world on a daily basis. It's a bunch of New York rag merchants relocating to Hollywood to create an empire of their own and Tin Pan Alley and the Catskills and vaudeville and the Chess brothers and sly old Irving Berlin selling goys perennial Christmas classics. Last and almost certainly least, it's Matisyahu sending out a message of universal hope to blue-eyed trust-fund heathens with fake dreadlocks. That, dear reader, is the Jewish tradition I identify with.

In the end my summer among the Hasidim had little lasting effect on me. But I can't hear Matisyahu's music without feeling a tinge of nostalgia for the Lubavitchers and the profound spiritual awakening that might have been.

The Genius of Escapism

Sullivan's Travels
Nathan's Bogus Journey Through the Awkward Years

Preston Sturges's *Sullivan's Travels* is an elegant Hollywood fable about a pampered director (Joel McCrea) who has made a fortune off trifles like *So Long, Sarong; Hey, Hey in the Hayloft;* and *Ants in Your Pants of 1939* yet longs to make a stirring proletarian message movie called *O Brother, Where Art Thou?* (has a nice ring to it, eh?). Eager to learn about the suffering underclass firsthand, McCrea goes undercover as a hobo and through a series of complications winds up on a chain gang.

The chain gang ends up at a Pentecostal service where the preacher shows a Disney cartoon that sends shivers of joy and laughter rippling through the dispirited convicts. In that ecstatic moment of revelation it becomes apparent McCrea can do more good for the downtrodden masses cranking out escapist comedies than he ever could directing somber message movies. People will always need laughter. They'll always need escape. They sure as shit don't need lefty agitprop about the nobility of the proletariat.

When I first saw *Sullivan's Travels* I found it irresponsible if not downright amoral. How dare Sturges suggest filmmakers don't have a solemn obligation to expose the sad plight of the working class? Where did Sturges get the unmitigated gall to suggest that filmmakers are better off focusing on entertainment than politics?

But the older I get, the wiser *Sullivan's Travels* becomes. These days the worst thing a film can do is uplift the human spirit. Politics and good intentions have ruined more filmmakers than drugs and success combined. When I watch *Sullivan's Travels* now it seems not only moral but wise. I'll take Preston Sturges over Sergei Eisenstein any day.

My initial condemnation of *Sullivan's Travels* is even more perplexing considering I'd already experienced my own version of the famous chain gang/cartoon scene. But maybe that's what being a deluded preteen would-be Marxist is all about: denying firsthand experience in favor of abstract ideals you can never quite bring yourself to believe in.

When I was twelve years old my family took a steep, permanent tumble down the socioeconomic ladder when my multiple sclerosis–stricken dad got divorced and left his soul-crushing but comfortable government job to pursue exciting opportunities in the field of unemployment. So he packed up my older sister and me and moved from safe suburban Shorewood, Wisconsin— where the cops had so little to do that they handed out Milwaukee Brewers baseball cards to schoolchildren—to Chicago, where my dad's family long ago laid down roots after high-tailing it out of their native Russia one step ahead of the Cossacks. Yes, the names had all changed since my dad hung around, but the dreams, well, they quickly deserted him as well.

Growing up, my father was a firm believer in what F. Scott Fitzgerald called "the green light, the orgiastic future that year by year recedes before us." He was an inveterate daydreamer who believed, like all good Americans, that money, happiness, and endless upward mobility were inalienable birthrights.

In the go-go eighties my father heeded the siren song of "no money down" and quit his government job to test his fortunes in the real estate racket. He'd drive me to his Coldwell Banker office in the mall, where I'd take in double features and he'd explain the duplicity inherent in the real estate game and the skillful use of euphemisms. For example, if a real estate listing mentioned a "motivated seller," that meant the house was on fire. A "handyman's special" was a house where pit-bull-sized rats had chewed through the electrical wiring.

I'd like to share an anecdote with you that hopefully explains why my father never made it in business. When I was ten years old my stepmother grew alarmed that the Jewish private school I was attending mollycoddled me, that under its loving protection I had devolved into a mincing ninny, a fancy lad in velvet pantaloons unequipped to handle the cruelty and degradation of what she deemed "the Real World."

So she had me transferred to a public school, where, in a time-honored schoolyard tradition, I was viciously beaten by a pair of popular pint-sized fascists named Jack and Rob every day after school for the unspeakable crime of being "the New Kid." There was no logic to these post-school dustups. Nor was there anything to be gained from these spirited rounds of fisticuffs: it wasn't as if Jack or Rob would someday take me aside and confide, "Well, good sir, you have proven yourself to be a scholar and pugilist of rare courage and determination. From this day forth feel free to hang out at our homes, play our Nintendos, and make out with our girlfriends."

The only reward for holding my own with my prepubescent tormentors was the opportunity to repeat the feat all over again the next day. My stepmother grew concerned that I was regularly coming home bruised and battered. She wasn't buying my lines about constantly running into door handles. So she sent my father to school to put the fear of God into Jack and Rob. That day my dad came to school and after consulting with my teacher took Jack, Rob, and me into the hallway.

But as my father faced Jack and Rob in the hallway of Atwater Elementary School something strange happened. It was as if my father was regressing before my eyes. He was suddenly no longer a thirtysomething husband and father defending his flock but a terrified ten-year-old quaking in awe at the coolness of the popular kids. So instead of reading the bullies the riot act, he awkwardly tried to arrange a play date for Rob, Jack, and me. My stepmother had sent my dad to play the glowering enforcer. Instead he transformed into a flop sweat–covered schoolyard matchmaker.

"Nathan, he, uh, he's a nice boy who likes baseball and you should be friends with him. Maybe you could trade baseball cards or something," my father offered meekly as Jack and Rob shot me an icy look that said, "Not only are we going to continue kicking your ass, but now we're going to beat up your father too. Then we're going to dig up your grandfather's corpse and affix it to a meat hook so we can use it as a punching bag in our playhouse, just to convey the depths of our hatred of you and your family."

Jack and Rob's campaign of post-class terror continued unabated until my enraged stepmother came to class and told the evil little fuckers that if they ever touched me again they were headed to an adolescence-long stint in juvenile detention. Jack and Rob never touched me again. The moral? Never send a man to do a woman's job.

My father is a man who gets intimidated by ten-year-olds. So it didn't come as a surprise that he lacked the killer instinct necessary to succeed in business. My dad is a big pussycat. Late-period capitalism has a long history of not being kind to big pussycats. My father was so meek, in fact, that when our apartment experienced a rodent invasion he bought a trap that didn't kill mice, it just hurt their feelings. Incidentally, that last line was written by Gags Beasley, a veteran gagsmith from Great Neck, New York. Hit me up with five more zingers of this quality, Mr. Beasley, and a shiny silver dollar is headed your way ASAP.

Every child experiences their own distant echo of humanity's fall from grace when they realize that their parents aren't perfect, that the godlike creatures they grew up worshipping are all too human. For me that acute disillusionment came when I realized that my father was not only imperfect but incapable of providing for himself or his family. It wasn't his fault really. He simply didn't have the money or the resources. He was trying to raise kids with blockbuster dreams on a Roger Corman budget.

There is a tendency in our culture to romanticize poverty, to imbue it with a sepia-toned nostalgia that blurs its harsh edges and bathes every trauma in a reassuring golden glow. Sadly, that sentimental horseshit sells books. So I can assure you, dear reader, that even though my family often did without, we were always rich in poverty, financial and spiritual. Even when we were reduced to collecting food stamps, there was always enough class resentment to go around.

Food stamps, it should be noted, are fucking awesome. For me food stamps meant the difference between figuring out seventeen different ways to prepare the contents of a two-dollar bag of potatoes and a gaudy cornucopia of name-brand goodies: boxes of Dove ice cream bars and TV dinners and Twinkies and Cap'n Crunch, the bountiful harvest of capitalism at its peak.

As a young man, my father taught me a valuable lesson: never be afraid to accept a handout. Not a hand-up, mind you, as hand-ups invariably entail doing some sort of "work" at some later point. That shit's flat-out distasteful. But handouts are the best things in the world because—here's the really sweet part—you don't have to pay for them, nor do you have to exchange labor for goods somewhere down the road.

In a culture of more, more, more, my family suddenly had to deal with less, less, less. We skidded irrevocably from the neurotic middle class to the feral poor. It was hard to say which was sadder: that my dad was reduced to looking for the kinds of jobs college kids on summer break would consider beneath their dignity or that he never held them for longer than a few weeks.

Making ends meet and paying the rent every month suddenly became a perilous adventure. In desperation one month my father "borrowed" my life savings of six hundred dollars to pay rent. In hindsight I can see that my father was a good man pushed by circumstances into some pretty dark corners. But at the time the liquidation of my life savings struck me as a betrayal of biblical proportions. The vanished six hundred dollars came to symbolize the middle-class childhood that had been pulled out from under me.

I became pathologically obsessed with money. I was intent on stealing back my six hundred dollars from the wallet stashed away in my dad's underwear drawer in twenty-dollar increments. I bullied my father into letting me cash in my savings bonds for half their ultimate value.

When I was a small boy my generous and loving father had bought me complete sets of baseball cards for my birthday. God, how I loved those cards. But when the bottom fell out I'd trudge over to the local baseball card store, where a Jabba the Hut–like creature with oily Brylcreemed hair gave me pennies on the dollar for the most cherished artifacts of my childhood. I was selling away my memories and hopes for the future one card at a time. Two cards stood out: Rickey Henderson's 1980 Topps rookie card and Cal Ripken Jr.'s 1982 Fleer rookie card. When I close my eyes and think of the lost promise of my childhood, two images immediately take shape: Rickey Henderson, all coiled intensity and raw power in a batting crouch designed to shrink his strike zone into a fraction of an inch, and Cal Ripken Jr. looking lanky and impossibly young as he patrols the infield.

I became skilled at manipulating my father. At thirteen I became convinced that unless I acquired a copy of *Playboy* with Sherilyn Fenn on the cover I would die of sexual frustration, that my sperm would back up into my brain and my head would explode like something out of *Scanners*. Then at the funeral the two or three lonely mourners who'd forgotten what a bastard I was would tsk-tsk and bitchily murmur, "I guess his dad should have bought that smut magazine he so desperately wanted; no, needed; no, richly deserved. Then this senseless tragedy could have been avoided."

I had a deep, spiritual need to see Audrey Horne naked. So after weeks of badgering my father, he reluctantly took me to the corner store to buy a copy. It was probably the most significant victory of my young life. Yet when we reached the corner store my father lingered interminably. He rifled through the magazine rack, perusing *Sports Illustrated* and *Newsweek*. He contemplated buying a new toothbrush and explored the dazzling array of deodorant and mouthwash on display. This drove me mad. I lurked malevolently on the periphery, issuing the following persistent plea:

Buy the fucking magazine
Buy the fucking magazine
Buy the fucking magazine
Seriously, just buy the fucking magazine

Finally, after several lifetimes of lollygagging and dillydallying, he bought the magazine. Oh, but it was worth the wait! I didn't believe in God at thirteen but my concept of the divine looked an awful lot like Sherilyn Fenn's milky white flesh.

In those miserable early years in Chicago I was powered by the kind of bottomless rage and resentment that leads some people to become writers and express themselves creatively and others to become comic-book supervillains. Let's just say it's fortunate that this whole writing thing seems to be working out (so far) or my henchmen would probably be aiming a death ray at the eastern seaboard at this very moment.

My family's dwindling fortunes were reflected in the cars my dad drove and/or abandoned. Back in his high-flying days as a failed real estate agent, he bought a big new Pontiac 6000, which he promptly proceeded to wrap around a telephone pole, breaking his nose and ribs in the process. By the time we moved to Chicago he was driving a two-toned boat of a late-seventies domestic eyesore whose brakes eventually stopped working, so we had to come gradually to a halt instead of stopping automatically like fancified rich folk.

My father was such a terrible driver that I decided early on that driving wasn't for me. Nowadays I could tell people, "I don't know how to drive a car. And I rape babies," and nine out of ten concerned citizens would respond with a horrified, "Oh my God. You don't know how to drive? What are you? Some sort of sicko?"

The only thing more traumatic for me than watching my beloved father sink into unemployment and depression was his stumbling attempts to resurrect his love life. Not long after we moved to Chicago my dad started seeing a single mother named Miriam who was a seething mass of contradictions. She was an Orthodox Jewish woman of easy virtue who spoke in an obscene rasp redolent of cigarettes and sin and wore a ratty wig that haunted my dreams. In my nightmares Miriam's wig would come alive and chase me down the streets of Chicago, cackling maniacally as it flew through the air, animated by the black magic of my anxieties.

Miriam used to hang out at the twenty-four-hour Kosher Dunkin' Donuts on Devon, where she tried to persuade my dad to become a cab driver, a profession only slightly more suited to my father's, um, unique gifts than American Gladiator. Miriam had a daughter roughly my age who collected receipts. She once showed me her scrapbook. It was the single saddest thing I've ever seen. It was as if she collected this detritus to show the world that she existed and had the paper trail to prove it.

The first few years of my adolescence were marked by regular visits from Vice Admiral Phinneas Cummerbund but I could always find escape at the picture show. One summer day my older sister and I purloined a cup full of quarters from our apartment building's laundry room and used our ill-gotten gains to finance two matinee tickets to see *Bill and Ted's Excellent Adventure* at the Lincoln Village.

Once the lights went down and the curtains parted, the outside world disappeared. For an hour and a half I blithely forgot the grim realities of my existence. Suddenly it didn't matter that my father would never hold another halfway decent job. It somehow seemed irrelevant that I didn't have any friends. For a brief idyll it wasn't important that my life would grow so miserable over the course of the next few years that being shunted off to a group home for emotionally disturbed adolescents would constitute a big step up.

No, during those unforgettable ninety minutes all that mattered was that Theodore Logan and Bill S. Preston Esquire of San Dimas, California, pass history and save the world. In that darkened theater I had an epiphany, a Road to Damascus moment. I decided to make movies my life's work. I wanted to be part of something that could bring so much joy, however silly or ephemeral, to a callous world.

It was as if the only world that mattered was the fantasy universe I'd created for myself out of daydreams and movies and television shows. When I was twelve years old I came down with a case of pneumonia that felt like waking death. My fever soared. My body ached. I began to hallucinate. The world around me took on a trippy, hyperintense quality as the lines between my dreams, nightmares, and waking reality devolved into nothingness.

The squalid two-bedroom apartment I uncomfortably shared with my dad and sister quickly became a potent incubator for disease. My father begged me to go to the hospital but I refused to leave until I was done watching *West Side Story* on a tiny black-and-white television that only picked up two UHF stations: 50 and 66.

Back in suburban Milwaukee, my dad had routinely stopped by the video store and picked me up something. While other kids grew up on a steady diet of Chevy Chase smirks and Eddie Murphy cackles, my father immersed me in classic Hollywood musicals. He imbued in me at a young age a deep, profound love of Astaire and Rogers, Gene Kelly, Frank Sinatra, and the incomparable Miss Judy Garland. I disappointed him terribly by growing up to be a heterosexual.

Let others have their raunchy comedies and mindless action-thrillers. I knew early on that the legendary Freed Unit over at MGM was king shit of fuck mountain.

So it was of the utmost importance to me to see how things turned out for Maria and Tony, the star-crossed lovers of *West Side Story*. I'd read enough Shakespeare to know that things didn't turn out too well for ol' Romeo and Juliet but I hoped against hope that their singing, dancing counterparts were headed for a happy ending. After all, people don't die in musicals. Things might look grim but there was no crisis so profound that it couldn't be resolved via an elaborate production number or emotionally charged duet.

I'd read *Romeo and Juliet* that year in school. I even memorized Romeo's "But soft, what light through yonder window breaks" soliloquy and added it to a makeshift Shakespeare-Plus Super-Ultra-Mega-Mix inside my brain, where it mixed and mingled with Marc Antony's eulogy for Julius Caesar and Hamlet's "To be or not to be" speech and bits and pieces of the Gettysburg Address and the preamble to the U.S. Constitution.

So I should have known what I was in for. Instead I held out hope that there was a place for Tony and Maria. This was America, wasn't it? Surely they wouldn't deceive me in song. I wept openly at the ending. It was at that moment that my father realized, once and for all, that his only begotten son would never grow up to be an NFL lineman or Navy SEAL. Film critic? Maybe. Bounty hunter? No.

Soon my entire family was infected with pneumonia. My great-aunt Ruth and uncle Irving's condo became a makeshift hospital as we moved in en masse and were treated to heaping bowls of chicken soup and endless supplies of 7-Up, not to mention maternal love. Throughout my childhood Aunt Ruth and Uncle Irving functioned as a two-person volunteer social safety net. It gave my father great comfort to know that they'd bail him out of any disaster, no questions asked.

Still, there were problems even the unconditional love of Aunt Ruth and Uncle Irving couldn't solve. So, after I spent a disastrous seventh-grade year maligned by constant bullying, my father decided I might benefit from an academic environment with higher standards and fewer schoolyard beatings.

We applied for the pre–International Baccalaureate program at Ogden, one of the top magnet schools in Chicago. The prerequisite for admission was scoring in the upper ninetieth percentile in both English and math, but they were inexplicably willing to make an exception for me.

"Well, Mr. Rabin, it looks like Nathan scores within the upper ninety-ninth percentile in English and history and within the upper seventieth percentile in math. That's obviously problematic. But I'm sure that if Nathan studies really hard and receives rigorous math tutoring, that shouldn't be too much of a problem," the admissions officer told my father and me during a sit-down to discuss my application.

My eyes grew as big as saucers as she introduced one bizarre, inconceivable idea after another. Stu-dy? Tu-tor? It was hard to wrap my mind around these utterly foreign concepts.

If my father had been brutally honest with Ogden, he'd have leveled with the admissions officer and conceded, "Look, my son is reasonably bright but he is also lazy as fuck, so unless this 'tutoring' somehow involves hand jobs from Jennifer Connelly and frosty chocolate milkshakes, there's no way he's going for it."

Instead we meekly agreed that, yes, I would need extra help but that it would be worth it to attend one of the best middle schools in Chicago. I shook the admission lady's hand and instantly became the dumbest smart kid Ogden would ever know. My fate/doom was officially sealed.

I never did sign up for math tutoring. Nor did I ever grasp a bizarre concept known as "geometry," where letters and numbers intermingled in a manner both obscene and incomprehensible. The notion that letters might represent numbers seemed like black magic to me. Throughout eighth grade I routinely racked up test scores in the single digits. If I weren't in the superadvanced class, I probably would have repeated eighth grade a half dozen times.

Things weren't any better on the social front. At Dewitt Clinton my unpopularity had manifested itself in schoolyard violence. At Ogden it was more a matter of social invisibility. Even in a class of freaks and geeks, my sad little table stood out as Poindexter Central.

To my left sat Ignatius, a sullen, big-boned African-American who snuck copies of *Hustler* and *Black Tail* into class. He occasionally made a big show of covertly flashing me particularly gynecological layouts during biology. "Yeah, go on pretending like this doesn't make your dick hard," he'd sneer when I tried not to look at some unfortunate soul getting triple-teamed by hirsute studs. Ignatius nursed a rather unique life goal: he wanted to become a bestselling author of pornography featuring himself as the lead character. To my right sat Daniel, an affable science nerd utterly at ease with his own geekdom.

Less affable and at ease with my perversions, I specialized in petty acts of subversion. For eighth-grade graduation I was pegged to write a speech about the demise of Communist dictatorships in Eastern Europe. In a wonderful bit of irony, Ignatius, that dedicated acolyte of *Hustler, Black Tail,* and *Juggs,* was given the job of delivering my speech about the glory of democracy and the long-overdue flowering of political freedom following the destruction of the Berlin Wall.

To undercut the sentimental, flag-waving nature of my assignment I decided it would be really fucking funny to pretend that Nicolae Ceausescu, the despised dictator of Romania who was eventually murdered by his own people, was nicknamed Spanky. I expected my reference to Nicolae "Spanky" Ceausescu to get cut after the first rehearsal but nobody seemed to notice the seeming incongruity of a power-mad Eastern European despot nicknamed Spanky.

At graduation the reference to good old Spanky reverberated through the hall. My sister and dad chortled enthusiastically, earning disapproving stares from parents who wondered what was so funny about the death of a hated dictator. Slipping Spanky into Ignatius's speech sadly marked the apex of my Ogden career.

Yet my undistinguished stint at Ogden somehow didn't keep me from hoping that I'd be able to follow in my classmates' footsteps by enrolling in the International Baccalaureate program at Lincoln Park High School. A tense meeting my father and I had with the admissions director at Lincoln Park disabused me of that notion.

"Well, Mr. Rabin, I'm not entirely sure why you're even here, because it looks like Nathan never technically even applied to be a student here. And looking at his grades from Ogden, well . . ." The admissions officer paused as she tried to find a polite, gracious way of saying that my grades were the academic equivalent of the monsters in H. P. Lovecraft fiction: so vast and horrifying that the human mind can barely comprehend their true dimensions for risk of engendering permanent, uncontrollable insanity.

An unmistakable sense of déjà vu swept over me as she continued: "Let's just say that the best course of action would be for Nathan to start high school at a local school. Then, maybe if he studies very, very, very diligently and gets a math tutor, he can reapply to Lincoln Park his sophomore or junior year."

I ended up going to three different schools in my freshman year, but Lincoln Park was not one of them. First, I matriculated under the radar at Mather, a local high school that prided itself on a diverse student body that spoke over fifty languages. Unfortunately, none of them was English.

At Mather teenage representatives of the rich cornucopia of American ethnic variety glared warily at each other from a disrespectful distance. The Russian kids spoke Russian to each other and avoided everyone else. The Pakistanis hung with the Pakistanis. And so on.

Gym represented a special torment. It seemed like a class created solely to exploit the insecurities of teenagers. Terrified of the opposite gender and uncomfortable in your own body? Then enjoy mandatory square dancing! Painfully insecure about your scrawny physique and voluminous acne? Then strip down to your bathing suit for compulsory swimming! Horrified that people will find out you're secretly as weak and powerless as a polio-stricken little girl? Then expose your myriad shortcomings through weight lifting! Worried about your incredibly tiny penis? Then enjoy showering with your better-endowed peers!

During weight lifting I picked up a bizarre, insulting nickname that would haunt me for the rest of my high school career. I was standing in the general proximity of the free weights, trying to will myself invisible, when one of the Syrian toughs started shouting at me.

"Hey, Rabin, I saw you up on Devon working at one of those fruit markets. You were lifting one of those hundred-pound sacks of potatoes, weren't you, Potato? That was you up on Devon, wasn't it, Potato?" he jeered, to the delight of his friends.

I responded with a cryptic look I hoped said, "Whatever, dude," and also, "Please don't hit me." You'd think such a strange non sequitur would have a hard time gaining traction but "Potato" took on a life of its own. Four years later at graduation the selfsame Syrian kids drunkenly shouted "Potato!" as I went up to accept my diploma.

Freshman year at Mather I hit the trifecta, racking up three insulting nicknames in quick succession. Beyond the curiously deathless "Potato" there was also "Paperboy." That was a lot easier to explain. I always had my face buried in a newspaper, generally the *Tribune* or *Sun-Times*. I read during class. I'd read in the hallway. I even read walking down the street, leading to all manner of silent-film-style slapstick shenanigans involving collisions with stop signs and all sorts of other stationary yet deceptively wily entities.

My third insulting nickname came from Mr. Schmecklenberg, a crazy old Jewish history teacher who informed us the first day of class that our history books were largely decorative props designed solely to placate the fussy old busybodies at the board of education. We were free to read them if we liked but he'd be going "off book" to deliver long, rambling, wildly discursive lectures about the real essence of history: the sex lives of famous dead people.

Every once in a while Mr. Schmecklenberg would get a faraway look in his eye and begin talking about having an out-of-body experience during open-heart surgery. For a few glorious moments Mr. Schmecklenberg busted loose from the infernal prison of self and wandered the cosmos, or at least a goodly portion of the hospital, a holy spirit, a vapor, a glorious burst of light and weird old Jewish guy energy. Then he'd return to his lofty discourse on Cleopatra's struggles with gonorrhea or some similar matter of profound historical significance.

"Raven! Raven!" he'd squawk, oblivious to the somewhat glaring absence of a "V" in my name, when I'd drift off into a daydream or furtively try to sneak peeks at Mike Royko's latest columns or Roger Ebert's reviews. The quarterback of the football team thought it was the height of wit to ask me, "Hey, Raven: where's Lenore?" or happily exclaim, "Hey, Raven: nevermore! Nevermore!"

Mr. Schmecklenberg died a year or two later, as did a colorful substitute teacher named Mr. Hawkins, who moonlighted as an undertaker and drove a hearse with vanity plates that read HAWK. He looked like a sinister supporting player from a blaxploitation flick. Mr. Hawkins had the remarkable ability to transform any perceived slight into a grievous insult to the soul and spirit of black America. "You will not disrespect this black man by asking to go to the bathroom twice in one period! I'm not falling for any of that foolishness!" he'd angrily declaim. He always seemed to be shouting, mired in a state of apoplectic rage. So it's not surprising that some unforgivable act of disrespect finally sent him to his grave. The weird, creepy dude who hung out with dead people was now a weird, creepy dead dude himself.

Not all my teachers were creepy or crazy or wildly unqualified—just a sizable majority. You tend to remember your best and worst teachers. The rest disappear into the cobwebs of memory.

I vividly recall a young substitute teacher who arrived one day brimming with idealism and enthusiasm, eager to get his *Mr. Holland's Opus* on, *Dead Poets Society* style. He may even have worn a suit, or at least a dress shirt. He was writing a book, a book about young people, he happily explained, and he wanted to know what made us tick. How did we feel about politics? Popular culture? The world? The portrayal of teenagers in movies and books? He radiated curiosity and passion.

I gazed at him with pity. This poor, deluded soul genuinely seemed to think being a substitute teacher entailed something beyond babysitting glowering juvenile delinquents. Oh, he'd learn otherwise soon enough. It wasn't long before this formerly bright-eyed, energetic creature boasted the glum, emotionless pod-person expression endemic to employees of the Chicago public school system, a vacant glare that says, "Students = dumb, education = bad joke, only things that matter = pension, health insurance, retirement."

I strongly suspect that that substitute teacher was in fact Adam Langer and the book about young people he was working on was the bestseller *Crossing California,* which takes place at Mather. If so, I congratulate you on your literary success, Mr. Langer. More significantly I congratulate you on successfully extricating yourself from the soul-crushing machinery of the Chicago public school system.

As things devolved steadily from worse to worserer at Mather (I blame my alma mater for my sad reliance on made-up words) I retreated deeper into myself. I tried to block out the unwanted incursions of a hostile outside world by keeping myself ensconced in a protective bubble of media. I read *Variety* religiously and the *Sun-Times* and *Chicago Tribune* from cover to cover. On the rare occasions I ventured outside my apartment, I kept a Walkman glued to my ears to keep me from having to interact with strangers. I ditched school for the forbidden pleasures of R-rated movies at nearby theaters with magical names like Lincoln Village, Davis, Nortown, and Plaza with great regularity.

Movies like *Bill and Ted's Excellent Adventure* and *West Side Story* allowed me an invaluable space to forget my problems and lose myself in waking dreams, but I was nevertheless headed for a harrowing psychological reckoning just around the corner, from which there would be no escape.

¡El Pollo Loco, él es el hombre!

Girl, Interrupted
Cold Chillin' at the Nuthouse

In a world of convenient fictions and reassuring lies we're irrevocably drawn to art that tells the truth. *Girl, Interrupted*—Susanna Kaysen's haunting memoir of her stint in McLeans Hospital, a famous psychiatric institution that housed Ray Charles, James Taylor, and Sylvia Plath—bears powerful witness to the way mental hospitals have become dispiriting holding pens for nonconformists.

Reading *Girl, Interrupted* the first time around, I felt like Kaysen was telling my story as well as her own. That's what great art does: it makes the personal universal. Rereading *Girl, Interrupted* on a long, sleepless seventeen-hour train ride to DC to visit my sister for Thanksgiving, I was struck by how unexpectedly funny *Girl, Interrupted* is. I guess you have to have a sense of humor in a mental hospital or you'll fucking go crazy.

I was similarly struck by its rambling, discursive structure. In lieu of a strong central narrative, *Girl, Interrupted* offers vivid fragments, evocative snippets of time and place and atmosphere, fleeting remembrances retrieved a split second before they vanished into the ether, lost forever. There is a delicate minimalism to Kaysen's memoir that's quietly heartbreaking. Unlike a certain jackass, she didn't feel the need to water down the experience

27

with cheap wisecracks. No, she delivers her timeless truths straight. Kaysen's delicate black comedy emerges organically from documenting the upside-down absurdity of mental hospital life with spare, deadpan wryness, from the intricate dance of comedy and tragedy, not from anything as coarse as jokes.

My long, strange trip to the locked ward of a much less reputable mental hospital I will call Meadow Lane began the night I broodingly washed down a packet full of caffeine pills with a pitcher of icy grape Kool-Aid. I didn't want to kill myself, necessarily, but I wanted my life to do a whiplash-inducing 180 and felt like anywhere my suicide attempt led had to qualify as an improvement over the free-floating despair of my dad's garden apartment.

Instead of releasing me from my mortal coil, the caffeine pills made me vomit for hours. At around two thirty in the morning I impulsively decided to shave my head but just as impulsively decided to quit halfway through.

I knew enough about caffeine to realize that my chances of successfully committing suicide via a caffeine overdose were nonexistent, but my heartbeat was racing so fast and I was throwing up so violently that I feared for my life.

At four in the morning I started watching a 1986 sex comedy called *Stewardess School* on HBO. I remember thinking about halfway through, "Dear Lord, please don't let me die of choking on my own vomit while watching *Stewardess School*." I couldn't imagine a less dignified death. I silently vowed that if God let me live I'd never attempt suicide, or watch *Stewardess School*, ever again.

Besides, I couldn't die halfway through *Stewardess School*. I had to know how it ended. Would *Happy Days* alum Donny Most and his madcap band of wacky funsters triumph? Or would the forces of repression win out? I had a life-affirming need to know.

A month or two later I found myself sitting opposite my sad-eyed father while a professorial psychiatrist named Dr. Fassbender earnestly asked me questions about my life: Was it true that I'd tried to kill myself? Would I benefit from some time away to work through my issues? It was past eight o'clock on a weeknight but I still had no idea what was about to transpire. No matter how bad things get, you never wake up thinking, "Man, I bet today's the day I'm finally going to be dragged kicking and screaming into a mental hospital."

However, my life had reached such a nadir that I would sometimes daydream about the perfect mental hospital. In my fantasy world the mental hospital would be a rustic place of relaxation and reflection, full of immaculately tended gardens and rolling hills. It'd be an oasis of calm and tranquility away from the madness of the outside world, a place where classical music wafted peacefully in the background, where contented patients whiled away the hours playing croquet, painting, practicing tai chi, or sculpting when not achieving a hard-won sense of inner peace and contentment with the help of kindly, deeply empathetic round-the-clock psychiatrists. Who knows, once there, maybe I'd fall in love for the first time, make friendships that would last a lifetime, or find myself. You know, all that hackneyed coming-of-age shit. And the television would be something out of my wildest dreams: fifty inches at least! It'd be the perfect place to heal wounded psyches and tormented minds.

My fantasy mental hospital was a cross between an Ivy League campus and a pricey day spa, only with straitjackets and padded rooms and a wider selection of psychotropic drugs. How desperately sad do you have to be to fantasize about the perfect mental hospital? Sad enough to imagine that any change in locale would represent a step up, even one most people would consider a nadir.

But my fantasy mental hospital seemed a universe away that night as my father stared at me glumly, his brow furrowed, a permanent frown on his face as Dr. Fassbender continued his gentle but persistent questioning.

I responded with the caustic sarcasm that had become my

default mode of communication. At the end of the session two burly, stone-faced security guards grabbed me and carried me off to the locked ward. Tears and snot ran down my face as I screamed obscenities at a father who once symbolized everything humane and kind about the world. When I was young my father was my sun: the warm, life-giving center around which all good things revolved. My father and Dr. Fassbender drifted further and further from my field of vision until they disappeared entirely, leaving me more alone than I'd ever been before.

I was brusquely told to shower and given paper slippers and a fluorescent orange jumpsuit several sizes too big to wear by staffers whose identities all bled together into one big ball of sour authority. A staff member then led me to my room and introduced me to my new roommate, a boyishly handsome, corn-fed fourteen-year-old from Peoria named Brian, who earnestly asked me why I was there.

"They think I want to kill myself. I didn't before but now they've really given me a reason to want to end my miserable fucking existence," I responded bitterly as I wiped the remaining tears from my face, which was red and raw from crying.

Brian then politely excused himself, slipped into the hallway, and told an attendant that his new roommate had just threatened to kill himself. Moments later the staffer shone a flashlight in my face and coolly ordered, "Grab your mattress. You're on suicide watch tonight."

I was led to an oppressively lit hallway in front of the staff office where I put my flimsy mattress on the floor and started crying all over again. A woman sitting at a desk in the office across the hallway glared at me and hissed, "Crying isn't going to get you anywhere," as if I imagined that all I had to do was fake a few tears and I'd immediately be transferred to the penthouse suite at the Ritz.

This may have been a personal abyss for me, but for the employees of Meadow Lane it was just another day at work. Sobbing teenagers in orange jumpsuits sleeping on mattresses in

the hallway were nothing new. Prolonged exposure to the numb-
ing realities of mental hospital life stripped away any remaining
vestiges of empathy.

Some folks collect stamps, others the bashed-in skulls of student nurses. I collect bitter ironies. So I had to savor the moment
when the woman staring daggers at me bitterly groused to a
coworker, "I just don't see why everyone thinks *The Simpsons*
is so great. What's so funny about a father strangling his son
every week? I can't see why anyone thinks child abuse is something to laugh about."

Here she was conveying bottomless concern for an imaginary
cartoon boy who brought joy to millions while betraying nothing but contempt for the squirming bundle of humanity sobbing
softly six feet away. When I interviewed *Simpsons* creator Matt
Groening fifteen years later, I briefly considered mentioning to
him just how much his show meant to me during that dark
night. Then I dismissed it as the WORST OPENING CON-
VERSATIONAL GAMBIT EVER.

To keep myself occupied I started plotting revenge against
Brian for ratting me out. I'd seen enough prison movies to know
that snitches constitute the lowest form of life, lower even than
Young Republicans and baby-seal clubbers. Snitching violated
the G-code. It violated the code of the streets. It somehow even
violated Isaac Asimov's Three Laws of Robotics. There were no
two ways about it: if I was going to survive inside Meadow
Lane, I'd have to get my hands on a shiv and enact speedy
revenge on Brian the next morning in the yard.

If I were to attain any respect in this hellhole, I'd need to
deliver swift vengeance. But first I needed a nickname, one to
match the tough new persona I'd have to adopt instantly if I
were to make it inside the belly of the beast. "Crazy Nate" had
a nice ring to it, but it hit too close to home.

No, I needed something more exotic, more menacing, more
inappropriately, even offensively, ethnic. Drawing upon the six
or seven words of Spanish I knew, I came up with the nickname

that would transform me from Nathan Rabin the crybaby neurotic Jew into the swaggering badass I desperately hoped to become: El Pollo Loco. The Crazy Chicken. Granted, it didn't make much sense. But I was certain my new nickname would strike fear in the heart of the punk bitch who cavalierly ratted me out to the pigs. Only later did I learn that "El Pollo Loco" is also the name of a chain of modestly priced Mexican restaurants. Quite possibly a chain of modestly priced Mexican restaurants that strike fear into the hearts of snitches everywhere.

With my tears finally subsiding, I perfected my plan for revenge. Obviously I'd need to find something to turn into a crude shiv or shank. Easier said than done. With the pigs watching me I'd have a devil of a time locating a toothbrush, pencil, pen, or something similar I could sharpen into a deadly weapon. Fuck! Oh well. Since my plans for revenge were unlikely to ever evolve beyond escapist fantasy, I decided that for the purposes of my daydreaming I'd somehow magically happen upon a screwdriver. Maybe an incongruously violent sprite, malevolent elf, or ex-con fairy godmother with a bone to pick with humanity would magically appear out of nowhere with the perfect shank, coated in a cloud of pixie dust.

Then I'd wait until we were all out in the yard. Granted, I had no idea if the mental hospital even had anything resembling a prison yard, but again, this was my fantasy and I wasn't about to let reality ruin it. We'd all be out in the yard, maybe lifting weights or doing push-ups, and I'd slowly, silently sneak up on Brian like a panther or ninja or panther that's also a ninja and, with a single devastating motion, slash the back of his neck with my crude makeshift shiv. As pinkish blood spurted across my face I'd start yelling, "That's what you get for fucking with El Pollo Loco, *ese!*"

As Brian fell helplessly to the ground into a pool of his slowly accumulating blood he'd utter a meek, helpless, "*Dios mio!* I never should have ratted out El Pollo Loco. *Él es el hombre!*"

Él es el hombre indeed, motherfucker. But it'd be too late. I'd smear his snitch blood all over my face like tribal war paint and stand over his limp, bleeding body deliriously yelling, "El Pollo Loco, El Pollo Loco!"

That way when Brian entered the gates of hell and they asked him who sent him there, he would reply, "El Pollo Loco." And the gatekeeper of Hades would reverently reply, "El Pollo Loco. *Él es el hombre*" That's right, motherfucker. I am the man. El Pollo Loco is the man.

Exhausted from all the crying, kicking, and imaginary bloodshed, I fell asleep that night softly muttering, "El Pollo Loco, El Pollo Loco." I'm sure the glowering *Simpsons*-hater on duty that night thought I was nuts but I didn't give a mad-ass fuck. I was sleeping on the floor of a nuthouse. There was nothing more they could do to me.

Or so I thought. For on my first full day in the joint I made a mind-boggling discovery: the ward had no television. This blew my mind. I was devastated. If I were in a movie the camera would have repetitively zoomed in and pulled back accompanied by shrieking violins that could only begin to suggest the utter sense of dislocation and nerve-jangling terror I was experiencing.

This couldn't be happening, I tried to tell myself. In movies people in psychiatric institutions were always staring glassy eyed at television sets in a Thorazine haze. Along with mumbling to yourself while lurching zombielike in circles and screaming at fellow patients to stop stealing your thoughts, it seemed to be the most popular leisure-time activity among the crazy-person set.

During my adolescence, television was so much more than just a way to fill twelve to sixteen hours out of every day. Television made me laugh. It showed me a wide variety of consumer products that would make me irresistible to beautiful women and provide me with a deep, permanent sense of spiritual satisfaction. On certain channels, specifically those owned by Pat Robertson, it preached to me about the evils of fornication, homosinuality, and Hollywood liberalism. It showed me exotic faraway places, like Beverly Hills 90210. Most important, if I was very, very good or very, very lucky, it would sometimes show me the boobs of nubile young actresses.

In the midnineties there was an exquisitely dark television show called *Profit* about a charming, murderous sociopath who grew up inside a cardboard box with only a television set to keep him company. Finally, an antihero I could relate to! The idiot box may not have transformed me into a cold-blooded killer, but it did a bang-up job corrupting my values and warping my soul.

Oh how I loved my glorious, glorious television set! It was my lover, my friend, my guru, my financial adviser, my everything. And now it appeared I was stuck in the sole television-free mental hospital in the known universe.

Deprived of access to all media, my fantasies assumed a strangely Steven Seagal–shaped form. My daydreams began to revolve around seeing *Marked for Death* the day I left the hospital. I don't entirely understand why. I'd liked Seagal's previous exercise in Eastern-philosophy-rooted gratuitous violence, *Hard to Kill*, just fine, but I wasn't a Steven Seagal fan by any stretch of the imagination. Maybe I just fixated on *Marked for Death* because in a grim, joyless ward where anything remotely fun was considered an unwanted distraction and consequently verboten (hence the absence of a TV) I couldn't think of anything less wholesome than watching a ponytailed martial artist beat the holy living fuck out of crudely stereotyped minority heavies.

Every night before I drifted off into a fitful, unhappy sleep I'd replay in my mind's cinema what it would be like to see *Marked for Death*. I lingered fetishistically over every aspect of the experience, from sitting down in a plush seat to tasting the appealingly abrasive texture of freshly popped buttered popcorn rubbing up against my taste buds, to be washed down with ice-cold cherry cola.

I felt lost without my electronic best friend. I imagined that my television set would somehow sense my absence and embark on an *Incredible Journey*–like exodus to Meadow Lane, hitching rides, hopping El trains, and dragging itself arduously across the concrete until it was finally reunited with its beloved owner. When the staff saw what lengths my television set had gone through to be with me, they'd be sure to back down and let my cathode-ray soul mate stay with me, right?

It was not to be. To make matters worse, my mental hospital archnemesis was a staff worker who bore an uncanny resemblance to Chris Elliott, the star of one of those glorious, glorious television shows I wouldn't be watching anytime soon. Chris Elliott's evil doppelgänger introduced me to my peers, glum-looking teens from little shit towns throughout Illinois dressed in baggy jeans and outsized sweaters. The dress code at Meadow Lane was purposefully asexual. Girls weren't allowed to wear anything that might remind hormone-addled boys that they possessed breasts or hips or asses. Touching was forbidden. A sexless thrift-store aesthetic reigned, as dowdy and depressing as the cold gray corridors and bare walls.

"So, Nathan, do you want to introduce yourself and tell everybody why you're here?" Chris Elliott's evil doppelgänger implored testily.

"Well," I began, "I guess because I told my dad yesterday that I was sick, so instead of taking me to the real hospital he took me here. I had a bullshit conversation with a psychiatrist who apparently couldn't tell that I was being fucking sarcastic the whole goddamned time and then he had me dragged kicking and screaming into this horrible fucking place and now I guess I'm fucking stuck here God fucking knows how long."

This, dear reader, was not considered the appropriate answer. The desired response, I can say now with the benefit of hindsight, did not involve even a single use of the word "fuck," let alone a whole string of them.

"OK, now do you want to stop lying to yourself and the group and tell them why you're really here or do you want to spend some time in the time-out room?" Chris Elliott's evil doppelgänger asked with palpable irritation.

I once again delivered the wrong answer. "I guess I better spend some fucking time in the time-out room 'cause that's the only fucking answer you're going to get from me in this lifetime," I hissed. Next stop: the rubber room.

It was a locked room with padded walls and a video camera in the corner to make sure patients didn't, in a fit of superhuman rage, rip out their spinal cord, then use it to slash their wrists. Meadow Lane imagined that its inhabitants were the Mac-Gyvers of suicide, able to fashion ingenious homemade instruments of permanent self-negation out of plastic sporks, Popsicle sticks, or blunt lead pencils. So anything that could conceivably be used as a weapon was forbidden. The Shiv Fairy would not be paying El Pollo Loco a visit after all.

The rubber room, alas, is nowhere near as exciting or dramatic as the Porter Wagoner song of the same name makes it out to be. Mostly it's just boring. The day before, I was a free man. Now I was in the rubber room of the mental hospital. It all seemed vaguely unreal.

I was eventually let out of the rubber room but my behavior did not improve. Instead of the earnest display of humility and guilt the staff was looking for, I answered every question with vitriolic sarcasm. Everything was "motherfucker" this and "bullshit cocksucking piece of shit" that.

Early in the afternoon one of my new colleagues marveled, "You know, I've been in a lot of different mental hospitals and you're the angriest person I've ever met in any of them."

Wow: angriest man on the mental hospital circuit. Now, *there* was something to stick on a résumé. Of course I was angry. I was in a mental hospital. How did they expect me to react? That first day I shuttled back and forth between the day room and the rubber room like a Ping-Pong ball in play. I steadfastly refused to give the staff the answers they wanted. I zealously clung to my sarcasm like a psychological security blanket. My rage was at once the source of my power and my powerlessness. It set me apart and it ensured that I'd never acquire any of the privileges Meadow Lane doled out stingily to its prize pupils, like furloughs home. The hospital ran on a point system. My first week there I consistently scored near the bottom. I was going nowhere fast.

If you're going to be stuck in this movie, the point is to be Jack Nicholson, not one of the gargoyle-faced character actors stumbling around in a Klonopin haze. I couldn't let the mental hospital break my spirit. Not just yet.

I exploded with anger toward my fellow prisoners for not being angrier. "You're teenagers, for chrissakes! Anger is your sacred birthright!" I wanted to scream at them. I wanted to instill in my fellow prisoners that it was their solemn fucking responsibility to be angry at everyone and everything in this godforsaken place, this fluorescent-lit mausoleum where resistance and hope and individuality died horrible deaths. I wanted to rouse them from their glassy-eyed stupor, to get them to throw some shit, start fights, bum-rush the show, fight the power, do anything, really, anything other than meekly go along with the program. Show me you're alive, people!

In endless, interminable group therapy sessions, patients were encouraged to confront other patients over transgressions real and imagined. It was drilled into us that we were there because we were broken and diseased and wrong and had proved ourselves unworthy of freedom. We were taught that our salvation lay in renouncing our former selves and our past transgressions and remaking our psyches to fit the mental hospital's narrow conception of mental health.

At Meadow Lane stupid teenage shit was elevated to the level of dangerous pathologies. It was the stuff of Bruce Springsteen songs or Meatloaf pop operas: stealing cars and breaking windows and smoking weed and swilling Mad Dog before class and making out in the back seats of beat-up cars.

In other words, my fellow patients were living the dream. Verily, they were gods among men. They were living the lives I desperately longed to live. I envied the sordid glamour of their tawdry teenage transgressions. We were encouraged to judge them unstintingly for their lusty misdemeanors, to implore them to consider the gut-wrenching anguish their poor, suffering, guiltless parents must have experienced every time their beloved progeny cracked open a can of Pabst Blue Ribbon or let a boy touch their boobs. Instead I wanted these patients to be my mentors, to teach me their sinister secrets, to lead the way to the booze, weed, and sex-saturated good life.

At fourteen, I was a terrible excuse for a juvenile delinquent. I didn't drink. I didn't smoke. I didn't hot-wire cars or get girls pregnant or turn Grandma's life-support system into a bong. I had no prison record. All I ever did was ditch school, steal money from my dad, and treat authority figures abhorrently. I wanted to be James Dean, to brood sexily and dramatically exclaim, "You're tearing me apart!" but I wasn't even Sal Mineo. I wanted to be El Pollo Loco. Instead I was meek little Paperboy.

The second day at the hospital my father visited me. I'll never forget the first words out of his mouth as he gazed unsteadily at me in the dayroom. "So," he began absentmindedly as I fixed my thousand-yard glare firmly in his direction, "how are they feeding you in here? Is the food any good?"

I shouldn't have been surprised. We Jews are a people famously obsessed with food. We didn't have time for a properly leavened nosh in the bad old days back in Egypt and haven't stopped obsessing about food ever since.

My father was merely carrying on a proud Hebraic tradition of prioritizing food above all else. But that didn't matter to me as I glared at him in the visiting room and spat out, "The food in here is amazing. In fact, they fly in a different five-star international chef every day just to prepare our meals. Folks are getting institutionalized solely for the meals, the food here's so good."

My father responded with a guileless, relieved, "Really? It's that good?"

Frustrated with my father's inability to detect sarcasm after all these years, I snapped, "What do you think, Dad? It's a fucking mental hospital. The food's adequate at best. It's not a goddamned culinary academy."

Within two days the dispiriting universe of the mental hospital, with its soul-sapping fluorescent lighting and rigidly defined boundaries, began to feel like the only world I'd ever known. An outside world I once viewed with only withering contempt suddenly sparkled with boundless promise. If only they'd allow me to leave the fifth floor, I swore to myself over and over again, I'd never take anything for granted. Oh! I'd savor the taste of each salty French fry as if it were the finest caviar. I'd take the time to really appreciate the subtle nuances of every ounce of a Mountain Dew Big Gulp.

I tried to convince myself that the problem wasn't that I was a combustible ball of rage but that I had never truly appreciated the sacred gift of freedom. Freedom is wasted on the free. The problem, as I saw it, was that I was insufficiently grateful for all the bounties life had afforded me, something my brief time in the hospital would hopefully correct. If they'd only let me go I'd be the bestest, most grateful young man in the history of the world.

I decided to explain this to Dr. Fassbender. In my fantasies he'd be so swayed by my logic that he'd immediately sign my dismissal papers and escort me personally downstairs, where my father would have rented a chauffeur-driven limousine to take me home. I'd then have the limousine take me directly to the Plaza, where I'd take in Steven Seagal's latest masterwork, *Marked for Death;* recline in the decadent luxury of the plush seating; and gorge myself on a family-sized bucket of popcorn and a 128-ounce cherry cola.

Dr. Fassbender became an unwitting vessel for my hopes and dreams. He'd gotten me into this damnable place, I brooded, so he'd better get me out as well. Besides, I liked Dr. Fassbender. He had a warm, avuncular presence that contrasted dramatically with the arctic vibe of the locked ward.

During one of our weekly sessions Dr. Fassbender asked me what I feared most.

"Mice, I suppose. Mice or rats."

"Well, in his autobiography, *Will,* G. Gordon Liddy writes about how he used to be afraid of rats when he was a young man. Then one day to conquer his fear he caught a rat, cooked it, and ate it. After that he was never afraid of rats ever again."

That, dear reader, was the sage advice of my sole ally at the mental hospital. I'm just glad I didn't tell him that what I really feared most was women. If I'd employed the G. Gordon Liddy method to overcome my fear of women, I'd probably have ended up somewhere considerably worse than Meadow Lane.

My roommate, Brian, bought wholeheartedly into the system I raged impotently against. A strapping, true-blue all-American lad, Brian was a big believer in believing in things: Mom, God, church, country, apple pie, and the safety and reliability of American-made automobiles, just for starters. He'd gulped down the Kool-Aid and politely asked for seconds.

If you believed in the system at Meadow Lane, everything made sense. There was a reassuring logic to it. There were goals to be met, points to be earned, and a big shining reward (freedom! Glorious, glorious freedom!) at the end of the yellow brick road. Brian—whose sole transgression in life involved breaking the rearview mirror of an ex-girlfriend's family car in a drunken, jealous rage—genuinely seemed to believe that he was sick. He felt like he'd done something terribly, almost unforgivably wrong and could only atone for it by earning his release through hard work and good deeds. If he just followed the rules and did everything he was supposed to, then one day he'd be healed. He'd click his heels twice and then suddenly he'd be back in Peoria. And Auntie Em and Uncle Henry and the whole gang would be there! There truly *was* no place like home.

Even when he ratted me out to the staff, Brian had my best interests at heart. After all, he wouldn't want a dead roommate on his conscience, would he? I found Brian's old-fashioned moral code both touching and sad. He genuinely believed that Meadow Lane existed to help him get better, that it nursed no ulterior motives beyond helping troubled teens. For me Meadow Lane and institutions like it existed for two reasons only: to make money and to break the spirits of their patients.

If you believe an institution's ultimate goal is to help you, then it's easy to buy into its system unconditionally. But if you consider that system a Kafkaesque nightmare designed to transform spirited young people into docile conformists, then buying into the system is tantamount to conceding spiritual defeat.

Halfway through my stay at Meadow Lane we experienced a crisis. A tall, lanky seventeen-year-old car thief named Christopher had told his roommate, a blond, simian-featured surfer type I will consequently refer to as Monkey-Faced Snitch Boy, that he was going to bust out of the hospital and find a soon-to-be-released fellow patient named Crystal based on the strong conviction that "she'd probably let him fuck her."

An emergency group meeting was called to address this unforgivable transgression. How were we supposed to make Christopher realize that he was a horrible human being who must change every facet of his terrible personality in order to prove himself worthy of living amongst respectable people if he didn't want to spend his every waking hour being condemned and judged by us? What kind of hot-blooded seventeen-year-old male wants to have sex with a bosomy teenage girl and not live in a mental hospital? It just didn't make sense. Or, rather, it did make sense. And that was considered crazy.

We were told that Christopher's comments were an affront not just to Crystal's peerless virtue but to womanhood as a whole. At Meadow Lane we weren't supposed to have sexual impulses, let alone discuss or act on them. Sex was strictly for marriage and/or procreation. Like all other healthy, normal compulsions, it was drilled into us that this urge to merge was unhealthy and abnormal.

However, I couldn't help but think, "Yeah, I bet Crystal

probably would let Christopher fuck her." Crystal seemed like a sweet girl but she seemed destined to end up a hard-luck, well-traveled barmaid who looks cute in a slightly trashy kind of way at the beginning of a long, debauched evening but morphs magically into Ann-Margret in *Viva Las Vegas* after a dozen bottles of cheap beer.

Monkey-Faced Snitch Boy had clearly violated the G-code by ratting Christopher out. It was time to bust El Pollo Loco out of cold storage and have him unleash merciless vengeance on him.

Confronting Christopher and his repulsive, subhuman hunger for freedom and sexual release threatened to turn into a daylong ordeal. At one point we were given scraps of paper and asked to write down our choices for the funniest and most attractive people in the ward. At the risk of being terribly immodest I was voted the funniest person. Wow, another accolade to stick on the old résumé! Who wouldn't want to hire the funniest, angriest man in the locked ward? This was turning into quite the ego booster. I felt like I should get up and deliver an acceptance speech. Oh, but there were so many people to thank! Dr. Fassbender and Dad and Chris Elliott's evil doppelgänger. Even Brian. The list went on and on. More pointedly, Crystal was named the most attractive patient. We were sternly informed that humor and sexuality were both tools used mainly, if not exclusively, for evil.

Apparently my early use of sarcasm to delineate the infinite variety of ways the staff at Meadow Lane could, and should, go fuck themselves was considered a negative, destructive use of humor. Similarly, Crystal was chastised for driving Christopher to insane heights of depravity by suggesting, however unconsciously, that her shapeless, dishwater-gray sweatshirts hid a phenomenal rack.

El Pollo Loco never did get to enact vengeance on Monkey-Faced Snitch Boy. On the contrary, when Monkey-Faced Snitch Boy started crying in the hallway about a week later, I was on hand to comfort him.

"It's just not the same, Nathan. When I got here it was like we were a family, you know, like we were all pulling for each other. Now I just don't know what to believe," he whined between sobs. It would have been ungracious for me to point out to Monkey-Faced Snitch Boy that nobody fucking liked him in the first place and they liked him even less now that he'd snitched on his roommate.

My friend Keith says the two most powerful forces in the universe are sex and nostalgia. Nostalgia is so powerful it can create profound longing for a glorious past that never existed. For me, nostalgia had transformed an outside world I hated and feared into a wonderland as lush and wondrous as the setting of an MGM musical. For Monkey-Faced Snitch Boy, nostalgia had transformed a group of sullen strangers who feigned interest in his problems solely as a way of kissing up to the powers that be and racking up points, literally and figuratively, into a warm-hearted, loving, supportive surrogate family.

By that point, however, I had lost the will to fight. So I told Monkey-Faced Snitch Boy exactly what he wanted to hear. "Don't worry about it [Monkey-Faced Snitch Boy]. When new people enter a group it sometimes takes a little time for everything to jell. That's it. I wouldn't worry about it. People like you," I told Monkey-Faced Snitch Boy, which was untrue only in the sense that everyone hated him.

While my mind rebelled against the harsh realities of Meadow Lane, so did my body. Every night I would run to my room and throw up stomach acid along with that night's dinner. The staff thought I might be developing an ulcer. An appointment was made for me to undergo stomach X-rays at a nearby hospital.

I was overjoyed! I'd finally be leaving the hospital! Sure, it was just for an hour or so, and I'd be accompanied by a female staffer whose complete absence of warmth made her a female counterpart to Chris Elliott's evil doppelgänger, but I'd be out in the world again. I'd skip gaily about, luxuriating in the intoxication of freedom. I built up my magical trip to get stomach X-rays into such a joyous, life-affirming triumph that it couldn't help but register as a disappointment.

When I actually left the hospital with my stone-faced chaperone, the afternoon was as grim as the ward I'd left behind. After a wildly anticlimactic stroll to the hospital I slipped into an ill-fitting hospital gown and was ordered to drink "cherry-flavored" barium sulfate, a noxious substance that apparently makes your insides light up like glow sticks at a rave. Cherry-flavored barium sulfate has the taste and consistency of ground-up chalk, but with an almost imperceptible rancid cherry-cough-syrup aftertaste. Incidentally, barium carbonate is used to make both rat poison and bricks. I suspect it tastes better than barium sulfate. I was strapped into a giant moving X-ray machine. As the machine whirred and rotated I struggled mightily to keep from vomiting the contents of my stomach all over the X-ray machine or flashing the X-ray attendant with various naughty parts my gown strained to cover. I didn't have an ulcer, as the doctors suspected.

I then left the depressing world of a nearby hospital and returned to the depressing world of Meadow Lane. With no access to movies, I made up my own. My first movie was more of a fragment. It'd begin with Genesis's "That's All" blaring plaintively on the soundtrack and open in a mental hospital. A young man stares longingly out the window of his room, at a drab strip of sky that seems to mock him with its tantalizing suggestion of a big, beautiful world just outside his grasp. He longs for transcendence, for a way out of this whole messy business.

Suddenly the window flies open, seemingly of its own accord. Just as inexplicably the young man leaps madly out the window, to the shock and horror of the startled staff and his disbelieving roommate, and begins flying over Chicago, soaring majestically over his neighborhood and high school and the ratty garden apartment he shares with his helpless crippled father. Nothing and nobody can touch him anymore. He might be dead or he might just have catapulted to a higher evolutionary plane.

My second movie idea involved a fourteen-year-old in a soul-crushing mental hospital (notice a theme?) who comes to the horrifying realization that the adults in charge are all vampires feasting on the blood of their patients. One patient after another mysteriously disappears without anyone paying attention: they're just fucked-up kids, so nobody misses them much.

Eventually the snarling antihero escapes and hunts down and destroys the vampires one by one, except for a sympathetic female staffer who cannot resist his sneering Hebraic good looks and withering way with a one-liner. Lots of steamy, soft-focus, wildly acrobatic, and wholly implausible sex ensues. I tried to convince myself that these were serious screenplay ideas but they were really just daydreams riffing on the primary themes of my adolescence: release (sexual and otherwise), escape, and a lust for power commensurate with my overwhelming sense of powerlessness.

I didn't write much at Meadow Lane. It would have been an exercise in futility. I once tried to start a diary but Chris Elliott's evil doppelgänger must have seen a mischievous gleam in my eye as I jotted down my seething contempt for everything and everyone around me.

"What are you writing about?" he barked angrily.

"Nothing," I responded unconvincingly.

"You won't mind me reading it then, will you?" he insisted. At that point I very maturely made the decision to run away, clutching my sheet of paper to my bosom like a newborn baby. There was nowhere to run to at the hospital. So I raced back to my room fifty or sixty feet away. Chris Elliott's evil doppelgänger followed in hot pursuit. When he reached my room he grabbed the sheet of paper and read it in a furious rage.

"This is garbage. Just a pack of lies. Nobody's going to want to read this," he hissed as he tore it to pieces. I like to think of Chris Elliott's evil doppelgänger as my first, and perhaps harshest, editor.

If writing was a losing endeavor at Meadow Lane, reading

was my sole source of joy. I came to look forward to the hospital's makeshift version of high school. It was a chance to escape the endless blather about feelings and relationships. I really took to the hour of free time we had after dinner. One of my relatives gave me a pair of Dave Barry books that brought a little levity into my dour existence. I am so not making this up. So, if you're reading this, Mr. Barry, I would like to thank you. Your brand of literary tomfoolery brought me comfort and laughter when I needed them most.

At Meadow Lane I had a chance to finally escape the prison of self, to satiate my curiosity about the world by engaging with the suffering souls around me. But I was too paralyzed with rage to connect with my fellow patients. When you're depressed it's like there's an invisible wall separating you from the rest of the world. You long to make meaningful connections, yet there's an impenetrable barrier between you and the rest of humanity that makes that impossible.

That's why there is something safe and comforting about the passivity of moviegoing. Movies and television give and give and give without asking anything in return. There was no danger that at the end of *Pee-wee's Big Adventure*, Pee-wee would step down from the screen, empathetically place a hand on my shoulder, and earnestly inquire, "Why do you have so much anger toward your father, Nathan? He's trying his best. He really is."

Movies afforded the rewards of human interaction with none of the terrifying hazards of actual human contact. Looking back I wish I'd made more of an effort to connect with my fellow patients, to try to understand the poignant cutter girls with telltale purple scars on their wrists and the testosterone-poisoned roughneck boys. I was deaf to the poetry of their sad lives. I suffered from a fatal lack of curiosity about anything that wasn't on a big or little screen.

I never bought into the idea that Meadow Lane was anything but a cynical moneymaking enterprise, but, as the weeks dragged on interminably, my will to fight was replaced by a pragmatic desire to get out by any means necessary. I grew obsessed with the prospect that I'd spend Christmas and New Year's under the hospital's fluorescent lights. At night sometimes I'd hear the muffled screams of the patients who lived on the floors above us, no-hopers who'd be leaving the hospital only in a body bag. Every anguished howl was a bloodcurdling warning from the ghosts of Christmas future.

I finally accepted what is perhaps the quintessential compromise of adulthood: the need to sacrifice your will and desires in order to get what you want. I came to understand the practical necessity of what Elia Kazan calls the Anatolian Smile—the pragmatic grin that masks underlying bitterness and resentment. I realized that all I had to do to get out was say the words everyone wanted to hear—that I was sorry for all the hurt I'd caused my father (which was true), that I realized how out of control I'd been but vowed to be much better in the future.

At family therapy I tackled my most challenging role to date: reformed juvenile delinquent/good son. With Dad and the rest of the patients and their families looking on, I swallowed my pride and delivered an earnest little monologue I'd been practicing all week. "I just want to say how sorry I am for all the hurt that I've caused you, Dad. I've really been out of control. I now realize that. My time here in the hospital has made me understand just how patient you've been with me. When I finally leave the hospital I promise to make a concerted effort to be a better son and student and really appreciate all the wonderful things in my life. I'm sorry, Dad, I really am."

Everyone seemed impressed. I'd made such remarkable progress in just a few weeks! Little did they know that my internal monologue actually went something like this:

Fuck you, fuck you, fuck you

The minute I get out of here I'll burn this motherfucking place to the ground and murder everyone behind it, slowly and with great relish

Fuck you, fuck you, fuck you. In conclusion, fuck you all, burn in hell, etc.

In the end, I was sprung from Meadow Lane for the most mundane of reasons: my dad's health insurance had run out. Once the money stopped rolling in, I was magically deemed cured. My earnest/fake plea for forgiveness merely allowed the hospital to put a happy face on my departure. It allowed them to preserve the useful fiction that I was being let out because I was getting better and showing remorse, not because the filthy lucre had suddenly disappeared. It was commerce, not progress, that dictated my release.

My residency at the psychiatric institution ended with a whimper rather than a bang. I had been dragged kicking and screaming into the mental hospital. I thought there would be a perverse symmetry in getting dragged kicking and screaming *out* of the mental hospital as well.

I'd fantasized endlessly about the day of my release. Surely a Lincoln Town Car, a ticker-tape parade, and a key to the city were in order for an event of this magnitude. Instead I endured a chilly cab ride home with my father on a frigid fall afternoon. The silence was deafening. Whatever relief I felt at saying good-bye to Meadow Lane was offset by the still-burning rage I felt at being put there in the first place. It would take me years to move beyond my anger at my father.

For the record, when I finally saw *Marked for Death* at the Plaza, it was far worse than I could ever have imagined. And I'm pretty sure the popcorn was stale and the cherry cola flat. I had been placed in Meadow Lane so that I'd be able to live with my dad again. In a final, bitter irony, my days living with my dad were numbered. Meadow Lane wasn't just a cure much worse than the disease: it was a cure to a problem that wouldn't exist much longer.

A decade later I flew out to Los Angeles for the *Girl, Interrupted* junket. The whole point of Kaysen's book is that her eighteen months in the mental hospital are a season in purgatory.

There is no redemptive arc, no life lessons to be learned, no glorious epiphanies. But in the film version Kaysen's character learns valuable life lessons, engages in hard-core bonding with her peers, and ends the film older, wiser, and ready to face the challenges of life outside.

With intelligence, taste, and only the best of intentions, writer-director James Mangold transformed a book that told the truth into just another Hollywood lie. When I interviewed Mangold that weekend I asked him why he had blunted the book's political message and feminist subtext. He told me that movies like *One Flew over the Cuckoo's Nest* had covered that territory already.

I wanted to scream at Mangold that *Girl, Interrupted* wasn't just another book. It wasn't *The Da Vinci Code*. It was a book that spoke for people who have no voices. It contained truths that shouldn't have been flattened or ignored or twisted. But I couldn't. I wasn't that angry fourteen-year-old kid from the mental hospital anymore. And Hollywood movies are immune to the kind of raw, unvarnished truth telling that makes *Girl, Interrupted* so much more than just another bestseller.

The Awful Intensity of the Moment

The Great Gatsby
The Wolfsheims

F. Scott Fitzgerald's *The Great Gatsby* has the distinction of being not only the greatest novel in our country's history but also the most American. Fitzgerald's dazzling elegy for the jazz age captures everything that's wonderful and horrible about the United States through the tragedy of Jay Gatz, an incandescent self-made man who reinvents himself as Jay Gatsby, a playboy of impeccable breeding, in his bid to escape his past and win the heart of the only woman he's ever loved. He fails of course—this is a tragedy, not a comedy—and his violent death causes the gaudy empire he's created for himself to disintegrate instantly into nothingness. In the end Gatsby's entire world is little more than a shimmering mirage, beautiful but empty.

That's the triumph and tragedy of *Gatsby* and of American life: you can re-create yourself in the image of your wildest fantasies but you can never outrun your past. *Gatsby* is more than just the lyrical embodiment of the jazz age: in its musicality it *is* jazz, that most archetypally American art form.

Gatsby is the ultimate WASP but his plight echoes the aspirations of the Jewish people, a tribe that knows a little something about changing their names, distancing themselves from hardscrabble pasts, and re-creating themselves in the image of upscale WASP perfection. Just ask Ralph Lifshitz, the Jewish, Bronx-born son of a housepainter who overtly modeled his fashion empire on the über-WASP aesthetic of Gatsby and Steve McQueen's Thomas Crown after changing his name to Ralph Lauren.

When I was fourteen I spied my own version of Gatsby's eternal green light when my social worker arranged for me to live with a wealthy family I lovingly call the Wolfsheims in Winnetka and attend New Trier, one of the finest public high schools in the country.

The list of powerful and influential people who matriculated at New Trier is long, distinguished, and not particularly relevant to the narrative at hand, however meandering or digressive it might be. It includes Donald Rumsfeld, Charlton Heston, Rock Hudson, A. C. Nielsen, Liz Phair, Rainn Wilson, Christie Hefner, Ann-Margret, and John Stossel. The list of powerful and influential people, real and imaginary, who didn't matriculate at New Trier is even longer, even more distinguished, and has nothing whatsoever to do with my life story. It includes Moses of biblical fame, Malcolm X, all the kings of England, Count Chocula, the guy from the *Police Academy* movies who makes funny noises with his mouth, ABBA, George Lazenby, and the Smurfs.

Like Gatsby, I wanted to believe that history was not destiny and that under the right circumstances I could reclaim my tarnished American dream. My stay with the Wolfsheims represented a fierce tug-of-war between my bourgeois aspirations and simmering class resentments.

But first let's rewind a little and learn how I came to live with a family of wealthy strangers in the first place. Shortly before I left the hospital my father fell while walking to the mailbox to send me a letter. This was not unusual. Many of my memories of my father during this period are horizontal in nature. He was forever colliding violently with the ground, oozing blood and assuring passersby that he was just fine and would walk it off as soon as humanly possible. My father lingered under the misconception that as long as he didn't use a walker or wheelchair, nobody would know he was disabled. He seemed to think strangers would see him lying on the sidewalk after yet another graceless tumble and wonder, "Who is that strapping, able-bodied young man lying on the ground in a pool of his own blood? Surely an Olympic athlete running himself ragged preparing for a triathlon."

During his myriad unplanned collisions with the pavement my father developed an almost preternatural tolerance for pain. So he didn't bother going to the emergency room until the pain became unbearable. At a local hospital, my dad learned that during the fall his ribs had punctured his lung. The doctors gravely informed him that if he'd waited a few more hours before going to the hospital he would have died of internal bleeding.

After the fall, my father's health deteriorated until one morning he woke up and discovered he couldn't walk anymore. Just a week or so after I left Meadow Lane my dad checked into Chicago's Rehabilitation Institute. Our life together was effectively over. I was sent to live with my uncle Lou and aunt Judy in the northern suburbs.

There is never a good time to have an angry, belligerent, sarcastic fourteen-year-old fresh out of a mental hospital show up at your doorstep seeking food, shelter, lunch money, and emotional rescue. But my aunt and uncle had just had their second child, so the timing was particularly unfortunate. I was a pox upon their house, a sentient black cloud in slouching teenager form. Uncle Lou has the patience of a saint and is a kind, decent, deeply religious man, a consummate mensch in every sense. But even he had to wonder what he'd done to deserve having a screaming six-month-old (Seth), an older son just entering the terrible twos (Benjamin), and a sneering, glowering fourteen-year-old all living under his roof.

In a kinder era I'd become Benjamin and Seth's cool cousin,

the guy who sees all the big movies before anyone else, talks to famous people, and works for a counterculture institution revered by them and their friends. But in 1990 I was simply a festering problem in need of a solution. My overachieving sister had sensed an ill wind blowing and scored full scholarships for a number of top private and boarding schools before settling on Michigan's Cranbrook Academy.

My relatives understandably hoped I'd follow in her footsteps. But I was far too lazy and apathetic to muster up the hustle to score scholarships of my own. Besides, I doubt that even the least discriminating boarding school would be impressed by the D's and F's littering my eighth- and ninth-grade report cards.

I didn't live at Uncle Lou and Aunt Judy's so much as I haunted it. During the day I attended to the exhausting demands of truancy and low-level juvenile delinquency. If I was feeling perverse sometimes I'd go to class. More often I'd linger in greasy spoons reading the newspaper or go to the picture show.

So it felt like a godsend when my hippie social worker announced that a wealthy couple in the upscale suburb of Wilmette was interested in having me live with them.

At fourteen, I was capable of doing a passable impersonation of a nice, sane Jewish boy for up to two hours at a time. After those two hours, however, my facade of normality shattered and I went back to communicating largely through agitated, monkey-like screeching and angrily hurled clumps of feces. Thankfully my introductory meeting with the Wolfsheims lasted well under two hours. I moved in with them after spending an hour and a half with them playing Scrabble, which is a little like deciding to marry someone after sharing a reasonably promising trip to the malt shop with them.

Or perhaps that metaphor isn't particularly apt; apparently I came with a money-back guarantee. If the Wolfsheims found my personality or affect to be defective in any way they could simply return me after a thirty-day trial for a moppet more to their liking.

To this day I wonder what my social worker told the Wolf-sheims about me. I'm guessing the phrases "seething powder keg of rage" or "just out of the mental hospital" didn't come up, but if they did they were probably rushed out in a barely coherent blur alongside my admirable qualities. So my social worker might have told them, "Nathan is at heart a really nice boy. He's also a seethingpowderkegofrage but he's quite bright and though onlyafewmonthsoutoftheloonybin he loves history. He knows a lot about movies and hatesrichpeople but has excellent penman-ship and other than masturbatingcompulsively and ditching-schoolconstantly, he's quite well behaved for someone with such seriouspsychologicalproblems."

I decided between visiting the Wolfsheims one sun-dappled fall afternoon and going to live with them for what I foolishly imagined would be a permanent basis that I would cut off all ties with my past. I would cast off my old identity like a second skin and be reborn as someone new, different, powerful, and strong.

I had even selected a new name to accompany my new iden-tity. El Pollo Loco obviously had no place in my new surround-ings. My new name and persona would be the inverse of El Pollo Loco. He would bear the all-American moniker of Nathan Rock-well. Rockwell. N. Rockwell. It was akin to legendary Jewish producer Sam Spiegel renaming himself S. P. Eagle early in his career. The thinking was the same in both cases, a sad, self-loathing conviction that people would see a telltale name like Rabin or Spiegel and think, "Fuck that hook-nosed, money-grubbing, media-controlling Shylock Jew bastard and his kikey motherfucking name."

But a name like Eagle or Rockwell: goddamn! Those were just good old-fashioned American names, the kind of moniker that'd belong to a real live nephew of Uncle Sam, born on the Fourth of July. An Eagle or Rockwell probably spends their free time nursing wounded baby bald eagles to health. But a no-good Jew like Rabin or Spiegel? That guy would sell his mother for pocket change.

Names have a talismanic quality in the United States. We are a nation of Gatsbys, die-hard believers in the magical powers of personal reinvention. Change the name and change the past. Change the name and change the present. Change the name and instantly, permanently negate the past, obliterate the historical record, create a phantom being that exists only in the present and future tense.

Just as Nathan Rockwell was the antithesis of El Pollo Loco, he was likewise the opposite of Nathan Rabin. If Nathan Rabin was awkward and defensive, moody and introverted, then Nathan Rockwell would be affable and extroverted, quick with a jocular "old sport" or pat on the back. If Nathan Rabin was a virginal compulsive masturbator who lived in mortal fear of women, Nathan Rockwell would be a dashing, self-confident ladies' man, the kind of incorrigible womanizer who whiles away the hours finger-banging little Susie Homecoming Queen under the bleachers. If Nathan Rabin was self-conscious and guilt stricken about growing up poor and reviled, Nathan Rockwell would be a carefree son of privilege. Even his servants would have servants and even the servants of his servants would have money. After all, you wouldn't want them getting their poor-people germs all over your sprawling mansions, now would you, old sport? It just wouldn't be sporting. And Nathan Rockwell was nothing if not sporting. There was just one thing he wasn't: me. Some folks have a genius for reinvention but I'm stuck with my one crappy personality.

Like many poor, anonymous Jews, I grew up dreaming of someday becoming a wealthy, famous gentile. For a brief shining moment, that seemed partially within my grasp. Like many relationships, my tenuous bond with the Wolfsheims was built upon a solid foundation of mutual deception. I pretended not to be a seething powder keg of rage. In return the Wolfsheims pretended they possessed the godlike patience and compassion necessary to make an angry, belligerent fourteen-year-old stranger feel like a welcome, secure member of their family.

The Wolfsheims hoped that my stay with them would be like a Jewish version of *Diff'rent Strokes* or *Webster* where the poor orfink lavishes love and affection on the nice liberals who have deigned, in their infinite generosity, to save him from a life of poverty and hopelessness. Instead it was like one of those French art films where estranged family members glare contemptuously at each other from across an ocean of alienation and an unbridgeable class divide.

Mr. Wolfsheim, a prickly corporate attorney, viewed me as a fixer-upper, a human reclamation project. "You know, Nathan," he told me not long after I moved in, "you can tell a lot about a person by the condition of their fingernails. You can tell whether they care about how they look and whether they're clean or not and whether they have the sort of job where appearance is important."

I instinctively looked down at my ragged, chewed-up fingernails, which had enough dirt under the cuticles to start a small mushroom farm. Mr. Wolfsheim's fingernails, however, were a thing of beauty (and consequently a joy forever): manicured, clean, and perfectly symmetrical.

Another of Mr. Wolfsheim's you-can-tell-a-lot-about-a-person life dictates was aimed at my caveman strut. "You don't even walk right, Nathan," he fumed. I was the first to concede what a horrible failure I was as a human being, how utterly useless I was in every facet of everyday life, but criticizing the way I walked seemed unnecessarily cruel. My manner of perambulation might not have been graceful but the old one-foot-in-front-of-the-other method of forward movement had always gotten me where I'd needed to go. What was he going to critique next? My ragged, uncouth manner of breathing? The ugly, blatantly proletarian manner in which my blood circulated?

"You walk like this," he spat as he hunched his shoulders down and dropped his head forward, stuck his hands sullenly into his pockets and shuffled awkwardly, the soles of his feet dragging over the concrete. It was a nasty burlesque of my Neanderthal body language and movement that was all the more painful for being entirely accurate. I was horrified because it doubled as a cruel parody of the way my father walked as well. Mr. Wolfsheim had never met my father. He never would meet my father. But in that agonizing moment he seemed to be taunting me, "You move exactly like your helpless, crippled father, you feral, ignorant working-class fuck."

I wanted desperately to escape where I'd come from, but Mr. Wolfsheim's ugly little impersonation screamed that I would always be my father's graceless son. It was in the blood. It was in the way I moved. I could no sooner change it than I could alter my DNA.

At Mather I'd been one of the best and brightest, in the sense that I knew how to read and write and refrained from attacking my teachers with a spiked bat. At New Trier I was so behind the curve academically I worried I'd be forced to ride to school on the short bus and given a 'tarded helmet and drool cup my first day of class. At Mather my ACT score of 25 was auspicious enough to earn me an invitation to geek it up on the Academic Olympics team. At New Trier the average ACT score was a little over 26. By comparison, at Mather it was 15; you get thirteen points just for spelling your name correctly.

I was utterly overwhelmed by New Trier, which was more like an elite college campus than a public high school: a sacred cathedral of education, daunting and holy. I felt unworthy to enter its doors, let alone matriculate there. I was afraid that someone would spot me as a truant juvenile delinquent from a poor family and have me rudely ejected for impersonating a student.

Maybe that's why I chose to spend most of my school days as far from New Trier as possible. After saying good-bye to the Wolfsheims I'd sneak out to the video store and rent soft-core epics to further my study of which R-rated movies contained naked boobs. It was harrowing, thankless work, enlivened only by constant masturbation, but I soldiered on regardless, convinced that my findings would benefit mankind as a whole. So instead of going to school, I'd rent *Private School for Girls* and peruse my ill-gotten finds after everyone else had gone to bed.

Or I'd wander aimlessly around Winnetka and Wilmette and daydream about the perversity and intrigue that lurked inside all those cozy, immaculately preserved houses. I guess I'd seen *Blue Velvet* a few too many times. In that respect being an inveterate teenage daydreamer was excellent preparation for being a film critic. Or a Peeping Tom. The windows to every stately suburban enclave were like little movie screens waiting to reveal baroque suburban secrets. To be an adolescent boy is to fall in love on a daily basis with beautiful women forever outside your grasp, to pine hopelessly for impossible dream girls you can never hope to possess. To be a movie lover, on the other hand, is to fall in love on a daily basis with beautiful women forever outside your grasp, to pine hopelessly for impossible dream girls you can never hope to possess.

During one of my increasingly rare visits to New Trier I was assigned to do a big presentation about the Middle Ages. Being a morbid soul, I decided to do a presentation on the bubonic plague, the only event in history more excruciating than my adolescence. I asked Mr. Wolfsheim for help and he gleefully acquiesced, encouraging me to dress entirely in black and go as a plague doctor, one of those shameless quacks who'd don beaklike masks and proffer bogus remedies for the black death.

Mr. Wolfsheim began to leap about joyously while regaling me with stories about how he studied improvisation in college. His stiff, authoritarian demeanor softened and an impish, conspiratorial twinkle entered his eyes. He seemed for all the world like a man reborn. For a brief idyll he was no longer a stodgy square but rather a fearless performer. In that strange hour I got a glimpse of who Mr. Wolfsheim was before he was a husband or father or corporate lawyer, when he was just a young guy with a glorious future lying ahead of him, a real-life Choose Your

Own Adventure. Like many rich people, he seemed vaguely embarrassed by what he had become. When he talked about college I got the sense that he was reconnecting with something pure and fierce and untamed. He was a young man once, and when he discussed his youth, his eyes afire, his movements sprightly and manic, he seemed for the first and last time wholly, poignantly, unmistakably human.

It's fitting that the sole moment of genuine emotional connection I experienced with Mr. Wolfsheim revolved around the bubonic plague. It was that kind of a year.

When I first met the Wolfsheims it felt natural to call them "sir" and "ma'am." It was the polite thing to do. But after I moved in, those terms of nonendearment felt chilly and remote. What could I call them? "Mom" and "Dad" felt creepy and weird. Though a woman was nice enough to carry me in her womb for nine months and then go through the agony of childbirth, I never felt like I had a mother. A biological parent? Yes. A mom? No.

When I was growing up, my dad always wanted me to call him "Pa." That's what the son on the sixties Western *The Rifleman* called his single-father dad. My dad liked to pretend that our relationship eerily mirrored the wholesome father-son dynamic on *The Rifleman* but I don't recall Chuck Connors's true-blue lawman ever having his son institutionalized.

I had a dad but he sure as shit wasn't a corporate lawyer in tailored suits. "Mr. and Mrs. Wolfsheim" sounded sycophantic. Calling the Wolfsheims by their first names would have felt insulting and irreverent, so I persisted in calling them "sir" and "ma'am" until those words came to underline the vast emotional distance between us. It was a compromise that made no one happy.

After an increasingly tense month at the Wolfsheims', an emergency meeting was called between myself and my social worker, in which the Wolfsheims were conspicuously absent.

I knew things were going badly but I failed to grasp the

extent to which our relationship had deteriorated. Just before my social worker arrived I asked Mrs. Wolfsheim if she was disappointed in me.

"Nathan," she began in her best maternal-martyr tones, "I'm *beyond* disappointed in you."

From the way she spat out her words you'd think she'd come home to find me fucking the family dog while wearing her wedding dress, not that I'd ditched some classes and rented R-rated movies. I wanted to explain to her that being surly and sullen to adults, ditching school, and thinking up new ways to look at naked women constituted the three immutable cornerstones of my crappy personality, not deviant aberrations.

A little later my social worker dropped by for a conference in my room.

"Nathan, how do you think things are working out here between you and the Wolfsheims?" she began nervously.

"Well, to be honest, not so good. I think they're really angry at me for ditching class. And I don't think they're too happy about me calling them 'sir' and 'ma'am.' It's really not going that well."

"Yeah. They agree. They want you to leave immediately. Take only what you need for tonight. We'll send for the rest later," my social worker said as unemotionally as possible, trying and failing to defuse the awful intensity of the moment.

I silently loaded my belongings into a cardboard box and prepared to leave the Wolfsheims' house for the last time. But to do so I'd have to face Mr. Wolfsheim, who stood near the door with a steely glare, his arms crossed in the classic defensive position. When I approached he told me, "Nathan, I'm sorry things had to work out this way. If you ever want to come back and talk about it, I'd be open to that."

Standing in the Wolfsheims' kitchen, I could not bear to let Mr. Wolfsheim feel like the bigger man. I couldn't stand the idea that he'd walk away from our month together feeling like a Good Samaritan whose attempt to do something noble was fatally compromised by the demon child the Jewish Children's Bureau saddled him with.

So I glared at him with as much evil as I could muster and deadpanned, "Yeah. I'll do that. I'll come back," and then, after a dramatic pause, continued, "And I'll burn down your mother-fucking house."

I had no intention of returning to Wilmette to set the Wolf-sheims' home ablaze. But it felt good to be genuinely malevolent rather than impotently passive-aggressive. In that moment Mr. Wolfsheim and I dropped the flimsy facades of gentility we'd intermittently adopted for each other's sake and the ugly human-ity of our fractious relationship bubbled to the surface.

Mr. Wolfsheim turned angry and defensive. "You better not!" he screamed. "If I so much as catch sight of you I'm call-ing the cops! I know your kind!"

With that melodramatic flourish I departed the Wolfsheims' life forever. When I reached my mortified social worker's car my false bravado wore off as I timidly asked her, "What am I going to do now?"

"It's OK. There's a group home called the Winchester House where you'll stay the night. It's not ideal but it's only temporary. You'll be there at most five or six days until we figure out what to do with you."

My life with the Wolfsheims was as dead as Gatsby in his swimming pool. I had no way of knowing my temporary stay at the Winchester House would last not five or six days but five or six years.

The Burrito Pimp of the Soup Kitchen and Son

The Catcher in the Rye
Crash-Landing at Winchester House

If every novel high school teachers assigned spoke to teenagers as directly as *The Catcher in the Rye,* recreational reading would be a more popular adolescent pastime than video games and masturbation combined. Where most novels that pop up on high school syllabi come off as dead books written in dead tongues by dead people, *The Catcher in the Rye* is like the charismatic kid with the anarchy symbol scrawled in permanent marker on his jacket who wants you to sneak out of class early so you can smoke weed and listen to Hüsker Dü on his boom box in the woods. Like so few adults, J. D. Salinger understands the teenage psyche: the heightened sense of drama; the alternating currents of self-pity, self-aggrandizement, and serrated, free-floating rage; and the utter disillusionment with the lies and compromises of the adult world.

The rambling, episodic adventures of Holden Caulfield—an aimless, endlessly profane teen who goes AWOL from his stifling boarding school after being expelled and spends a lonely few days carefully cultivating his contempt for humanity like a dark psychic bonsai tree—elevate teen nihilism to the level of existential philosophy.

Because Salinger disappeared following *The Catcher in the Rye*'s release, he achieved a strange pop-art transubstantiation with his most famous creation. In the public mind Salinger *became* Caulfield, the archetypal outsider raging passionately against a hopelessly corrupt world. Salinger, like Caulfield, remains frozen forever in a perfect state of eternal adolescent ennui. He's a brooding question mark for which there is no answer.

I don't trust anyone who never went through a Holden Caulfield phase. But I fear for anyone who never made it beyond their Holden Caulfield phase. It's no coincidence Mark David Chapman and John Hinkley were both huge *Catcher in the Rye* fans. When taken to their logical extreme, Caulfield's grim views on the emptiness of adult society can lead to some pretty dark places. For Holden it leads to a mental hospital. By the time I read *Catcher* I knew just how dark a place that could be.

My own Holden Caulfield phase nearly got me expelled. In honors freshman English we were assigned a final based on John Knowles's *A Separate Peace*. In a fit of Salinger-inspired belligerence, I wrote on my final exam that *A Separate Peace* was such phony, sentimental bourgeois bullshit that it didn't even merit being read, let alone written about. The really sad part is that I wasn't adopting a hipper-than-thou pose to cover up not doing the assigned work. I'd read the book, but I refused on principle to complete the all-important final exam solely to make an exceedingly fuzzy, ill-considered point about how, I dunno, everything was fucking bullshit or something. So I failed freshman English and ended my freshman year with a robust 1.6 GPA.

By that point I felt like nothing mattered anyway. I'd fallen through the cracks and was free-floating into oblivion. The grim realities of my new existence crystallized that fateful night I was first driven to Winchester House. The worker on staff that night was Dwayne, a handsome black man in his early thirties with a hustler's soul and a regrettable fondness for leather baseball caps and leaving IOUs in the petty cash box.

When I walked through the door that first night, Dwayne

eyed me wearily and said, "Hey. I warmed up some leftovers in the microwave. You're bunking with Noah tonight. Welcome," with a notable absence of enthusiasm. The other boys looked at the fresh meat glumly. The friendliest was my bunkmate, Noah, a preposterous-looking ten-year-old imp who followed me around like a lost puppy.

"Hi, I'm Noah. What's your name?" he asked eagerly.

That shouldn't have been a difficult question. But for me it was a matter of profound significance. Who was I? Who did I want to be? Who did I think I was? Why was I always in such a goddamned hurry to be someone else?

Just as I'd done in the mental hospital and with the Wolf-sheims, I created a half-assed alter ego for myself. "Uh, Larry Miller. My name's Larry Miller," I responded waveringly, inexplicably borrowing the name of a stand-up comedian and character actor for my nom de idiocy. My ruse did not last long.

"His name's not Larry Miller," Dwayne scoffed indignantly at my pointless charade. "His name's Nathan Rabin."

El Pollo Loco and Nathan Rockwell both served valuable psychological purposes. El Pollo Loco helped protect me from a scary and hostile new world. Nathan Rockwell was the vessel that would lead me to über-WASP glory. But Larry Miller was just a stupid name I pulled out of my ass to deny the realities of who I was and where I'd landed. I suppose it's possible that I labored under the delusion that my stay at Winchester House was going to be temporary. What's the point in getting too settled if you're only going to be leaving in a week anyway?

But I knew damned well that I wasn't going anywhere, that Winchester House was my home for the foreseeable future, not a way station en route to someplace better. I'd burned plenty of bridges, most recently by threatening arson of a less metaphorical sort. First I was my mother and father's problem. Then I was my dad's problem. Then I became the mental hospital's problem and my family's problem and then the Wolfsheims' problem. Now I was officially society's problem. So they sent me to a place for boys who had run out of options. I was no different from anyone else there. Nobody ever ended up at Winchester House because their family was too wealthy or stable. We were an island of misfit boys.

My first night at Winchester House, Noah kept me awake by dry-humping the wall of our modest room just off the kitchen on the first floor. "Boofing the wall, boofing the wall," he repeated over and over again in a singsong voice, "boofing" being his homemade euphemism for humping. His aim, as I would soon learn, was to annoy and enrage, but there was something hypnotic and tribal about the way he chanted it, something almost reassuring in the way his soft, protruding, curiously external belly and crotch hit the wall in a crude pantomime of sexual aggression.

Noah was born without a protective wall of stomach muscles, so his belly hung low and out like a kangaroo's pouch, a deformity that seemed to preclude ever leading a normal life. It similarly helped explain the bottomless rage that fueled everything he did.

The day before, I had been the ostensible scion of a wealthy Jewish family in a tony suburb, attending a high school that represented the unassailable apogee of public education. Twenty-four hours later I was living in a group home and being kept awake by a manic ten-year-old Puck dry-humping the wall. 'Tis truly a strange and beautiful world.

I found a certain sad solace in the knowledge that my housemates had even less to feel hopeful about than myself.

There was, for example, Edgar, a chubby-cheeked misfit with a hideous rattail and a maddening habit of chewing on his tongue so that it poked out just past his lips and resembled a tiny little bubble of Bazooka Joe. Edgar fetishized normality because it represented an impossible ideal. Where most teens daydream about being prom king and banging the head cheerleader, Edgar fantasized about not going to a special education school and working part-time as a bagger at a grocery store.

Edgar's parents seemingly emerged whole cloth from an early John Waters movie. Edgar's mother was a meaty lass whose second husband tolerated her as long as she stayed away from his gun collection. His father was the most effeminate homosexual in the known universe, with an obscene, leering lisp that rocketed light-years beyond self-parody. I've long been able to reduce my father to fits of uncontrollable laughter with an unconscionably mean impersonation of Edgar's dad.

After lights-out one night Edgar told me about a Christmas where his dad got him a bike, an almost inconceivably generous gift given his family's abject poverty. He was overjoyed and celebrated with a big glass of Tang. The next morning he awoke to find that someone had broken into their apartment and stolen his bike. The unwashed glass of Tang was now filled with cockroaches. That succinct little snapshot told me more than I ever wanted to know about Edgar's pre–Winchester House existence.

A spirit of half-assed anarchy ruled over group home. People drifted in and out, leaving behind only the faintest of footsteps. When I moved in, the house was dominated by nineteen-year-olds Stan and Fred, a complementary twosome with a Jay-and–Silent Bob thing going: Fred was tall, wiry, and perpetually agitated. Stan was shorter, chubbier, and perennially chill.

Not long after my arrival at Winchester House, Fred decided to give me an impromptu crash course in social skills.

"Dude, do you even got any friends at all?" he barked accusingly. Before I could answer he continued. "Do you even know anybody at school? I'm not even talkin' 'bout friends or shit like that. I'm talkin' 'bout people you see in the hallway and are like 'whaddup' to."

Fred then demonstrated the near-imperceptible head-nod of friendly acquaintanceship he would send a semichum to reaffirm their bond. "See? You ain't even gotta say nothing. You just gotta let people know you're seeing 'em." Fred would have continued with his discourse on how to win friends and influence people if Stan hadn't shot him a look that said, "Dude, go easy on the guy."

During my first year at Winchester House my roommate was first Noah and then Luke, a fourteen-year-old self-described "hillbilly" ("'cause I was born on a hill," he confided with delicious literal-mindedness) who liked to say he was from "down south in Burnham, Illinois," even though Burnham was technically only about twenty miles south of Chicago and several thousand miles north of the Mason-Dixon line. Luke's dad was a security guard who got shot in the face and died in the line of duty.

Luke had a strict, oft-stated policy of not talking about what he broodingly referred to as "shit that happened in the past," but every once in a while he'd get a weird gleam in his eyes and swear bloody vengeance against the proud Nubian gods of Africa he held responsible for his dad's murder. Luke used less empowering, culturally sensitive language to describe his father's killers but I won't trouble your delicate sensibilities with the actual terminology employed.

Luke was funny, sometimes even intentionally so. He was ridiculous and ultimately deeply sad, haunted like Hamlet by a ghostly father forever demanding vengeance. The highest/only praise Luke ever gave was that someone was a "cool kid." Luke and Leona, a vivacious girl who lived at one of our sister group homes, were the Frank Sinatra and Ava Gardner of the JCB, perpetually squabbling soul mates whose on-again, off-again *l'amour fou* had everyone riveted. I remember once impishly asking Luke if he'd be OK with me asking Leona out.

"That'd be, you know, OK, 'cause you're both some pretty cool kids," Luke replied with strained casualness that suggested it'd be anything but OK. It was a moot point anyway since I was far too terrified of women to ask anyone out, let alone the great love of Luke's life.

Our sister group homes were a source of endless fascination. The outcasts who lived there were genuine bad girls, teenage hellcats with bad attitudes and worse reputations. They drank beer and smoked cigarettes and ran away from home and got pregnant and cussed out adults and did all the nasty, antisocial things I wished I'd had the balls to do.

Going out with a group home girl had distinct advantages. First, girls from our sister houses by definition couldn't look down on us for living in a group home. We never had to explain the group home universe of rules and restrictions and group therapy and social workers and weirdo roommates and absent moms and deadbeat dads and the ever-present specter of the mental hospital to group home girls because they were locked into it just as irrevocably as we were.

Group home girls also had a reputation for being easy, loose, and wild. But there were drawbacks. For example, group home girls had a maddening habit of being shuttled off to mental hospitals every other month or so. You had to act quickly if you were interested in a group home girl, or impregnable mental hospital walls would stand defiantly between you and your unstable object of desire. One afternoon I heard through the group home grapevine that an almost feral new girl named Carrie had told one of her housemates that she wanted to "fuck me." I was horrified. And delighted. And confused. And frightened in the way teenage boys invariably are when confronted with the full force of female sexuality. It was a nonissue, however, as Carrie was shipped off to a mental hospital before anything happened.

The Winchester House boys unsurprisingly developed a series of epic, unrequited crushes on girls from our sister homes. Luke had his melodramatic dalliance with Leona. Edgar nursed a painful, intense crush on Tamika, a tall, skinny, bookishly pretty, and very sweet black girl with an elegantly elongated neck. Then there was Noah's equally poignant, equally hopeless crush on Daisy, a willowy, ethereal wrist cutter several years his senior.

In addition to its sister homes, Winchester House boasted a brother house in Clampett, a group home that catered to African-Americans, Hispanics, and other non-crackers. The house was lorded over by a striking middle-aged African-American woman who looked like a young Eartha Kitt, with all the sexiness, scariness, and sexy-scariness that that entails. She perversely had the macho, painfully image-conscious teenagers in her charge paint the walls of Clampett a garish shade of pink. I can't imagine which was more embarrassing: living in a pink house or living with the knowledge that you were indirectly responsible for such a girly eyesore.

If my Winchester House brethren were like perpetually squabbling stepsiblings, the Clampett House boys were more like cousins you see a couple of times a month. We went on trips together, most notably camping expeditions to Lawrence, Michigan, or Galena, Illinois, played together in the big inter-group-home softball and volleyball leagues, and experienced the magic of group therapy together.

My favorite among the Clampett boys was Maurice, a tall, good-looking African-American jock who, in a moment of Yogi Berra–like profundity, once groused, "Man, I hate living in America. When I grow up, I'm moving to California."

But it was with my Winchester housemates, especially my roommates, that I formed the strongest, weirdest, most unlikely bonds. Luke and I had almost nothing in common. But one ridiculous summer we'd get dolled up in the finest threads our modest clothing allowances would permit and head over to Indian Boundary Park under the laughable delusion that we were cruising for chicks. Every afternoon I'd put on an Ocean Pacific bathing suit and an Ocean Pacific jacket with no shirt underneath (I have no idea what made me think I could pull off the no-shirt look) and slick back my hair with pink mousse the slippery consistency of ectoplasm. Then Luke and I would head to Indian Boundary Park, lounge next to a miniature zoo that marked the last stop for its inhabitants before the slaughterhouse or hot dog factory, and chillax in a manner we inexplicably imagined honeys would find irresistible.

During our summer of getting no love, Luke became enraptured by Missy, a tawdry temptress in a purple Hornets starter's jacket, a resplendent vision of white-trash loveliness with a bleached blonde perm and gum-smacking attitude to match. Luke felt he lacked the eloquence to adequately convey the profundity of his affection for this lissome stranger, so he asked me to play Cyrano and ghostwrite a love letter to his would-be paramour.

I acquiesced and, in a characteristic fit of maturity, we rolled up our love letter into a tight little ball and hurled it in the general direction of what we quixotically hoped would soon be Luke's new girlfriend, then boldly ran away once she safely retrieved it.

In retrospect I probably should have included something in the letter to indicate that it was coming from the creepy blond white-trash dude with the pubic-hair child-molester mustache and not from me: three years later, I had the misfortune of having a locker directly next to Missy's thuggish boyfriend Syed.

Missy sent icy glares in my direction throughout high school but it somehow never occurred to me that she labored under the misconception that the love letter she received at Indian Boundary Park came from me rather than Luke. Then one late afternoon before the first night of Passover, Syed and his posse of brooding ne'er-do-wells accosted me outside a baseball card shop.

"Hey, asshole, you wanna fuck my girlfriend, huh? You in love with her? You gotta write her a fucking love letter?" Syed sneered as he and his gang started pummeling me with their fists.

I pleaded ignorance but by that time they'd knocked me to the ground and were taking turns kicking me. I tried to explain to Syed that it was all just a big misunderstanding. But it's prohibitively difficult to reason with someone who's kicking your head against a fire hydrant.

Late in the beat-down one of the hoods tried to add a little larceny to their assault and battery by rifling through my clothes for money but thankfully missed the two hundred dollars I had rolled up in the inside pocket of my leather bomber jacket.

That's the great thing about bullies: they're mean and nasty and impervious to reason but they're also, for the most part, really fucking stupid. That's one of God's great consolation gifts to us Poindexters.

At school the next day the meekest member of Syed's crew took me aside and, in a voice quaking with nervousness, sputtered, "You're not mad about yesterday, are you? You know we were just kidding, don't you?"

Now, I like to think I have a very dark sense of humor, but I've never endured a beating I found amusing. I've never found myself reflecting, "I sure didn't feel that way at the time but in hindsight that hilarious prank my peers played where they kicked me in the face repeatedly was quite droll. The horrific cranial swelling I experienced afterward was a particularly wry touch."

When I told my old boss Stephen Thompson that anecdote, he observed, "That's the problem with all your stories, Nathan: they begin really cute and end with you getting viciously beaten."

That wasn't the only time someone tried to pass off a brutal beating as a harmless practical joke. Junior year I had a particularly hapless geometry teacher who spoke to us in baby talk and was biding his time until he made it through grad school and could teach real students. During class one day an Irish kid named Tom who I considered a friend decided it'd be hilarious to tell people it was my birthday.

"Hey, everybody, it's Nathan's birthday. Free licks on the birthday boy!" were his exact words. It wasn't even my birthday but my classmates nevertheless decided they had a perfect opportunity to punch me really hard for each year I'd been born, a dark tradition at my school and many others. Once again a whirlwind of flying fists descended upon me in a furious eight-on-one onslaught. After several minutes of indifference Mr. Lee eventually asked my tormentors to stop, but not before I had purple-black welts all over my arms, neck, and torso and my head felt like a lead balloon.

The next day at school Tom nervously tried to explain that my beating was, in fact, a harmless practical joke gone awry. I couldn't really be mad at Tom, who was fundamentally a good guy. I can't say the same of Mr. Lee. Years later I ran into him at a 7-Eleven and he "encouraged" me to attend a Bible-study group with him. While he enthused on the glory of learning the Good News together, I couldn't help but think, "Hey, you know when I really needed Jesus? When I was being viciously beaten during your class and you were standing there doing nothing, you baby-talking, condescending, hypocritical piece of shit. Also, I'm Jewish, so fuck you two times with a tractor rape chain and die a slow, agonizing death, motherfucker." I am a big believer in the power of forgiveness, in letting go and moving on. But not with Mr. Lee. Fuck that guy.

You never knew where the day would take you that first year at Winchester House. You might end up locked in a car for an hour in the South Side while a none-too-reputable staffer handled his business at a pawn shop, or you might end up whiling away a giddy night playing the Teenage Mutant Ninja Turtles video games alongside black Muslims clad entirely in white.

At Winchester House I learned to work the angles. Countless afternoons spent watching *Yo! MTV Raps* and listening to Chicago's all-hip-hop station had imbued me with an innate respect for the art of the hustle.

I made the most of the meager crumbs thrown my way. During the waning days of my disastrous freshman year I was sent off to Mather every day with an unthinkable bounty of four dollars and twenty-five cents. To me this was a small fortune. My daily windfall was explicitly earmarked for bus rides to and from school, at a buck-fifty apiece, with a dollar thrown in for school lunch and twenty-five cents for milk.

I furtively chortled with glee every time I received my daily scratch. What fools the JCB were! In what universe did they expect me to pay the princely sum of three dollars just to avoid walking a mile and a half to and from school? For that matter, why did they expect me to go to class? Or eat the swill the lunch ladies dished out? Or drink this distasteful "milk" product?

So instead of taking the bus to school, I'd walk to a convenience store about a block away from Mather where an oil painting of a fierce-looking mullah glared down at a motley aggregation of truants playing hooky. The store's primary attraction was a back room where snarling hoods gathered to play video games like *Double Dragon, Shinobi, The Simpsons, Wrestlemania, Altered Beast,* and *Ninja Gaiden.* It was a strange ecosystem unto itself, complete with its own rituals and codes of conduct. Placing a quarter on the left-hand corner of the screen, for example, ensured that you were next in line to play said game.

The cry of "Lemme get a quarter" was a ubiquitous mantra among young toughs with a serious video game jones but insufficient funds to scratch that itch. When uttered menacingly, the phrase took on a threatening quality: "Lemme get a quarter. Or else." But when uttered softly, it took on a desperate, even pleading edge, as if to say, "If you can find it in your heart, dear sir, I would very much appreciate you lending me a quarter so that I might play this video game I'm terribly fixated on."

The convenience store proprietors fed our low-level criminality out of financial necessity: if they were to eject every truant waging video game war during school hours, their customer base would shrink to nothing. Besides, I never saw a nondelinquent frequent the store. There was the occasional can of questionable-looking soup or beans on display, but I always assumed they were there for purely decorative reasons. Nevertheless, every once in a while the cops were called to eject a particularly rowdy or disagreeable patron and us ne'er-do-wells would scatter like cockroaches under a bright light.

The convenience store/truant heaven was a grim, unwelcoming sphere where lost boys sneered at each other rather than attempt small talk, but I was hopelessly drawn to it all the same. For at the nasty-ass convenience store my four dollars and twenty-five cents allowed me to live like a king, albeit a monarch with perversely downscale tastes. For that generous allotment I could play eight video games, buy my daily copy of both the *Sun-Times* and *Chicago Tribune,* and still have enough money left over for two cans of Mountain Dew and a bag of Cheetos, essentials that satisfied my daily requirement of highly caffeinated beverages and fluorescent-orange foodstuffs.

At Winchester House my relationship with my dad entered a new phase. Long gone were those dark days when I vowed to excise him from my life completely. I'd never forgiven my father for not living up to the image I had of him growing up. But at Winchester House I was able to accept him for who he was: an imperfect but big-hearted man doing his best with the bum hand life had dealt him.

Before we moved to Chicago my father worried about losing his shaky foothold in the neurotic middle class. He worried that his wife would leave him. He worried that he wouldn't be able to provide for his children. He worried that he'd never be able to find another steady job after leaving the comforting, deadening womb of government bureaucracy. He worried about losing his station in life. He worried about car payments and insurance and making ends meet.

Then my father's second wife left him, he tumbled down the socioeconomic ladder, his brakeless car was towed by the city, he gave himself over to permanent unemployment, and his children became someone else's responsibility. A lot of people would have crumbled under the crushing weight of such an unfortunate series of events. I would have. But my dad was made of sterner stuff. Something exceedingly strange and unexpected happened inside him as his world fell apart: he got happy. More than that, he achieved a Zen state of contentment.

Everything he'd worried about had come to pass and he was still standing. Furthermore, he was liberated from any responsibility beyond finding ways to occupy himself in lieu of work and familial obligations. If freedom's just another word for nothing left to lose, then my father was the freest creature on God's green earth.

My father became a connoisseur of life's simple pleasures. Buying a shirt with a designer label at a thrift store or riding in one of his brothers' cars gave him profound joy. In Madison, years later, he began to rhapsodize about the water my sister brought him. "Oh, this water, it's so good. It's so crisp and clean and refreshing and delicious. Thank you. Thank you."

My sister and I looked at each other and, without saying a word, broke out in laughter. Our dad, the Zen master of Rogers Park, had done the impossible: he'd found sensual rapture in a humble glass of tap water. The Dalai Lama would have been proud.

My dad entered a second childhood. He began attending groups for manic depression despite not being bipolar himself. He reembraced Judaism and listened to self-help tapes and lectures from snake-oil salesmen masquerading as inspirational speakers. He developed a new set of friends so destitute he couldn't help but look like a Bill Cosby–like exemplar of wealth and stability by comparison. He learned to play what he lovingly calls "the Crip Card" to secure kick-ass seats and cheap tickets and taxi vouchers and all sorts of goodies available only to the fun loving and downtrodden. My father is prominently involved in philanthropy: he just happens to be on the receiving end of it.

My father took to poverty and unemployment with shocking ease. He found a second home of sorts in Ezra, an establishment that can charitably/inaccurately be called an exclusive dining club for the moneyed elite and less charitably called a soup-kitcheny-type deal.

Years later I lived in a yuppie apartment complex with one of those built-in junk-mail receptacles under the mail slots when I made a joyous discovery: seven or eight of my neighbors had mistaken a mailing containing a coupon for a free burrito at a new Chipotle franchise for junk mail and haphazardly tossed them in the junk-mail receptacle.

With visions of burrito gold dancing madly in my fevered imagination, I greedily scooped up the coupons, then headed to the other mailboxes in my apartment complex and collected Chipotle mailers until I possessed well over a hundred dollars' worth of burrito coupons.

If I were capable of human emotions, tears of joy would have been streaming down my face. You know that feeling you experience upon witnessing the birth of your first child? It was like that, only a thousand times better, because free burritos were involved.

I immediately thought of my father and the deep reverence for free shit he'd imbued in me. Feeling wistful and proud, I was convinced that my father would officially be the burrito pimp of the soup kitchen once I gave him my overflowing bounty of Chipotle coupons. People at Ezra already thought my dad was the coolest motherfucker on the planet. Once he began sharing his free burrito stash, his peers would begin worshipping him as a god. I was right. You might think the apex of my relationship with my father came when I professed my love for him on national television or dedicated this book to him. No, the high-water mark of my relationship with my dad came when I proudly presented him with twenty-three Chipotle free burrito coupons.

The good people of Ezra were similarly overwhelmed by my Chipotle bounty. To them I am the miracle man with a fistful of free burrito coupons first and an author, critic, blogger, and failed basic-cable television personality a distant second.

When I moved into Winchester House my old man stopped symbolizing all my shattered dreams and thwarted ambition and became more like a fun uncle. He became a reluctant coconspirator in my exciting adventures in truancy. On the rare days I didn't skulk around the convenience store, I'd head over to Dad's place to watch television or read the newspaper, confident that he'd write me up a note excusing my absence from class. In his mind it made sense. I might not have been "going to school" or "passing my classes" or "trying" but I was doing something far more important: spending time with dear old Pa.

Our relationship took on a level of informality that bordered on perverse. For a year or so I addressed my father exclusively as "Shorty the Pimp." Why? Because I could. Then again, when I was a neurotic little kid, my dad used to admonish me to "duck down" whenever we heard a police siren because the fuzz were after me, so maybe it was just a tardy form of black-comic revenge. In a similarly bizarre adolescent linguistic quirk I adopted "Stay black!" as my default parting line to any and all non-African-Americans. The unexpected upside to living in a group home for emotionally disturbed adolescents is that nobody looks at you askance when you behave in an emotionally disturbed manner.

If my dad compared himself to his fellow University of Chicago graduates, it'd be easy to feel like a failure. But since his new social circle prominently featured people who lived in cardboard boxes and nursed strong, frequently aired suspicions that the CIA was stealing their thoughts, he felt pretty damn good about himself and his station in life.

My dad's guilt over not being able to take care of me was assuaged by his unshakable, if delusional, belief that living in Winchester House afforded me a quality of life rivaled only by the jet-set lifestyles of the Kennedys and Rockefellers. My father had a hard time wrapping his mind around Winchester House's unthinkable luxuries. Imagine, three meals a day! Made from nongeneric ingredients! With side dishes even! And beverages! Several kinds of beverages! And enough air conditioners to comfortably cool the entire house! And color television! With cable! And a Nintendo! And vacations!

But nothing impressed Dad more than the fact we got a seventy-dollar seasonal clothing allowance. That blew his mind. Imagine, his very own son wearing clothes without holes in them! New clothes even! That hadn't even been donated to charity or worn extensively by people in the seventies! For seventy dollars a season my father believed I could afford to fly all the finest tailors from Savile Row to Chicago to personally craft an outsized wardrobe for me made out of the finest satins and silks.

At Winchester House, our humble furnishings represented the ghosts of tax write-offs past. The crown jewel of our library was a semicomplete set of Nixon-era encyclopedias the end of the Cold War rendered wildly inaccurate. Someone was kind enough to donate an arcade-ready stand-up video game that would have been inconceivably awesome if only it worked. I was no longer in free fall but only because I'd sunk to the bottom.

It took the arrival of a strangely charismatic ex-life-insurance-salesman named Herschel to end the anarchy and aimlessness of my Holden Caulfield period. But after an auspicious beginning Herschel's reign would end in madness and disorder as well.

The Blood-Splattered Punchline

In Utero
The Prepubescent Trickster God of Rogers Park

By the early nineties rock music had famously devolved to an unprecedented level of suckitude. But with a few power chords purloined from the Pixies, an ulcer-ridden loner from Seattle named Kurt Cobain single-handedly made rock feel raw and real and relevant all over again. Misfits and outsiders around the world felt as if Cobain was channeling their rage with every guttural scream and cryptic lyric.

We at Winchester House embraced Cobain as a kindred spirit. Cobain was the perfect spokesman for a generation that expressed itself with upturned middle fingers rather than peace signs and was deeply suspicious, if not downright contemptuous, of the idea that writing great rock songs entitled a man to speak for his entire g-g-generation. Like Bob Dylan before him, Cobain wore the title of generational spokesman like a crown of thorns, an unbearable, unwanted, and ultimately fatal burden.

He was the boy with the thorn in his side. Behind the hatred there lie a murderous desire for love. On the surface his lyrics were oblique to the point of meaninglessness. But it's not what Cobain sang so much as how he sang it that mattered. Cobain articulated what it was like to be angry and sad and scared and lonely and desperate and vulnerable and defiant all at the same time. He was an icon with a direct line to everybody's wounded inner child. He was a seething, squirming mass of violent contradictions. He played macho, ballsy hard rock while wearing a dress. He was a pop star who loathed the concept of pop stardom, a feminist whose music was coopted by frat-boy misogynists.

Cobain's lyrics hid behind layers of irony, sarcasm, and obfuscation yet seemed ripped from the innermost recesses of his soul. His quiet songs were exquisite sighs of world-weary resignation. His loud songs were apocalyptic howls of rage. Like all self-disrespecting Gen-Xers, including the inhabitants of Winchester House, that rage was directed largely toward himself.

At Winchester House everybody loved Kurt Cobain but nobody identified with him more than Noah. In every facet of his life Noah was uncompromising, an interpersonal Dadaist locked in perpetual combat with the world around him.

Where I pragmatically used humor to win friends, Noah used humor as a weapon in his lifelong quest to alienate people. The whole point of his comedy, and his existence, was to angry up the blood. His idea of a knock-knock joke, for example, went:

NOAH: Knock, knock.
ME: Who's there?
NOAH: It's me, the rapist. I've come to rape you.

So you can imagine how delighted Noah was when he discovered a song called "Rape Me" on *In Utero*, Nirvana's incendiary, uncompromising follow-up to *Nevermind*. *In Utero* was seemingly designed to lose the millions of mallrats and teenyboppers who flocked to Nirvana after *Nevermind* by making an album so extreme, bleak, and uncompromising, it'd scare all but the hardiest souls away. It was a massive commercial suicide attempt that of course made Noah love Nirvana even more. It was an album with lyrics like "I wish I could eat your cancer when you turn black." And that was from the single.

At the group home we stitched together a homemade vernacular out of bits and pieces appropriated from songs we liked, whether it was Beck sarcastically drawling "I'm a loser, baby, so why don't you kill me?" or Cobain screeching "Rape me!" or Henry Rollins accusingly screaming "Liaaaaaar!" or Snoop Dogg insisting he "don't luuuuhvvv deez hos." Whenever Noah smoked pot he would run around with a crazed look in his eyes and, quoting Onyx in "Slam," scream, "Oh my God I'm so high," before insisting that never in his entire misbegotten existence had he ever been as high as he was at that very moment. Until the next time he got high.

We Winchester House boys were ferociously verbal. Not intelligently verbal or even coherently verbal, mind you, but ferociously verbal all the same. If someone said something stupid, their verbal blunder was entered into a collective memory bank, never to be forgotten or forgiven. Since we were teenage boys we were constantly saying incredibly stupid shit.

Edgar, for example, was a peerless mangler of the English language. Sometimes he'd merely insert phantom letters where they didn't exist. One-handed pitcher Jim Abbott became "Jim Albott," while legendary fastballer Nolan Ryan morphed into the whimsical "Nome Ryan" (or would it be "Gnome Ryan"?). If you were concerned that you might have overestimated your abilities, Edgar would say you were "doubting your overconfidence." If you were nervous, Edgar would say you were feeling "yanxious."

Now, I don't want to suggest that the people I grew up with were feral subliterates. But the people I grew up with were feral subliterates. For all his semantic playfulness, Noah was frequently subverbal. In his never-ending bid to enrage the universe, he'd repeat a series of nonsense noises in various combinations until he reached that magical combination of sounds that threw whoever he was antagonizing into a murderous rage. He wasn't content until people wanted to wring his skinny little neck. He was forever searching for that semantic G-spot that would trigger the maximum level of irritation.

That was the process by which I received the nickname "NOY." Like a mad scientist of annoyance, he experimented with endless variations ("NIE," "NEE," "NOO," "NOY," "NIE," "NOY," "NOY") until I couldn't take it anymore and exploded with anger. Then he knew he had a winner. Others were even less fortunate.

"Pee Stains" was the undying nickname for Dwight, perhaps the saddest character ever to darken Winchester House's hallowed halls, a bed-wetting, bucktoothed, retainer-chomping eleven-year-old with a high-pitched, spastic, easily enraged girly voice and Bill Laimbeer–style goggles that served as a visual exclamation point to his overbearing geekiness. Pee Stains had a deliciously short temper that made him a perfect victim for Noah.

Noah boasted a tricked-out arsenal of weapons of mass irritation. Simply calling Dwight Pee Stains was enough to enrage him. But there was also Noah's oft-threatened but never-employed threat of an "all-night scare," a dark night of the soul where Noah would wake Dwight up at random intervals to terrify the living bejesus out of him. Noah derived an unseemly pleasure from winding Dwight up and watching him go. So did the rest of us.

My most treasured memory of Dwight happened at the gym of the Jewish Children's Bureau therapeutic school. We were playing something that vaguely resembled basketball and Dwight stopped dribbling and cocked back his arm and hurled the basketball with one hand as if it were a javelin. Having a good foot and a half on Dwight, I calmly intercepted the ball on its lazy, meandering flight to the basket and swatted it hard against the wall.

"Boo ya! Get that bullshit out of here! Shaq-Fu, bitch!" I taunted belligerently. In those days if you made an impressive offensive play you'd yell "Jordan!" If you made a primo defensive play you'd yell out something Shaquille O'Neal–inspired. Dwight spazzed the fuck out. He wound up his skinny little arms and legs like a cartoon character and ran away sobbing and yelling, "Oooh, I hate you, Nathan! You big meanie!" I am not proud of the way I treated Dwight.

Now, if this were a Mitch Albom heart-tugger, Dwight's geeky, easily mocked exterior would hide a noble soul and a treasure trove of hidden wisdom. We'd bond slowly but surely as he taught me invaluable life lessons about never judging a book by its cover. Then someone would die and the cash registers inside my opportunistic mind would begin ch-chinging joyfully. But it's not that kind of book. If anything, beneath Dwight's geeky, easily mocked exterior lay an even geekier, even more easily mocked interior. At Winchester House no life lessons were ever taught or learned. The noble business of uplifting the human spirit lagged far behind the pragmatic necessity of surviving adolescence with your sanity relatively intact. We collectively earned zero points toward sainthood.

For all his bluster and bad behavior there was something fundamentally boyish about Noah's antics. He was a mutant Huckleberry Finn, Bugs Bunny rendered flesh and blood, a prepubescent trickster god. His shenanigans were irritating but harmless, goofy bits of boyish bluster, all-night scares, and slapstick chases around the house.

Noah lingered far too long at the humping-random-things stage of his sexual development. Walls, stuffed animals, horrified roommates: no one and nothing was safe from Noah's unwanted sexual advances, although to be fair, Winchester House's walls shamelessly led Noah on with their whorish, fading coats of white paint and come-hither cracks.

The only creatures safe from Noah's raging, incoherent sexuality were girls his own age. Noah feared no one except, you know, girls. Noah's sexuality, like his gleeful promise of an "all-night scare," ultimately constituted an empty threat. So perhaps it's not surprising that when a genuine sexual transgressive entered our humble home, Noah was unhealthily obsessed with him.

The outlaw in question was a skinny, fine-featured fourteen-year-old black kid with an enigmatic personality and a sardonic sense of humor. His name was, well, let's just call him Ezekiel (note: that is not his real name). One surreal afternoon the staff at Winchester sat us down and gravely explained that Ezekiel had done something unspeakably awful, criminal, and unforgivable to his housemate Gilbert, who was like Edgar in miniature, right down to his Coke-bottle glasses and gangly awkwardness. Gilbert was the one human being in the universe to whom Edgar could safely feel superior. Gilbert idolized Edgar. So of course Edgar treated him with contempt. Such is the way of the world.

As a result of his heinous crime Ezekiel now faced the ultimate punishment: he was cruelly and unusually being forced to live with us before being shuttled off to juvenile detention, or kiddie jail.

I know that I am destined to roast in hellfire for eternity, because upon hearing this, my first reaction was "Gilbert? Really? Wow. He could have molested better." Ezekiel was definitely molesting below his station. We were understandably not told the precise nature of Ezekiel's crime. They didn't even act it out for us with anatomically correct dolls like they do in Lifetime TV movies. We were just told that Ezekiel was the scum of the earth and we'd suddenly be spending a whole lot more time together. Then he'd disappear and we'd never see him ever again.

Noah and Ezekiel got along famously. They shared a secret language of cryptic looks and sly half smiles, a nonverbal vocabulary designed to frustrate anyone who tried to invade their private universe. They were like creepy identical twins who communicate telepathically. I was a little jealous of Ezekiel's bond with Noah. I was supposed to be the one Noah had a weird, unquantifiable connection with, dammit. But how could I compete with Ezekiel and his "unforgivable crime" and "one-way trip to juvenile detention" and "pedophilia"?

For two very strange weeks Noah and Ezekiel were salt-and-pepper brothers from other mothers, psychic twins pumping out double-barreled mischief and shenanigans. Then he was gone.

Noah was an anarchist by personality and inclination. He considered it his duty to create chaos everywhere he went, to afflict the comfortable and then afflict the afflicted as well. He didn't discrimihate.

There I'd sit in the Winchester House living room, innocently trying to masturbate to the grinding, spandex-clad posteriors and gyrating cleavage of *Club MTV,* when out of nowhere Noah would haphazardly chuck an encyclopedia in the general vicinity of my head. Or, if Ezekiel was there, they'd take turns chucking encyclopedias at my head, then running away. There was no rhyme or reason to it. Cause and effect may be conjoined twins everywhere else but they were strangers where Noah was concerned. His moods and motivations defied explanation and shifted without notice or warning. Being friends with Noah in the morning was no guarantee that he wouldn't hate you several hours later.

Noah was a man with a message. Unfortunately that message was "Fuck you, authority figure! You're not the boss of me." Noah often acted as if he was put on Earth solely to bedevil me. I was masochistic enough to consider that a worthy goal.

Noah symbolized freedom. He was the little voice inside everyone that wants to scream, "No!" when faced with life's billion dispiriting compromises. "No!" was the only tool he had, but when spoken loud enough, that "No!" became empowering and even righteous.

When Noah learned of Kurt Cobain's suicide he threw a makeshift vigil for him. He laid out all of his Nirvana CDs and magazine covers and photos and lit candles. We sat there listening to Nirvana music in uncharacteristic silence. It was as if a part of us had died along with Cobain. Like Cobain's ascension to superstardom, there was something strangely inevitable about his suicide. He'd been trying to kill himself since he tumbled out of the womb. He even wrote a song called "I Hate Myself and Want to Die," an unlistenable dirge I'd nominated for prom theme at my high school. It wasn't chosen. Oh well, I didn't go to my prom anyway. I did go to the special ed prom, but that's another story entirely.

The day Cobain died I pledged to Noah that if Dave Grohl ever started a band I'd come back to Winchester House and take him to see it. A year later I took Noah to see the Foo Fighters play the Riviera behind their first album. It felt good to be able to make good on my promise.

Noah, meanwhile, promised to throw a gang party at my dad's apartment. I didn't take Noah's threat/vow seriously. He was a determined little bugger but there were limits even to his dark powers. Then one night my college girlfriend and I returned to my dad's apartment after an Ani DiFranco concert and I was horrified and more than a little amused to find that Noah, Edgar, and at least a dozen surly no-goodniks had commandeered my dad's garden apartment and were sulking about, drinking cheap beer and smoking cigarettes.

"Hey, Nathan, your friend Noah came by with some of his friends and they're hanging out," my father offered cheerfully. I had to hand it to Noah: he said he was going to throw a gang party at my dad's apartment and now there he was, presiding over a gang party at my dad's apartment.

"Ohmygod, Nathan. I have no idea who half these people are. I'm scared," Noah told me in panicked tones. It was hard to tell whether he was being sincere or if it was just another bit of gonzo performance art. Noah was a living, breathing, one-man theater of the absurd. As he frantically tried to contain the madness, Noah became the sorcerer's apprentice, desperately trying to control the black magic he'd unleashed. The next thing I heard was Edgar screaming. I ran over to see blood spurting out of Edgar's head and onto the walls and floor of my dad's apartment.

Edgar had pissed off the wrong hooligan. The young ne'er-do-well registered his dissatisfaction with Edgar's antics by smashing a beer bottle over his head. Finally my father had had enough. "Out, out! Everybody out!" Pa yelled indignantly. Edgar and Noah offered to clean up the blood but my father ushered them out angrily. As I washed the blood from my dad's floor I couldn't help but admire Noah's audacity.

These dual final memories of Noah epitomized our strange relationship. I tried to do nice things for him. In return he subjected me to a never-ending gauntlet of bizarre, inexplicable, yet really creative abuse. It was as if Noah was punishing me and himself and everyone else for crimes that existed only in his imagination.

That's the kind of guy Noah was. He was the singular breed of lunatic who could conceive and execute a gag whose punchline could only be written in blood on my dad's wall.

A couple of months ago I was wandering through a Best Buy when I heard a hauntingly familiar sound. I wandered over to a flat-screen TV where a black teenager lay on a beanbag chair with the simultaneously bored and intense look endemic to video game aficionados. A do-rag covered his head. His legs sprawled out lazily from his beanbag chair. The game was *Guitar Hero*. The song was "Heart-Shaped Box." As the virtual guitar god mashed the buttons, his face betrayed no emotion. His toes didn't tap. His head didn't nod. At no point did he throw up the devil's horns to indicate that Nirvana, or at least a cheap soundalike, was pleasing Satan with its rock. The music seemed to mean nothing to him. A razor-blade howl of anguish from a man murderously in love and hate with his wife was reduced to background music for a video game.

It's easy to rail against the commodification of art. But the music business has never been pure. It's been corrupt since the first caveman beat out a primal rhythm on a rock with his club and the first caveman agent figured out a way to screw him over. But there will always be idealistic souls who try to conduct themselves with integrity in a business dominated by liars, con men, and thieves.

I imagine that when Kurt Cobain stared down oblivion, the future he'd never experience sprawled out in front of him. In that final moment of clarity he could see "Heart-Shaped Box" becoming background music for video games, a Nirvana-scored "rock opera" episode of *Cold Case,* and "Smells Like Teen Spirit" becoming fodder for karaoke game shows. In that final moment he could see all too clearly an era where rock stars talk about "diversifying their brand," "synergy," and "maximizing ancillary revenue streams" without shame, where Kurt Vonnegut could shill for American Express and Elvis Costello could wax rhapsodic about the genius of Beethoven in a Lexus commercial without being branded corporate whores. He could foresee a world where selling out is only considered heresy if the sellout fails to secure a good price for their soul.

Cobain raged against the commodification of his art in ways that only underlined his powerlessness. He famously wore a "Corporate Magazines Still Suck" T-shirt on the cover of *Rolling Stone,* the granddaddy of corporate rock magazine suckitude. It was an act of sublimely passive-aggressive subversion at once pointed and pointless. It's hard to rage effectively against the machine when you're caught up in its gears.

Cobain killed himself so he'd never again have to be complicit in the exploitation of his music. He pulled the trigger so that he'd never have to unsteadily rest his electric guitar on a fat, bloated belly and gush about how perfectly goddamned delightful it was to have Volkswagen on board as the official automotive sponsor of the twentieth-anniversary *Nevermind* stadium tour (coming to an auditorium near you in 2011!).

He robbed his wife of a husband and his daughter of a father so that he'd never have to face Barbara Walters's Vaseline-smeared lens and tearfully recount how Scientology or born-again Christianity allowed him to finally overcome a lifetime of drug addiction and self-hatred. He pulled the trigger so that he'd never experience the joy of performing before yuppies texting their friends and holding up their camera phones to document the moment for posterity. He died a martyr. He died a hero. He died a coward.

A month or so after my trip to Best Buy, I got an e-mail from Noah via MySpace. It was friendly in the slightly strained, awkward way e-mails from long-lost friends often are. Noah was living in Utah and working in retail.

I've thought about Noah often since I left the group home. Yet the prospect of a twenty-seven-year-old Noah who worked in retail was unbelievably depressing. When you're a trickster god at eleven there's nowhere to go but down.

I don't want to imagine a twenty-seven-year-old Noah for the same reason I don't want to contemplate a fifty-year-old Kurt Cobain. Like Holden Caulfield and J. D. Salinger, I want them to exist in a state of perfect adolescent rebellion, frozen in time in the moment before the world had its wicked way with them. Sooner or later everyone breaks down and accepts the compromises of adulthood. It's inevitable. In my memory Kurt Cobain and Noah are eternally larger than life. But the world has a way of shrinking everyone down to size.

Kurt Cobain will have his revenge on Seattle. He'll come back as fire and burn all the liars and leave a blanket of ash on the ground. As for Noah, well, perhaps it's best that I leave him fleeing the blood-splattered walls of my dad's garden apartment following his greatest, most pointless triumph, his magnum opus of meaningless, Dadaistic cosmic destruction. It somehow just seems right.

Lukewarm Crawlspace Vermouth

The Chronic
The Group Home

NWA laid the foundation for the mainstreaming of gangsta rap, but Death Row Records took the genre to nihilistic extremes. The label's logo—a hooded man strapped into an electric chair—said it all. These motherfuckers were dangerous. They were going to hell and taking everyone with them.

Death Row's albums trafficked in fantasies of power and freedom that struck a chord in white teenagers oppressed less by cops and the prison-industrial complex than by the everyday tyranny of teachers and parents. On wax at least, the studio gangstas of Death Row could do anything: shoot motherfuckers, smoke a pound of weed a day, guzzle gin and juice, and treat women abhorrently. Even more exhilaratingly, they could do anything and never suffer any negative consequences. The denizens of Death Row were worshipped for the very qualities that made us group home kids outcasts: our contempt for authority, our profanity, our nihilism and misplaced aggression, and above all, our undying contempt for the white man.

Albums like Dr. Dre's *The Chronic,* Snoop Doggy Dogg's *Doggystyle,* and NWA's *Straight Outta Compton* and *Efil4zaggin* did more than just blatantly glorify criminality. They gave an entire generation of white teens invaluable, poisonous lessons in manhood. Chief among the philosophical tenets espoused by West Coast gangsta rap philosophers was the innate duplicity of women.

Songs like "Ain't No Fun" tore down in four misogyny-filled minutes what it took romantic poets centuries to create. Teenage boys as a genus live in mortal fear of teenage girls. Gangsta rap taught us that the worst thing any man could do was to fall in love with a woman. A woman you love can break your heart. A woman you love can make you want to die. A woman you love can turn your world upside down. But if gangsta rap teaches us anything, it's that a bitch ain't nothing but a bitch and a ho ain't nothing but a ho. *The Chronic* preaches that bitches ain't shit but hos and tricks. Kurupt extrapolated on this point when he legendarily reasoned, "If Kurupt gave a fuck about a bitch I'd always be broke. I'd never have no motherfucking endo to smoke."

I took these words to heart. I didn't know what endo was but I feared that if I were to give a fuck about a bitch, I too would "always be broke" and never have no motherfucking endo to smoke. Just as previous generations of black musicians adopted royal monikers like count, king, and duke to compensate for being treated like second-class citizens on the road, rappers depict themselves as all-powerful gods to compensate for growing up feeling poor, powerless, and anonymous. The misogyny and criminality endemic to gangsta rap is a reflection of weakness and insecurity rather than strength.

At Winchester House my roommate David—who smoked weed, had a pager and cell phone (which he invariably answered with a barely comprehensible "Jee-yuh. Whodis?") back when that meant something, wore low-slung jeans with enough fabric to clothe a small island nation, and spoke fluent Ebonics despite being a chubby asthmatic Jew—and I would listen to *Efil4zaggin* and *The Chronic* furtively after lights-out, grooving hard on their transgressive cartoon fantasies of power, violence, and sex. David at least came upon his Wafrican-American affectations honestly: until he ended up doin' time at Winchester he lived on the South Side and went to Kenwood Academy, a predominantly black high school where R. Kelly, Da Brat, Chaka Khan, and, uh, OG Mandy Patinkin all matriculated.

There was a subtle but unmistakable class system at Winchester House. David, Noah, and I were all private placements. Our social workers had sensed an ill wind blowing in our family lives and placed us in the safe confines of what my father likes to call Winchester Preparatory Academy for Boys. We were the children of college graduates, refugees from middle-class existences gone awry, the collateral damage of exploding nuclear families and bitter divorces where custody wasn't an issue since one parent disappeared.

David's dad was a drunken accountant. I never quite mustered the courage to ask what happened to his mom. Noah's mom, ironically, was a social worker. Noah never knew his father, which lends further credence to my theory that he is the only begotten son of the devil. I was the son of a University of Chicago graduate. We were smart, angry, Jewish, and alternately blessed and cursed with senses of humor blacker than a landlord's soul.

Luke, Edgar, Pee Stains, and the others were gentile wards of the state from the feral working class, products of the kinds of families that pop up on the media radar only if they're willing to hurl chairs at each other while screaming profanities. Where we private-placement kids were ineffably haunted by our middle-class memories, the wards of the state had never known anything better than Winchester House and had experienced far worse.

You might expect that the wards of the state would be the troublemakers. Instead it was the private-placement kids who seethed with hostility. Like most Americans, we labored under the delusion that we were owed a solid middle-class existence and burned with anger at having it pulled out from under us.

Even more than the rest of us, David was a powder keg of barely suppressed rage. I once made the mistake of saying something incorrigibly smartass to him and without saying a word, he punched me hard in the stomach. As I struggled to catch my breath and refrain from crying, I made a quick mental note never to say anything that might cause David to punch me ever again. Being a sucker for self-preservation, I kept on David's good side. He seemed like someone who'd inevitably end up beating someone to death in a bar fight. I didn't want to be that person.

At Winchester House the music you listened to defined who you were. The music inside my Walkman wasn't just the soundtrack to my life, it was my life. Johnny Rotten's poisonous sarcasm and David Byrne's art-rock weirdness and De La Soul's Daisy Age hippie-hop utopianism were realer to me than the bullshit my teachers were feeding me.

David, with his hip-hop bravado, brute strength, and nihilistic sense of humor, was *Efil4zaggin* and *The Chronic*. Noah, with his genius for absurdism and provocation, embodied Nirvana's *In Utero, Incesticide,* and *Nevermind*. Because we had so little access to music each cassette was treasured disproportionately. Today I probably have five thousand CDs in my collection that collectively don't matter as much to me as my adolescent memories of listening to the Coup's *Genocide and Juice* or A Tribe Called Quest's *Low End Theory* until the tape broke.

Oh good Lord, I'm starting to sound like an old fuddy-duddy: now, back in my day technology was perfected in the form of the cassingle, a marvel of practical science that combined the durability and quality of the cassette tape, a medium that only breaks 30 to 40 percent of the time, with the decadent luxury of being able to listen to an entire three-minute song *and* its instrumental on the B-side. My beloved cassingle of Bruce Hornsby singing "The Old Valley Road" meant infinitely more to me than any iPod stocked with the great canon of Western music.

As a teenager, I lived for all-ages shows at the Metro. It shames me deeply to admit this, but I was an enthusiastic participant in mosh pits throughout the early nineties. There's something liberating about losing your sense of self and disappearing into the writhing mass of hormones and bodies and aggression and joy of the Crowd. At seventeen, I was lonely enough to relish any kind of human contact, even if it was just a random stranger's body pinballing off my own in the mosh pit of a Blur or Oasis or Elastica show. Yes, I was that pathetic.

I became a fan of the breathless hyperbole of British music tabloids *Melody Maker* and *New Musical Express*. There was no middle ground for these venerable hype machines. Every hot new band, whether it was Sleeper or Cast or Ash or Supergrass, was total fucking godhead, an incomparable collection of supergeniuses that made the Beatles look like a third-rate bar band. Everything else was utter shite, downright Stingian in its crimes against music. These magazines fed my bone-deep adolescent superficiality. I dreamed of a future where I'd be the intrepid *NME* reporter doing shots and trading bong hits with skinny white boys who would imminently change the world with their impossibly jangly hooks and tastefully déclassé wardrobes. In none of these rock and roll fantasies did I ever actually play music myself: I was always just the guy with the notebook along for the ride, the kicks, and/or the leftover skanks. Even my aspirations had limitations.

We mutant white boys at Winchester House fell in love with the totality of hip-hop: the anger, the joy, the knee-jerk antiauthoritarianism and bottomless rage, some of it righteous, most of it anything but. Around the same time David started bumping *The Chronic*—an album-length celebration of the powerful strain of marijuana that inspired its title—he and many of my housemates began experimenting with weed.

I, however, refrained from taking secret tokes in the middle of the night for a very mature reason: I thought getting high with guys my age was totally gay. Actually much of my adolescent behavior was motivated by a pathetic desire to avoid looking gay. When I went to the movies with my dad I would leave an empty seat between us so nobody would think I was a gay hustler and my father a crippled trick. The muddled thinking behind this phantom buffer seat of overcompensating heterosexuality went thusly: why would two men sit next to each other except to facilitate sucking each other's cocks more easily?

Turning down weed was another way of distancing myself from my housemates, of preserving the fiction that my presence in a group home was a cosmic fluke and not the product of having run out of options. If *The Chronic* made the deplorable practice of smoking pot look like the apex of outlaw cool, my housemates' cannabis consumption made it seem dangerous and lame. Noah's oft-repeated mantra, "Oh my God I'm so high," was bad enough. But it paled in comparison to watching a wacky tobaccy–addled David puke his lungs out on Mather's front lawn. Out of feigned concern for David's health I dutifully snitched on him to Herschel. Older boys could get kicked out for weed but David got off easy with a few weeks of grounding.

I was no better than Monkey-Faced Snitch Boy or Brian, my mental hospital roommate. If I had a time machine I'd be honor-bound to travel back in time and have El Pollo Loco enact swift vengeance on me for violating the G-code. This time it'd be me getting righteously shived in the yard.

But if I fancied myself too cool, heterosexual, and moral to smoke the demon weed with my Winchester House brothers, I somehow wasn't too cool to purloin ancient half-empty bottles of vermouth from my dad's apartment, stash them in the squirrel-infested crawlspace of Winchester House's second floor, and sneak secret swigs of sickeningly sweet liquor whenever I needed a pick-me-up. Why couldn't Dr. Dre have followed up *The Chronic* with an album titled *Flat, Lukewarm Crawlspace Vermouth*? Then my secret passion would finally have had a little hip-hop credibility.

One of the most insightful things anyone has ever said about rap is that hip-hop is funny but that if you don't see the humor in it, then it's scary. If you take gangsta rap's tales of drug dealing; gleeful, indiscriminate homicide; and virulent misogyny literally it's easy to lapse into a state of Bill O'Reilly–like hysteria (they're coming for our children with their crunk juice and baggy pants and mysterious Negroid ways!), but when has it ever been a good idea to take pop music at face value?

I hate to be the bearer of bad news but Justin Timberlake doesn't really want to rock your body, Johnny Cash never shot a man in Reno just to watch him die, and despite what the lyrics to "Jailhouse Rock" suggest, Elvis never witnessed a homoerotic prison-yard rock and roll freakout. To me gangsta rap was theatrical. It was black comedy. It was role-playing writ large, but it was not, in fact, documentary realism no matter how many rappers mouthed empty bromides about "keeping it real" or speaking truth.

Though I couldn't articulate it at the time, I sensed that Ice Cube and NWA's first-person narratives of drug dealing and guilt-free mass murder had more in common with Jim Thompson writing from the perspective of homicidal, sociopathic lawmen and Vladmir Nabokov channeling the world's most romantic and clever pedophile than the genre's detractors would ever acknowledge.

At the same time the idea that rappers might actually be living the life they talked about in songs gave their music a frisson of excitement and danger. I came of age at a time when the lives and music of many of the most revered rappers became hopelessly blurred. Snoop Dogg would rap about weed and guns in his songs, then Kurt Loder would pop up on television to joylessly drone that Snoop Dogg had just been busted for weed and guns, then Snoop Dogg would shamelessly exploit his run-ins with the law on projects like his "Murder Was the Case" long-playing video.

We responded to the anger in gangsta rap and to its antiauthoritarian extremism. Dr. Dre and NWA taught us to hate not just cops but all authority figures and authority in general. I don't love the holice. To me doctors are just cops with stethoscopes. To kids who grew up feeling poor and alienated, the simmering class resentment that fueled political and gangsta rap was incredibly empowering.

Growing up impoverished and filled with rage wasn't a liability when it came to pursuing a career as an MC: it was a goddamned job prerequisite. Albums like *The Chronic* presented a seductive new kind of Horatio Alger story where getting high and uncorking your anger to a dope beat was enough to propel your meteoric rise from ashy to classy. Though the MCs we idolized were blacker, cooler, and more talented than us, we felt like they were expressing our every tangled, ugly emotion.

We all wanted to be Snoop Dogg when we grew up, but then 2Pac came along and made Snoop look like Pat Boone. What powerless teen doesn't daydream of being, to borrow a particularly resonant 2Pac lyric, "a self-made millionaire, thug-living out of prison, pistols in the air"? Only an evil-hearted Nazi robot, that's who.

Like the inmates of Death Row, we used words as weapons, mainly against each other. And like so many gangsta rappers, we internalized the contempt we felt from mainstream society and perpetually disapproving neighbors who viewed living next door to a group home as only a quick step up from living next door to a crack den. We luxuriated in self-hatred. We had no way of knowing that our heroes on Death Row were, in many ways, just as powerless and impotent as we were. They were fucked by duplicitous record executives, by shitty publishing deals, and by the all-consuming sleaziness of the music business. But at Winchester House we treasured the vicarious fantasies put forth by Snoop, Dre, Daz, Kurupt, 2Pac, Nate Dogg, and everyone else stranded on Death Row with nowhere to go. Nothing kills a top-notch adolescent fantasy quite like a cold, bracing dose of reality.

The House Slave and Nat Turner, or It All Comes Out in the End

Apocalypse Now
The Long, Strange Reign of King Herschel

Francis Ford Coppola famously said that *Apocalypse Now* wasn't just a movie about Vietnam; it was Vietnam— a statement that succinctly captures the genius, madness, ambition, and incredible hubris of Coppola's classic update of Joseph Conrad's *Heart of Darkness*. In Coppola's film Martin Sheen's Captain Benjamin L. Willard must terminate "with extreme prejudice" Marlon Brando's AWOL Colonel Kurtz when Kurtz stops playing soldier and starts playing God.

One of the reasons *Apocalypse Now* remains resonant for multiple generations is that everyone knows someone like Colonel Kurtz, a visionary overachiever who began with only the best of intentions but was gradually, inevitably corrupted by power.

I've known my share of Colonel Kurtzes but the one who made the most indelible impression on me was Herschel Feingold. For three years Herschel was a father, coach, drill sergeant, buddy, therapist, nemesis, and tireless advocate to us Winchester House boys. Then one day he was gone, never to return. That's how it was at Winchester: relationships were intense yet incredibly tenuous.

The wind that blew Herschel into our warped little axis was a tiny help-wanted ad advertising a low-paying full-time position running a therapeutic group home for emotionally disturbed, learning-disabled, and behaviorally disordered boys. The ad made the gig seem comically unappealing. But Herschel pursued it all the same. I suspect Herschel needed us as much as we needed him.

Herschel saw in the Winchester House position an opportunity to redeem a life full of squandered potential and abandoned dreams. Before he took over Winchester House, nothing had quite panned out for Herschel. He went to college but dropped out. He got married, then divorced. He had a daughter he doted on but had to fight to see. He was apparently extraordinarily successful at selling insurance (once a salesman, always a salesman) but hated his job.

Herschel nevertheless radiated cockiness. The world might look at Herschel and see a fat, balding, asthmatic Jew with Coke-bottle glasses and werewolf-like tufts of hair sprouting out of his ears, nose, and neck. But when Herschel looked in the mirror he saw Cary Grant in *To Catch a Thief*.

There was something strangely reassuring about Herschel's cockiness. In this sick, sad, unknowable world, Herschel's cocksure strut implicitly suggested not only that the world is knowable but that he'd mastered it. Herschel was a natural salesman. The product he was invariably selling was himself.

Herschel's reign began as a benevolent dictatorship. But history teaches us that dictatorships seldom stay benevolent. I'm sure Colonel Kurtz was a pleasure to work with in the beginning as well.

After years of chaos Herschel brought a much-needed stability to my life. In my own inimitably crappy, half-assed way I blossomed under his tutelage. Herschel cultivated the image of a man who could get you anything. He was a cross between a genie and the world's most efficient concierge. He was the magic man. He could make anything happen.

One glorious afternoon the entire Winchester House gang drove down south to Burnham, Illinois, along with the sum total of Luke's earthly belongings, to deliver him permanently into the care of his ever-loving mother, who looked disconcertingly like an older, uglier, distaff version of Luke, only with a slightly less pronounced mustache.

More than anything, Luke longed to hunt down his father's killers and execute them with a flurry of awesome karate chops and sweet-ass kung fu moves. Beyond that, however, he longed only to leave his Jew-run prison and be reunited with his mom. Luke got his happy ending. From Luke's descriptions of Burnham, I anticipated a Deep South Neverland populated by mint julep–sipping Southern belles, beefy power brokers who answered to "Big Daddy" and subsisted on sweet tea and deep-fried food-stuffs, and at least a few working plantations, with or without indentured servants. But Burnham was like every other shit town in Illinois.

Luke's departure was bittersweet. I was happy for Luke and touched by his joy at finally going home permanently. But I was also cognizant that happy endings and joyful reunions were rare at Winchester House. I knew I wouldn't be leaving anytime soon.

Luke desperately pined to be reunited with his mother. I nursed less noble ambitions. At fifteen, my life's goal was to someday touch a girl's boob. As a tentative step toward helping me achieve that lofty ambition, Herschel scored me my first date ever, with Winona, the daughter of a woman he was seeing. Winona's mother was a wry character who once counseled me, "Nathan, there are two keys to getting along in the world. First: lower your standards. Second: settle."

On our maiden date, at Second City on New Year's Eve, 1991, my anxieties conducted a fevered symphony of self-loathing inside my fevered brain bone. My terrified heart beat out a crazy bebop rhythm, fast and loose and wild and free. Not to be outdone, my insecurities arrayed themselves into a merry conga line and started chanting, "You're not going to make it / No, you're not going to make it." Concomitantly self-doubt rumba'd merrily while chiming in with a steady, propulsive chorus, "You suck-suck-suck-suck-suck," adding, "And also you-are-gay / Yes oh-so-incredibly gay." As usual my insecurities and self-doubt made valid points with infectious musicality. I wasn't about to second-guess a force as mighty and all-knowing as my self-hatred.

With this cacophony throbbing in my psyche, I had a hard time concentrating on the task at hand. Winona could have been spouting anti-Semitic conspiracy theories while expectorating wildly and I would have been far too wracked with self-consciousness to even notice. I was oblivious to anything but my own abject terror.

As midnight approached I sucked down a Diet Coke for courage, closed my eyes, puckered up, and lurched unsteadily in Winona's direction. I vaguely recall entering into something that could generously be called a kiss (my first) but it's entirely possible that I ended up slobbering all over the Second City stage, a cross-dressing midget, or a nearby stool.

On our second date I went to Winona's Bat Mitzvah party. Once again crippling self-consciousness was the theme of the evening. I was only two years older than Winona but those two years were filled with transformative, life-changing milestones, from my first half-assed suicide attempt to that halcyon moment I was dragged kicking and screaming into a mental hospital. At the risk of sounding melodramatic, I crammed at least sixteen years of trauma into my fifteen on the planet.

Besides, Romeo and Juliet were fifteen and thirteen, right? Things certainly worked out well for them. But as a six-foot-tall fifteen-year-old I towered over Winona and her friends like Gulliver among the Lilliputians. I would duck into the bathroom throughout the night and look pensively at my gangly frame in the mirror and think, "What am I doing here amongst decent, respectable people? I should be in a cell somewhere being beaten upside the head with a nightstick for my own good."

Our third and final date took place at a matinee of *JFK*. At the risk of being controversial, I gotta say, *JFK*: not much of a make-out movie. Date movie of the year my ass. Since Herschel broke up with Winona's mom around the same time, that pretty much spelled the end of my relationship with Winona and, for good measure, my entire high school dating career. Boobs untouched.

I envied Herschel's fearlessness and ease with women, the way he'd bat his eyelashes playfully and wink and flirt shamelessly with anyone with a vagina. Herschel epitomized a personality type I call the Big City Jew. The Big City Jew fancies himself an insider everywhere he goes. He's the guy who flirts with every waitress, who plays the percentages with women, figuring, usually correctly, that if he hits on a hundred reasonably attractive women, there'll probably be at least three or four who are lonely enough to go out with him. The ninety-five rejections incurred don't bother the Big City Jew. He just figures they don't know what they're missing. He's the guy who learns the name of the proprietor of every store he frequents, since you never know when you're going to need a favor and the Big City Jew is never afraid to ask for favors.

I cringed every time Herschel switched into flirtatious mode, yet I desperately wanted some of his mojo to rub off on me. At fifteen my mind and body were in a perpetual state of guerrilla warfare. My raging hormones angrily demanded that I mate with a female of the species every half hour or so, or at least simulate said mating with a nearby pillow. My deeply repressed Jewish brain, however, tried to convince my body that I was 100 percent asexual and would be overjoyed to go to my grave a eunuch. I reconciled these violently contradictory urges by having sex constantly, but only with myself and while immersed in near-fatal levels of shame. My hormones yelled, "Fuck! Fuck, while the spirit is strong within you, you crazy fool! Fornicate for the sake of your species! Fornicate or all is lost!" My neuroses droned, "No, sex isn't really your thing. You're more of a fatal-heart-attack-at-fifty-one-due-to-pent-up-sexual-energy kind of guy."

Herschel tried to get me to come out of my shell but I was far too self-conscious to acknowledge that I was a sexual being. I was too neurotic even to accept invitations for dates from girls I was attracted to. During my senior year two separate girls got Wenner Exius, the sole black gay intellectual at Mather, to ask me to the prom on their behalf. I had crushes on both girls yet very gravely informed Wenner, and by extension my two potential prom dates, that I did not *believe* in the prom.

I meant that I did not believe in the prom as a social construct or excuse for promiscuity or binge drinking (though at seventeen I longed for an excuse for promiscuity and binge drinking), but I like to think that I meant it literally as well, as in "I've heard of this 'prom' thing and even seen news segments about it, but I ultimately think of it as a fantastical figment of the imagination, like Santa Claus, the Easter Bunny, or the Hannukah Zombie." If I were to be honest with myself, something I strenuously avoided doing throughout my adolescence, I would have replied, "I'd love to go to the prom but I'm desperately scared of girls and if I ever did go on a date I'd probably soil myself, then begin sobbing uncontrollably, then curl up into a fetal ball. Then things would get ugly."

So I ended up skipping my prom yet attending what I like to affectionately call the Emotionally Disturbed Prom thrown by the Jewish Children's Bureau's therapeutic day school. Not surprisingly, Herschel was the catalyst. A very sweet, very smart girl with the squirmy, sad vulnerability of a wet puppy who lived in one of our sister homes asked me to the prom after her intended date was incapacitated by a car accident.

Being what mental health professionals diplomatically call "a giant fucking pussy," not to mention "a total dickweed," I initially said no, until Herschel lovingly bullied me into saying yes.

It was a weird, deeply uncomfortable night. I don't envy any girl unfortunate enough to have tried to date me during the height of one of my self-loathing phases. So, Michelle, if you're reading this, I'm deeply, deeply sorry that I ruined the emotionally disturbed prom for you. If I could do it all over again I'd be considerably less of a douchebag.

Herschel helped get me a job at Blockbuster. He fed my nascent identity as a critic in training by asking me which movies he should see or rent. "What's good, Nathan?" he'd ask brightly. When I was fifteen Herschel and my wonderful social worker, Mary Lou Coyle, enrolled me in a class on film noir and gender studies at Facets Multimedia, a film school, video store, and theater that played a crucial role in my burgeoning film education.

Mary Lou instantly sensed that movies were one of the only ways to get through to me. It was unmistakably something of a leap to imagine that just because I loved movies I'd want to discuss their psychological, gender, and political underpinnings in an unmistakably adult context. But Mary Lou and Herschel saw something in me that I didn't see in myself, a rapacious curiosity about the world that could be cultivated. They believed in me when I didn't believe in myself.

If *Bill and Ted's Excellent Adventure* hipped me to the joys of movies as escapism, the "Film Noir and Gender Roles" class illustrated the dizzy, intoxicating power of film as art. Watching movies like *Sunset Boulevard, Double Indemnity,* and *Scarlet Street,* I felt the same glorious burst of identification I felt upon reading *The Catcher in the Rye,* that transcendent, life-affirming feeling of "My God, this speaks to me in a way nothing else does."

The world of noir was a realm I instantly recognized as my own. It was all about shadows and sensuality, about the elegant curve of a female calf and the divine architecture of a pair of gorgeous gams. It was sex. It was death. It was the American dream as a sucker's bet and love as an invitation to ruin. It was American life pitched somewhere between stylized tragedy and dark comedy.

Though I was far too timid to talk during class, the Facets course made me look at movies in an entirely different way. A new world of subtext opened up to me. The more I knew about movies, the more I got out of them. There were layers of meaning and inference visible only to people who took the time to really explore.

My fascination with the kinky world of noir dovetailed with my obsession with existentialism. This was back in olden times when you had to journey to long-forgotten places called "libraries" and pore through musty antiquities called "books" to acquire information instead of merely hitting some buttons on the trusty computer-box.

What I learned about existentialism at the library made sense of an insane world by acknowledging its inherent absurdity. Of course the world is absurd and irrational. Anybody at Meadow Lane could tell you that. More important, I sensed that understanding existentialism would really impress hot beatnik girls who looked like Audrey Hepburn in *Funny Face*.

I was at that age when everything seemed somehow interconnected, where the hard-boiled protagonists of noir and 2Pac and Sartre all seemed to be espousing the same bleak, fatalistic wisdom about the cruelty and randomness of the universe. As a critic I've spent my career trying to connect those dots.

Herschel and Mary Lou made me feel safe and stable enough to cobble together a homemade philosophy held together with duct tape, logical leaps, and adolescent bullshit. I was a teenage intellectual scavenger, taking what I wanted from various philosophies and discarding the rest. From Marxism and a decade and a half of class resentment I borrowed the idea of class warfare and the innate cruelty of late-period capitalism.

The staunch feminism of my beloved older sister and intellectual mentor led me to embrace its notions of white male privilege and the oppressive male gaze. I like to think my fierce feminist convictions at least partially offset my raging misogyny.

My newfangled intellectual pretensions engendered a subtle but unmistakable snobbishness toward my housemates. I imagined that I was somehow fundamentally different from my Winchester House peers, that I was an outsider, an observer, a writer-in-training taking in the whole strange, sordid spectacle for future reference. I deluded myself into thinking I was a writer until my writing career inexplicably became a reality. I faked it until I made it.

Some anonymous soul was kind enough to donate a primitive computer to Winchester House. I spent long hours sequestered in our basement writing what I foolishly imagined was a screenplay.

My housemates found less productive ways to while away the hours. One of my favorite memories of Winchester House is of Herschel huffing and puffing as he furiously chased Noah around the house, his Buddha belly bouncing up and down rhythmically. They were a study in contrasts, Noah tall and skinny and Herschel short and stout. Noah was a human cyclone of chaos and disorder. Herschel was an equally headstrong force for repression and order. Together, Noah and Herschel constituted one of the all-time great comedy duos, like Abbott and Costello, Laurel and Hardy, Hitler and Mussolini.

Within the hermetic universe of the group home I was an obedient house slave to Noah's torch-wielding Nat Turner. I was teacher's pet to his bomb-throwing revolutionary. I secretly enjoyed being Herschel's special little man, the willing sidekick he'd play poker with at night for spare change and send to the gas station to pick up smokes. It seems a little odd that we were regularly dispatched to pick up Herschel's Salem Lights but it didn't seem weird at the time. Herschel had deputized us Winchester House boys as smokes-gatherers in good standing and if Herschel said something was OK then it became OK. That was the force of his personality. I wore the beat-up, ancient leather bomber jacket with a torn-up lining and a fur collar that Herschel had given me with pride. I hoped to attain some of Herschel's bravado through osmosis.

I craved Herschel's approval and validation but I could never forget that there was an innate limit to our friendship. We could laugh and joke and be pals but at the end of the day he was the boss of me. In the cosmology of my halfhearted Marxism he was a bourgeois manager to my ever-sufferin' pubescent proletarian. Sometimes I'd push too far with Herschel and the warmth of friendship unceremoniously gave way to the bracing chill of arbitrary authority. At times like that I retreated back into myself, imagining, not without reason, that Herschel's friendship was fundamentally pragmatic.

Noah's relationship with Herschel was equally complex but far more freighted with bile and contempt. Noah was preternaturally gifted in the dark art of mischief. Herschel felt the full force of his contempt daily. I envied antithetical aspects of Herschel and Noah's personalities. I admired Herschel's unselfconscious ease in maneuvering his way through the world, the effortless way he got what he wanted through charm, guile, and persistence. But I also envied Noah's indomitable will, the way he sneered insouciantly at the little carrots the world offers those who play by the rules.

Herschel would sometimes whine, "You know, Noah, I work hard to get you nice things and make life easier for you, and how do you repay me? By kicking me in the head." Then one day in the midst of one of his patented orgies of mindless destruction Noah suddenly stopped and, in a pitch-perfect imitation of Herschel, whined, "You know, Herschel, I work hard to make you angry and make your life difficult, and how do you repay me? By giving me punishments." It was fucking genius. Even Herschel had to laugh.

Herschel had the misfortune to embody every corrupt authority figure and absent parent in Noah's life. Noah would sometimes answer one of Herschel's orders with a poisonously sarcastic, highly theatrical "Yes, *Mother*" or "Yes, *Father*," and it became apparent that Noah was intent on making Herschel pay for the sins of his absent parents.

Over time Herschel's benevolent dictatorship grew increasingly less benevolent and more dictatorial. There were ironclad rules for everything. You didn't just have to make your bed every morning: you had to make it with military precision, then have it inspected. There was a three-point system to accepting feedback or instructions: you had to make eye contact, smile, and say, "Yes, Herschel," without a trace of sarcasm. That last part was particularly difficult for Noah and me.

Herschel, however, was free to use sarcasm with impunity. He was quick to point out he was using sarcasm *to make a point,* a distinction that was generally lost on us. Herschel could be quite the smart-ass but his preferred mode of comic discourse was running gags that wore out their welcome the first time around.

Herschel had a groaner for every occasion. If a car approached him as he walked across the street he'd sneer, "Hit me! I need the money!" (If he were a cinephile he could have substituted *Midnight Cowboy*'s "I'm walkin' here! I'm walkin' here!") If he caught one of us with our fingers up a nose he'd quip, "Pick me a winner." If one of us wanted to use the bathroom he'd smile serenely and announce, "It all comes out in the end."

If we were running late he'd adopt a mock-grave tone and jape, "We're on a mission from God," in homage to *The Blues Brothers*. Incidentally, if you grow up in Chicago you are legally required to see *The Blues Brothers* at least a half dozen times. Failure to comply can result in penalties up to, and including, being force-fed Polish sausages until your stomach explodes. Hey, it's a tough, toddling, my kinda town.

After delivering one of these witlesscisms Herschel would wink and flash a big shit-eating grin that said, "Ain't I a stinker?" The wink and grin were the raison d'être of the mothballed gags, yet another way of saying to the world, "Ain't it great bein' me?" It was simultaneously maddening and ingratiating.

Whenever I visit somebody's home for the first time I'm irresistibly drawn to their CD collection. You can tell a lot about a person by what they listen to. Herschel, for example, was a greatest hits guy. He had no time for the B-sides, album tracks, and instrumentals of life. No, he wanted nothing but the hits and he wanted them now.

When Herschel got a dog he didn't settle for a flea-bitten mutt from the pound. No, Herschel got a dog that would be a status symbol, prizewinner, and cash cow all at the same time. With visions of flashing dollar signs spinning in his head, he bought a purebred French herding dog called a briard he was intent on breeding for a big payday. The briard was very sweet and incredibly stupid. It was adorable watching him herd Herschel's wayward little flock on our trips to Indian Boundary Park.

When faced with a conflict between two desirable outcomes, Herschel's default answer was always, "Why not have both?" So we had elaborate Passover dinners with lots of guests *and* a big, gaudy Christmas tree in the living room every December. Rather than live in a shit hole, he transformed the group home apathy built into a place fit for decent human beings.

He had the scratched-up, piss-colored kitchen floor torn out and replaced with glistening new black and white tiles. It was a statement of purpose with enormous symbolic significance: he was ripping out the old and bringing in the new. Even more impressively, he trained us apathetic delinquents to do the job ourselves. It amazes me that at various points in my life I was able to read and speak Hebrew, break a wooden board with my hand, operate a sander without incurring grave injuries, and read from a teleprompter without making a complete ass of myself. Herschel deserves credit for at least one of those quickly forgotten skills.

Herschel was a larger-than-life figure of Falstaffian appetites. And by "larger-than-life figure of Falstaffian appetites" I mean "fat sack of shit who loved to eat." Hastily conceived, indifferently executed meals of hot dogs and peanut butter and jelly gave way to giant pots of baked Mostacholi with homemade meat sauce and mozzarella and Italian beef with baked mozzarella. Like all good Midwesterners, Herschel subscribed to the notion that every dish can benefit from baked or fried cheese. Partially out of self-interest, he taught us how to cook. I learned that the key to extra-creamy mashed potatoes was sour cream and the secret to succulent French toast was Hawaiian bread.

Herschel started a volleyball team called the Underdogs for the Winchester House and Clampett boys that competed against other group homes. It takes chutzpah to call yourself the Underdogs when your competition consists exclusively of former runaways, refugees from abusive homes, and wards of the state. But anyone who saw the JCB's motley assortment of misshapen misfits trudge dispiritedly onto the court in three-dollar dishwater-gray team shirts and sweatpants had to concede that the name was richly deserved.

I loved away games because they meant taking the creaky old JCB school bus to dusty, faraway gyms musty with tradition. Life had taught me to always be on the lookout for the world's next devastating onslaught, so I became a defensive specialist on the court and off, a sturdy defender skilled at wearing down my opponents through steady play and persistence.

However, during a game against a team representing the Maryville City of Youth, my modest defensive skills were completely useless against a tall, lean Maryville standout who bombarded us with one explosive strike after another until we were ready to throw up the white flag and mutter, *"No mas."*

So we were both horrified and guiltily relieved when we faced off against Maryville City of Youth in the state group home championships in Springfield, Illinois, and discovered that Sir Strikes a Lot, the bane of our existence, was missing a leg following a car accident. Without their star player we ended up defeating Maryville City of Youth handily en route to a fourth-place finish. But I felt guilty: it was as if we had telekinetically willed our stiffest competition out of commission.

After years of hitting on everything that moved, including our social workers and teachers (awkward!), Herschel started dating a pretty, tough single mother named Julia. Julia's son had been bitten in the face by a dog as a baby. The dog bite scarred him emotionally as well as physically: he had a tough, brittle exterior, as did his mother.

They'd both been kicked around by life. The boy's father had been MIA since his birth and Julia was coming out of an abusive relationship. So she must have been a ripe target for Herschel's brazen self-confidence and dogged persistence. There was something irresistible about the ease with which Herschel carried himself, which seemed to say, "Stick with me and everything will be just fine."

After a whirlwind courtship they got married, though I don't remember whether I attended their wedding. Memory has a way of reducing even seminal experiences into abstractions that grow fuzzier with each passing day until they disappear altogether. I do vividly remember an impromptu Winchester House class in sex education where Julia confided that Herschel satisfied her sexually while we struggled to keep from projectile-vomiting at the thought of Herschel's sweaty middle-aged gut slamming against her.

To provide for his new dependents, Herschel lovingly bullied the JCB into building a stand-alone apartment in our backyard for his instant family, a private sanctum he could retire to at the end of a long day with a glass of merlot and a *New Yorker*. It was a bold maneuver, even for Herschel. On one level it made all the sense in the world. Finding a sane, college-educated adult willing to spend forty or more hours a week babysitting disturbed adolescents for wages that made inner-city schoolteachers look wildly overcompensated represented a daunting challenge under the best of circumstances. But offering caretakers a room of their own to decompress, handle grown folks' business, cuss, fuck, smoke, and talk shit about us demon spawn must have made it seem a whole lot more manageable.

From another, less generous angle the unit in the backyard looked like a tremendously expensive monument to Herschel's bloated ego. There was always a touch of the con man in Herschel, with his brazen cockiness, gift of gab, and genius for manipulation. The less charitable among us wondered how Herschel suckered the rubes at the JCB into building his lady friend a castle in the backyard.

Herschel's wife, meanwhile, must have wondered how exactly her new husband had managed to sucker her into quitting her job, marrying him, and building a life based around caring for surly teenagers. Herschel had promised her the world, then delivered a thankless, exhausting, modestly compensated job and a dream home in the backyard of a glorified holding pen for juvenile delinquents. What had she gotten herself into?

As his marriage started to crumble and he battled his bosses, Herschel's confidence and authority started fraying at the edges. His cocksure strut disappeared. He suddenly seemed uncharacteristically vulnerable. Like a dog, Noah sensed fear and went in for the kill. Ending Herschel's authoritarian reign would be Noah's greatest triumph, but I unwittingly ended up playing a more substantial role in Herschel's eventual ousting.

As Herschel's tenure at Winchester House stumbled erratically to a close, my high school career ended on a singularly bleak note. At graduation I experienced nothing but eviscerating emptiness, the sum total of four interminable years of bitterness and ennui, sadness and alienation, truancy and constant, vaguely simian masturbation. The meaninglessness of my miserable high school career descended over me like a dark cloud. It was all so goddamned pointless, such an exercise in futility. While everyone around me beamed from ear to ear or shouted drunkenly at the kids getting diplomas, I found myself wondering how I survived four fucking years with these people.

To paraphrase Winona Ryder in *Heathers,* if looks could kill, my teen angst would have racked up quite the body count.

My black mood persisted after graduation ended. My family took me to the Gold Coin, a greasy spoon in Evanston, where I watched with rapt fascination as a white sport-utility vehicle led police on a surreally slow chase on every television in the restaurant. Devoid of context, the scene seemed utterly bizarre. Why was this considered news?

Of course this wasn't just any sport-utility vehicle: it was a Ford Bronco with O. J. Simpson in the back seat with a gun to his head. I had no way of knowing that Simpson would indirectly help determine the future of Winchester House.

In the midnineties there was a craze among sports card collectors for insanely expensive new cards that promised autographs, sports memorabilia, and bits of the Dead Sea Scrolls in every pack. In 1994 the most sought-after card was a voucher for a Signature Rookies football card O. J. Simpson autographed while in jail awaiting trial for double homicide. For collectors willing to spend seven dollars on a pack of cheaply produced cards, this voucher became the sports equivalent of Willy Wonka's Golden Ticket. Its value skyrocketed to the four-to-five-hundred-dollar range.

This was when the public still labored under the misconception that O. J. was somehow responsible for the death of his ex-wife just because he was a jealous coke addict with a violent temper and a history of domestic abuse. It was before the cloud of suspicion enshrouding the Heisman winner magically dissipated with the jury's "innocent" verdict. The public hadn't yet embraced Simpson as a heroic real-life answer to *The Fugitive*'s Richard Kimble, an unjustly accused man devoted to stalking golf courses, nightclubs, and the hotel rooms of sports memorabilia dealers in search of the "real killers" behind the brutal slaying of Nicole Brown and Ronald Goldman.

Herschel knew that I collected Signature Rookie cards and stopped by the baseball card shop and picked me up a pack. I greedily opened it and experienced a surge of childlike joy upon discovering a voucher for an autographed O. J. Simpson card inside. Oh, happy day! Oh, how the herald angels sang! Yes, everything was finally coming up Milhouse. In a business deal of Shylockian dimensions, Herschel arranged to sell my O. J. card for four hundred dollars in exchange for half the profits.

If Herschel and I were simply buddies, as I had once deluded myself into thinking we were, this transaction wouldn't have raised eyebrows. But we weren't buddies: he was the boss of me, with all the responsibilities and restrictions that entailed. When the JCB brass found out about Herschel's sale it was furious. Herschel had pushed and pushed but now it appeared he had finally crossed the line.

A meeting was called and Herschel's bosses at the JCB explained to us that for reasons they could not go into Herschel would no longer be working at Winchester House. He'd done a world of good for us but the ugliness surrounding his firing washed all that away in an avalanche of rumors, innuendos, and accusations. Nobody ever talks about Colonel Kurtz's decades of distinguished service to the U.S. military, just the unfortunate business about going crazy, playing God, and severed heads.

The bitter irony is that everyone at Winchester ended up there because at least one parent had abandoned them, a formative trauma that scarred each of us in different but profound ways. Now, at the behest of the Jewish Children's Bureau, another parental figure was leaving us, never to return. Herschel had long tried to infect me with the idea that if you close yourself off to the world to avoid getting hurt, you also close yourself off to all the good things in life. You won't feel the agony of rejection but you'll never know love or real friendship. It was a lesson that took a long time to take. I nevertheless got close enough to Herschel to get hurt by his absence. Herschel never quite accomplished the Herculean goals he set out for himself.

But that doesn't make him a failure or a bad guy. It just makes him human.

I never saw Herschel again. Every once in a while I wonder what he's up to. My guess is that he's probably out there somewhere charming someone who's surprised at how easily they're allowing themselves to be seduced.

Wayne the Video Store Vampire

Reservoir Dogs
Blockbuster

When you're a disturbed sixteen-year-old, *Reservoir Dogs* is the greatest movie ever made, if not the single defining triumph of Western civilization. If you're over or under sixteen, *Reservoir Dogs* is still a damned fine movie, but it no longer seems like a seismic cultural event.

Reservoir Dogs hit me like an atom bomb. It seemed like the most explosively original movie I'd ever seen, which is ironic given how indebted it is to cinema's past. In a sense Tarantino does in his movies what I'm doing in this book: he takes the art and trash he loves and makes it his own. He's an insatiable cultural magpie picking out the shiny ephemera he likes and disregarding everything else.

As a movie-mad teenager, I was intoxicated by the idea that being a filmmaker could be an extension of being a cinephile, that the world's best film school wasn't USC or UCLA but rather watching every half-assed seventies B-movie or quirky French art film. It was downright life-affirming to think you could go from watching movies to making movies. Tarantino somehow made being a socially retarded chatterbox movie geek with a giant head (literally: I'm downright Charlie Brown–like in my encephalitis) full of trivia, pop culture references, and old movie lines seem cool, for which I am forever grateful.

So I was overjoyed to follow in my hero's footsteps by landing a job as a video store clerk. My first day on the job at the local Blockbuster, I watched an instructional video that began with a blow-dried smoothie gushing, "Congratulations! You're in the entertainment industry!"

Gosh, for some reason when I think about "the entertainment industry," the image that springs to mind is of Tom Cruise swaggering down the red carpet, not a sixteen-year-old mopping floors and ringing up microwave popcorn. In that respect a more accurate spiel would be "Congratulations! You're now making little more than minimum wage! Now get to work! Those toilets aren't going to clean themselves!"

I nevertheless felt like the Blockbuster uniform, as well as Tarantino's shining example, gave me permission to paradoxically both slip out of my skin and become a flamboyant performer, and be my true self every time a shift began.

Talking about movies freed me from my crippling self-consciousness. Movies were liberating. They made me feel alive and pointed to a wonderful world outside the group home where I could be whoever I wanted to be.

At Blockbuster I learned that the ability to entertain oneself is an invaluable lifelong gift. To while away the hours, I transformed my register into a makeshift vaudeville stage where my "Strangely Overenthusiastic Clerk Routine" was enjoying an indifferently received open-ended run. I became known throughout a twelve-block radius for the quantity, if not quality, of my humor.

For example, when a customer called and inquired, "Do you have any *Sniper*s in your store?" I would feign shock and reply, "Good Lord, I hope not. I'm not even wearing a bulletproof vest!" Ba-dum-bum! When a customer asked if we had *A Few Good Men,* I'd quip, "That depends on who you ask." My coworkers quickly came to know and grudgingly tolerate my humor.

It was during those endless shifts that I first developed a deep and passionate love affair with the sound of my own voice, a romance that continues to this day. More important, working at Blockbuster gave me an opportunity to be around my beloved movies. It was a tawdry, for-profit cathedral of film. Every video box radiated promise. As a kid, I used to go to video stores and fantasize dreamily about all the films I'd see someday. Now I had unfettered access to a treasure trove of classics. I quickly plunged into cinephile romances with the oeuvres of Jean-Luc Godard and Brian De Palma, two filmmakers with decidedly adolescent-friendly sensibilities.

I have an unfortunate habit of staying places for exactly one year too long, whether it's the group home or Blockbuster. Blockbuster and the movies it peddled were my salvation during high school. But when I went away to college in fabulous Madison, Wisconsin, sophomore year, working for Blockbuster became an ordeal.

I couldn't secure an actual transfer to a Blockbuster in Madison, but on my first day in Madison I ran into my old store manager Matt eating outside an establishment promising "burritos as big as your head." Matt now worked as a district manager in Wisconsin and promised to put in a good word for me with the branches he oversaw.

At that time there were four Blockbusters in the greater Madison area. There was a downtown Blockbuster about a block away from where I lived. There was an east-side Blockbuster about a block away from where I matriculated at glamorous Madison Area Technical College. Then there were stores in Sun Prairie and Monona, suburbs out in the middle of the boonies reachable only by two half-hour bus rides.

"Now, here's the thing," Matt told me after talking with the various store managers. "Because you've worked at Blockbuster for so long, you make far too much to work at either the downtown or east-side stores. I probably shouldn't be telling you this, but you actually make more than some of the assistant managers at the downtown store." It should be noted, dear reader, that the gaudy wage that priced me out of working at Blockbusters within stumbling distance of where I lived and went to school was four dollars and sixty-five cents an hour. Or forty cents more than minimum wage.

Wayne, the manager at my new store, was a gray-skinned, dead-eyed automaton with straw-colored hair and the personality of a calculator. He spoke in a bloodless monotone that sucked the air out of the room one dead syllable at a time.

I suspected that Wayne was secretly a vampire or zombie. He had all the telltale symptoms: a ghostly white complexion; a complete dearth of humanity; a vacant, empty stare; and most important, an insatiable hunger for blood and human brains. But more than anything, Wayne was a monster of banality, a sentient corporate instruction manual brought to life through the darkest forms of capitalist black magic.

To ingratiate myself with this inhuman beast who walked amongst the living yet belonged amongst the dead, I gave him an affectionate nickname: Petey Wheatstraw, the Devil's Son-in-Law, after one of my hero Rudy Ray Moore's most beloved characters. What soulless supercracker doesn't secretly pine for a nickname paying homage to the self-proclaimed "King of the Party Records"?

"Uh, Nathan. Could you please stop calling me Petey Wheatstraw, the Devil's Son-in-Law? It's disrespectful and unprofessional. If you continue I'll have to write you up and I don't want to have to do that," Wayne droned at me one day.

Wayne feared my mild shenanigoats would distract him from his all-consuming war of wits with prepubescent evil geniuses he was convinced were out to destroy his livelihood.

"Up until now we've been accepting elementary school IDs as proper identification, but it has come to my attention that children have been making up fake school IDs to set up bogus accounts so they can steal videos and video games. So from now on we'll only be accepting legal ID from children," Wayne warned us gravely at a staff meeting.

If there really was some diabolical nine-year-old criminal mastermind defrauding Blockbuster with his sinister schemes, I think I'd be better off throwing in my lot with him than working at BBV. He certainly wouldn't chafe at paying my decadent four-dollar-and-sixty-five-cent-an-hour wage. Yes, being the sidekick of a prepubescent supervillain would definitely be a big promotion from being a lowly customer service representative.

One day Wayne walked into Blockbuster wearing a tiny little stud in his left ear, stonewashed jeans, and a black T-shirt, a look that screamed "sullen twelve-year-old circa 1986." Seeing Wayne out of uniform was a jarring experience, like watching your rabbi stumble out of a leather bar at two thirty in the morning.

Wayne, who, it should be noted, is in no way related to the devil, either through birth or through marriage, was such a soulless corporate drone that I just naturally assumed he ate, slept, lived, and even showered in his regulation blue oxford shirt and khaki pants. But Wayne wasn't just a man who had sold his soul to Blockbuster Video. No, he was a rocker as well.

"So is your group like Night Ranger?" I asked him one chilly afternoon during a rare moment of semi-informality.

"Sort of, but we're not as eclectic. We're more toward the light rock side of things," Wayne droned. I'd never encountered anyone who listened to Night Ranger, let alone copped to playing in a group that sounded like a wussier, less diverse version of them.

Wayne was engaged to Holly, an assistant manager at the downtown store. Holly was a cool, pot-smoking, rock and roll kind of gal, the kind you suspect has a tiny butterfly tattoo on the small of her back. Holly was far too cute and charming to be seeing a sentient corpse like Wayne, so we speculated that he was simply Holly's sugar daddy. Holly was pregnant and the rumor sweeping Blockbuster was that Wayne wasn't her baby daddy.

I cherished the idea of Holly cuckolding Wayne. I spent hours daydreaming about the countless different ways Holly might be cuckolding him: with a rough-hewn delivery boy in the back room while children banged on the front door in fevered anticipation of the store opening, getting fucked from behind against the new-release wall, her sweat-drenched face bashing inelegantly against a row full of *Top Dog* videotapes, and last but not least, getting banged over Wayne's desk after closing time while the special Blockbuster edition of *Entertainment Tonight* whirred mechanically on the monitors.

I never learned whether or not Wayne was Holly's baby daddy. I guess if the baby displayed an early predilection toward drinking blood or hungered for the brains of the living, it was probably Wayne's progeny after all. The assistant managers were a lovably loserish lot. I remember one middle manager happily showing me a newspaper with a headline that read RABIN ASSASSINATED.

"I guess you must have pissed off the wrong customer, huh, Nathan?" he joked with the enthusiasm of someone who'd been waiting for hours to unleash a particularly wicked zinger. The assassination of Yitzhak Rabin may have been a defining trauma for Israel, a disaster for peace-loving people everywhere, and an international tragedy, but for my assistant manager it was just an excuse for a tasteless joke. As someone who would never engage in comedy of questionable taste or derive humor from human suffering, I just find that sad.

After a good eight months I finally received my transfer to the east-side Blockbuster but I lasted only a couple of months there. My Blockbuster career ended with a whimper, not a bang, but it did lead to my next video-store job, which led to writing for *The Onion*, which led to doing a national television show, which led to writing this book. So while I understand people who see Blockbuster as a cultural parasite, I'll always be grateful for the chance it gave me.

As a cinephile, I love Netflix and see it as a vital step in cinema's evolution. But I also mourn the imminent demise of the brick-and-mortar video store. Video stores are so much more than just a place to get movies. They're also potent breeding grounds for future filmmakers and critics, as well as meeting places and makeshift community centers for cinephiles and movie buffs. I know my four years in the video-store trenches proved essential to both my film education and my professional career. So much more than late fees and long lines will be lost if the local video store goes the way of the dinosaur.

I fear that Netflix will breed a generation of cinephiles and filmmakers who will be more obsessive and informed than their predecessors but also even more removed from human contact and likely to view the world exclusively through the prism of film rather than personal experience. I similarly fear that the films these wunderkinds will eventually produce, no doubt on (ugh) digital video, will become ever more synthetic, insular, and self-referential, ever more removed from the everyday struggle outside the multiplex.

At Blockbuster I didn't just cultivate my passion for film: I found myself. It was there that I first realized that by being funny and smart and knowing more about movies than anyone else I could trick people into liking me, or at least into thinking I wasn't completely worthless. In a very real way my entire career in entertainment—and the long, strange road to basic-cable television cancellation—began in the air-conditioned comfort of a Blockbuster on the north side of Chicago.

She Really Worked Me Over Good, She Was a Credit to Her Gender

"Maggie May"
Emma G

Even more than Ice Cube and Sting, Rod Stewart is the poster boy for squandered potential. Stewart has been a cancerous boil on the face of popular culture for so long that it can be hard to remember what a ferocious talent he was at the beginning of his career.

Long before he slaughtered standards with easy-listening renditions of the great American songbook, Stewart was writing standards himself. No song embodies his early genius better than "Maggie May." The ultimate coming-of-age song, "Maggie May" is a love letter written with a poison pen, a bittersweet story song about an older woman who drags the protagonist from boy to man and the profound psychological damage incurred in the process. It's a song that careens between affection and bitterness, nostalgia and regret, love and hate. In a line worthy of Elvis Costello, the protagonist tells his mentor in the wicked ways of the world, "The morning sun when it's in your face really shows your age," before quickly defusing the lacerating nastiness of that observation.

Every man has his own Maggie May, a worldly woman who broke his heart and taught him valuable life lessons about how love is an evil succubus that will devour your soul, destroy your life, and compromise your credit rating. Maggie Mays tend to be older women, but that isn't always the case. When I was nineteen, for example, I experienced my very first Maggie May in the form of a seventeen-year-old with the preposterous name Keely Maurice Zuckerman.

For years we maintained a strange video-store, customer/ employee quasicourtship. Every time Keely stepped into my Blockbuster Video wearing perilously low-slung jeans and slinky tops, my always rapid banter rocketed far past the rate of comprehensibility and I freaked the fuck out.

I wanted more than anything to take Keely in my arms, declare my undying love for her, and spirit her away to a reasonably priced nearby motel so I could finally rid myself of my cursed virginity. But I was far too much of a pussy to do anything more forward than give Keely free rentals on my employee account. After literally waiting years for me to make the first move, Keely finally bit the bullet and asked me out.

After work that night I hung out with her and her rich bohemian friends from one of those highfalutin alternative high schools where students didn't have to worry about getting beaten up during class. While I fought back an encroaching panic attack, Keely told me about this guy she met at a Stone Temple Pilots concert who she made out with 'cause he kinda sorta looked like Weiland even though he already had a girlfriend and tried to pressure her into appearing in a homemade porno. In other words: Mr. Right!

It's quite possible that she was telling me these things to let me know that she was not, in fact, a waiting-for-marriage kind of gal, but I was far too paralyzed by fear to take notice. Not only was I a virgin at the time but I'd never so much as touched a girl's boob. I was convinced I was the last nineteen-year-old virgin in existence. I went through high school feeling like the world was a giant orgy only I hadn't been invited to.

My anxiety about dating Keely manifested itself in agonizing constipation. It was as if my disgusted bowels had gone on strike to protest my fatal inability to get laid. I forget the circumstances but at one point I mentioned my gastrointestinal turmoil to Keely's mother. Like a true Jewish mother she immediately sprang into action: it didn't matter to her that my relationship with Keely wasn't going anywhere; there was a nice Jewish boy whose gastrointestinal system required her assistance, so I was soon inundated with home remedies for indigestion.

Sadly, I think Keely's mom had a deeper connection with my tormented bowels than her daughter had with the sum of my being. Throughout my adolescence I found myself drawn irrevocably to surrogate mother figures. It took all the restraint I could muster not to fix my puppy-dog eyes in Keely's mother's direction and meekly ask if she would be my mommy, too.

After three or four dates where I lacked the courage to go in for more than a chaste farewell hug, Keely decided she'd had enough of me, my pussyfooting and dillydallying. We made plans to see the Chris O'Donnell/Drew Barrymore vehicle *Mad Love*, but when the time came for her to pick me up at the group home, she was nowhere to be found. I knew things hadn't been going well but I was devastated. Of course the whole picking-me-up-at-the-group-home thing was probably a deal breaker. Nothing says "stud" quite like not knowing how to drive and living with an aggregation of misshapen misfits.

For weeks afterward I lay in bed all day, the air conditioner turned up full blast, playing Radiohead's *The Bends* over and over and over again in a masochistic orgy of self-pity. In my fragile, depressed state I imagined that every tortured syllable Thom Yorke howled secretly mourned the death of my relationship with Keely. Sure, the words might be different, but I fantasized that in the title song Yorke was really singing, "Why couldn't you go to the movie with Nathan? / Woah woah woah / You would have had so much fun / Yeah yeah, yeah / Watching Drew and Chris fall in love." I roused myself out of my depressed stupor just long enough to masturbate and work my eight-hour shifts at Blockbuster. No matter how bad it got, I always had time for masturbation and work.

Keely standing me up was the worst thing that ever happened to anyone in America. Puffed full of the self-importance endemic to teen life, I imagined that the banal misfortune of a cute girl ditching me was a tragedy on par with the Trail of Tears and the Tuskegee Experiment. I must have been the first heterosexual teenage boy ever dumped for not being sexually aggressive enough.

But my thwarted romance with Keely was ultimately a warm-up for an even more disastrous flirtation just down the road. When I was an eighteen-year-old freshman at the University of Illinois at Chicago, I fell in love for the very first time, with Emma G, a twenty-two-year-old who drank and smoked and slept around and seemed to hold the key to all the secrets in the world behind her big brown eyes. We had a pair of courses together and after class we'd make fun of the way our South African teacher pronounced the word "issues" "ith-use" and talk about politics and classes and how thoroughly ridiculous everyone seemed. I was gobsmacked by her worldliness as only an eighteen-year-old virgin can be.

"So, how many girlfriends do you have?" she asked flirtatiously after class one day. All I could think was, "You're allowed to have more than one?" followed by, "You're allowed to have even one?" She was a Communist in a post-Communist world, an adorable political anachronism. I pretended to be a Marxist-Leninist to curry her favor. And though she professed not to have much use for bourgeois concepts like "love" and "monogamy," she was clearly still in love with her ex-boyfriend, who not so coincidentally was the head of the local Communist Party.

My father taught me at an early age that Republicans only cared about rich white people and businesses while the Democrats cared about women, blacks, Jews, Hispanics, gays, and the poor. It wasn't until much later in my political education that I came to realize that the Republicans *and* Democrats only care about rich white people; the Democrats just do a better job of pretending to care about everyone else. Not that it helps them get elected.

When the government shut down my dad's office in the mideighties, my father told me that Ronald Reagan had put him out of a job. In my youthful imagination, it was as if Reagan literally flew *Air Force One* to Milwaukee, dressed down my dad for being a fat-cat government bureaucrat and a pawn to the welfare queens with their pink Cadillacs and baseball-sized diamonds, and personally kicked my dad out of his office and sent him spinning madly, permanently, toward poverty. I became convinced that Ronald Reagan, that glad-handing phony on the television with his Colgate smile and Big Lies, was personally, single-handedly responsible for my family's misfortune.

As a twelve-year-old, I volunteered, for one magical day, for Michael Dukakis. I manned the phone banks at Dukakis's Chicago headquarters and told people to watch him that night on *Nightline*. I was convinced that once America drank in the raw charisma and swarthy animal sexuality of Dukakis in action, they'd have no choice but to elect him in a landslide. It didn't work out that way, though I'll always treasure the moment in the '88 presidential campaign when a certain future California governor endorsed Bush the elder by barking, "Ah juhst played duh Tuhminator on da beeg screen. But Maaachuuuhhhl Duuuuikakakis eez duh real tuhminator of America's few-chah!" It's fortunate that Dukakis was defeated or his controversial "Operation: Terminate America's Future" program would have dispatched an army of killer cyborgs to America's major cities for a campaign of postapocalyptic robo-terror.

So I was understandably receptive to Emma's incendiary ideas, though I'd be lying if I said that my attraction to her was political. One fateful night Emma invited me to a Communist Party party. Buzzed off three beers—I had yet to develop my heroic tolerance for alcohol—I put my beloved tape of the Smiths' *Louder Than Bombs* into the nearest boom box and softly sang along to "Unloveable," my theme song.

As the liquor filled my body with a strange, unprecedented sense of well-being, I began to wonder if this would be my own personal D-Day, that ecstatic moment when I'd finally be deflowered. I was convinced that my problems would instantly vanish the moment I lost my virginity. The truth, of course, is that losing your virginity simply causes your problems to start taking steroids and lifting weights so they can do maximum damage at the appropriate interval.

Later that evening Emma very drunkenly told me she was way too hammered to drive and that I might have to spend the night in her apartment. Would I mind? Good Lord, I felt as if the answer to all my prayers had arrived. Then she stumbled into the coatroom and passed out, leaving me to catch a dispiriting ride home with her ex-boyfriend, who gave me the hard sell on becoming a foot soldier in a Communist revolution perpetually just around the corner. My nerves were raw. I felt like crying. I wanted to break down and confess that I had no real interest in Communism; I just wanted to get closer to Emma.

Things were never the same. My window of opportunity had passed. In class Emma would argue vehemently with a clean-cut Republican ROTC cadet. After class they'd flirt outrageously. I suspected they were having dirty, thrilling interpolitical hate-sex.

In a desperate attempt to resurrect our waning bond, I decided to confess my feelings to Emma. After class one afternoon I finally mustered up the courage to stutter, "Emma, I, I, love you." The words hung uncomfortably in the air for a seeming eternity.

She stared at me blankly with pity and discomfort. "Jesus, Nathan. You barely know me," was her horrified response. That was true, but it didn't make what I was feeling seem any less real or valid.

A year and a half later, when Judy, the girl I lost my virginity to, gave me a cat for Valentine's Day, I named her Maggie May. I told Judy I just really liked that Rod Stewart song. Some things are better left unsaid. Like "I love you."

You Must Be the Jew

"Brick"
Judy

When I interviewed Ben Folds he attributed the success of "Brick" to simple timing: alt-rock radio needed a power ballad. He provided it with one. Timing undoubtedly played a role in making the song an unlikely hit but I think that "Brick" resonated with the general public for a more profound reason. Like so little in popular culture, it told the truth. Like *Girl, Interrupted*, it tackled tricky subject matter with spare, understated eloquence.

"Brick" isn't a pro-choice song. It's not a pro-life song. The word "abortion" never even comes up, yet "Brick" captures the haunting, harrowing emotions surrounding the termination of a pregnancy with heartbreaking visceral force: the numbness, the loneliness, the pervasive shame and guilt, the way abortion binds people together while pulling them inexorably apart.

Also like *Girl, Interrupted*, "Brick" covers a topic I wish I didn't have firsthand knowledge of. Within weeks of leaving the group home and losing my virginity, I got my girlfriend pregnant. The abortion that ensued cast a pall over a relationship that never had much of a chance to begin with.

When I met Judy she was a Young Republican in conservative

sweaters who chain-smoked and radiated smarts, toughness, and brazen self-confidence. We lived in the same co-op and though she was ostensibly going out with an oppressively clean-cut, overachieving nineteen-year-old law student named Winthrop (he was in the fucking ROTC, for chrissakes) who lived on the floor below us, we'd drink beer and flirt and smoke cigarettes on the front steps of the co-op, reveling in the exhilarating freedom of being away from home.

The first time we hung out outside the co-op I took her to a meeting of Madison's International Socialist Organization, a quixotic organization whose crudely Xeroxed fliers promoted the violent overthrow of capitalist oppressors as the answer to everything from racism and sexism to male pattern baldness and spider veins. I suppose Judy found my Marxist Hebraic ways exotic. After weeks of flirtation and stolen glances we made out one bleary night after smoking pot, drinking too many bottles of Blatz, and watching *Pulp Fiction* in her room.

As I unfastened her comically unwieldy, burdensome old-school bra with a single deft hand movement—a fluke that led her to believe that I was far more experienced sexually than I actually was—my libido chanted, "Go, go, go!" while my neuroses fretted, "What about protection? Use a condom! For God's sake, man, cover up!"

But I was too drunk, stoned, horny, and naïve to insist on using a condom. I had no excuse. I'd grown up at the height of the AIDS scare and sex ed taught me that sex was death and that the only way to avoid pregnancy, AIDS, syphilis, and gonorrhea was to use a condom while praying to baby Jesus, saying countless Ave Marias, and fondling rosary beads while in the act of sexual congress. But, as is too often the case, my penis had the last word. He was convinced that if I hesitated for even a second the moment would be lost and I'd be doomed to a life of celibacy.

After consummating our relationship, then reconsummating it, then consummating it a third, fourth, and fifth time in case the first few consummations didn't take, we exchanged secrets. I told her about my month at Meadow Lane. She told me about the miscarriage she'd had after an ex-boyfriend kicked her in the stomach. Judy was an amazing storyteller and an inveterate fabulist, two inextricably interwoven qualities that endeared her to me immediately. That first night together she recounted the miscarriage in novelistic detail, recounting every tortured emotion.

The next morning there was a fussily written note on Judy's door from Winthrop explaining that while he thought Judy was a great girl and he would always treasure their week and a half together, he had decided, after due consideration, much soul-searching, and perhaps a visit to his pastor, that it would be best if they ended their abbreviated romance. At no point did Winthrop acknowledge, in the letter or elsewhere, that his deliciously moot gesture might have been motivated by the fact that his ostensible girlfriend was fucking the weird Jewish guy who lived ten feet away from her. No, Winthrop was intent on being gracious, gentlemanly, and civil, three qualities that had no place in the scuzziest co-op in Madison.

Judy read the letter to me with hilariously deadpan solemnity, mercilessly playing up the strained nobility to devastating comic effect. She then regaled me with an account of her last date with Winthrop, where he nervously sipped tap water and recounted every mundane detail of the night he went to a Jen Trynin show: what he wore, what he drank, what time he went to bed.

At a house meeting shortly thereafter Winthrop acted as his own legal counsel and asked the house to break his lease so he could move someplace less redolent of romantic heartbreak. It was adorable, really, that Winthrop thought he had to wage a legal campaign to get out of his lease. We were a fucking co-op, after all, not the goddamned marines. At Le Château the prevailing philosophy was "Dude, whatever, man," so Winthrop didn't exactly have to draft a legal dream team to break his lease.

Winthrop was smart enough to realize that things had deteriorated quickly and leave post-haste. I, on the other hand, realized that things were going south, then decided to stick it out for two more agonizing years.

A few weeks later I went to a Catherine Wheel/Belly concert with Judy's best friend, Diane. For some reason the topic of Judy's miscarriage came up. "What are you talking about? Judy never had a miscarriage. She had two abortions but she never had a miscarriage," Diane replied.

Suddenly those early days flirting on the porch seemed terribly far away. To paraphrase the Magnetic Fields, Judy was just like me: she was one big bruise. In the game of life she was playing to lose. I never looked at Judy quite the same way again. In time we'd grow to hate each other almost as much as we hated ourselves.

I started using condoms after the night Judy confessed to her two abortions but it was too late. A month later Judy called me at Blockbuster to tell me she was pregnant: "I'm pregnant." The words hit like a death sentence. *I'm pregnant. I'm pregnant.* My heartbeat slowed to a crawl. Time seemed frozen. I felt like I was walking underwater. Everything felt heavy and oppressive and shattering. So this is what they meant by "real life."

I looked over at Wayne the Blockbuster zombie as he sat obliviously at his desk, his face frozen in a look of grim concentration. Two little words had torn my world apart. I felt like a ghost moving through this earthly realm without quite being part of it, isolated, alone, damned. I felt like crying. But I was too numb to do anything but struggle to finish my shift without breaking down. I became fixated on the idea that I had gotten Judy pregnant during our first night together. It was all too perfectly awful to contemplate.

I spent my adolescence pining for the day I'd lose my virginity. Now the best thing in the world had turned into the worst. I had gotten my wish. It turned to shit before my eyes.

Just a few months out of the group home, I was suddenly faced with an agonizing decision: abortion, giving the baby up for adoption, or raising a child I couldn't afford. My convictions changed on an hourly basis. I made up my mind over and over again to do the honorable thing. I'd marry Judy, drop out of school, and get a second job. Then I'd come to my senses and realize just how impossible that'd be. I doubted Judy could abstain from drugs or alcohol for nine months. Besides, what kind of parents would we be? We were young, irresponsible, broke, and crazy. And doomed. Hopelessly, irrevocably doomed.

As I wrestled with the most agonizing decision of my life, two antithetical futures stretched out before me. In one, I was a harried father with big black rings under my eyes, two jobs, and a wife and child I hadn't chosen and couldn't support. In the other, I was freed from the responsibility and obligation of parenthood but burdened eternally with the guilt of having snuffed out something I had created through naïveté and stupidity. They were two different visions of hell. I couldn't envision a happy outcome to my dilemma. I couldn't foresee a future where I'd be a happy or successful teenage parent.

After the abortion Judy sank into a debilitating depression.

"She's a brick and I'm drowning slowly."

Judy would lie in bed all day crying. She dropped out of school. I woke up every morning knowing I'd done something I could never undo. I smoked pot every night hoping it would help me forget. It never did. All it did was numb the pain.

The abortion united and divided us. We had blood on our hands. We could never go back to where we were before. Our first weeks in the co-op felt like an impossible Eden we could never return to. The abortion had aged us. We could never be kids again.

Meeting a girlfriend's family for the first time is like learning the creation story of a favorite character. It answers two eternal queries: where did this person come from and how did they get so hopelessly fucked up?

Judy's main familial relationship was with her crazy grandma Cloris. Like many joyless, meddling biddies of her generation, Grandma Cloris spent her days reading *Reader's Digest,* sending televangelists money, dying her hair colors not seen in nature, and firing off an endless stream of incoherent, paranoid, hand-written letters to various relatives. The cornerstone of Grandma Cloris's, um, unique prose style was wild, erratic underlining. Underlining was to Grandma Cloris what exclamation points were to Terry Southern and footnotes were to David Foster Wallace. Let me assure you, dear reader, that underlining is to be used sparingly, if at all. Writers might like to think that under-lining a section of their work highlights just how crucial said portions are to their overall argument. But all you're really high-lighting is just how fucking crazy you are.

Grandma Cloris hated me long before we met. One of her first letters to Judy after we'd started dating warned her that if I were to marry a non-Jew my family would hold a funeral for me. Grandma Cloris made sure to underline the word "funeral" sev-eral times in a shaky, erratic hand.

Meeting Grandma Cloris did nothing to alleviate her con-tempt for me. "I was a nurse for many decades, Judy, and I can tell you firsthand that Nathan has the red eyes and the twitchy body language of a drug addict! Stay away!" she wrote soberly to Judy mere days after our first torturous visit to Grandma's house. Grandma Cloris underlined "drug addict" several times. One might argue that I had twitchy body language because I was visiting my girlfriend's ragingly anti-Semitic grandmother, not because I was all hopped up on Screaming Meanies, Red Devils, and Purple Poppers.

I was amused to discover Grandma Cloris had photocopied her letters to Judy and taped them all over her apartment. That way when I cold-bloodedly murdered Judy in a marijuana-fueled rage so I could use her life essence in my patented Matzo brei/Christian blood tofu scramble an archive would exist illustrating that Grandma Cloris had repeatedly warned her virginal straight-edge granddaughter all about me and my drugged-out Hebraic ways but Judy had tragically failed to heed her not-at-all-insane ramblings.

Judy hailed from the kind of Podunk shit town where domestic abuse and drunk driving are popular hobbies, not grievous social ills. On my first trip to Stoughton we went to a redneck bar where a raggedy dog licked up errant liquor from the dirt floor. As I exited the bathroom an inebriated redneck jabbed a finger provocatively at me and taunted, "I wanna fuck your girlfriend!"

The smart-ass in me wanted to respond, "What a coincidence. I wanna fuck my girlfriend too!" Thankfully the portion of my brain devoted to self-preservation took over. By the time the hillbilly left the bathroom my party had vacated the premises.

The very different existences of Judy's parents mapped out two possible destinies. She could follow in her mother's footsteps and use her looks and charm to snag a wealthy husband like her doctor stepfather, or she could emulate her father and pursue an existence wholly devoid of meaning and substance. Judy's dad lived in a trailer out in the woods, drank a gallon of cheap vodka every day, and raised Saint Bernard/golden retriever mixes he shot if they developed hip dysplasia.

I'll never forget Judy's father's first words to me.

"You must be the Jew!" he shouted gingerly from across an open field by his trailer. Now, I don't mind being a Jew. I'm almost inordinately proud of my religious heritage. But when I stop being a "Jew" and become "the Jew," images of Kristallnacht and burning synagogues begin swirling in my head. During that trip to Stoughton, Judy announced that our sprawling family would now have another member: an adorable Saint Bernard/golden retriever puppy. Judy insisted her father would take it out back and shoot it if we didn't adopt it immediately. What could I do? I knew damn well that we had no business getting a dog, let alone a giant puppy prone to hip dysplasia. It was blatant emotional blackmail: care for this needy, demanding future giant for the rest of eternity or an adorable puppy will be murdered.

We returned to Madison with the Saint Bernard/golden retriever puppy that we decided to name Betty, after Betty Friedan. During a rare moment of candor I asked Judy if she was building her menagerie of adorable animals to compensate for the shakiness of our loveless union.

"Yeah, probably," she said, then giggled nervously in a way that suggested she was joking and being serious at the same time.

It wasn't the first time Judy had attempted to fill the black hole at the core of our relationship where love, trust, and mutual respect were supposed to be with an adorable critter. As I mentioned in the last chapter, Judy had surprised me with an adorable cat that looked like a big gray mouse for Valentine's Day that I came to call Maggie May. I've subsequently come to love Maggie as dearly as anything in the world, but as a callow, selfish nineteen-year-old, all I initially saw was a furry little shit machine tethered to an unending series of responsibilities. It might as well have come with a card that read, "Congratulations! You're now obligated to feed me, clean my waste, and provide for my veterinary care for the rest of my life! Congrats, sucker!"

When I went to pick up Judy at work for our big Valentine's Day dinner she asked immediately about my furry, saucer-eyed new burden.

"So, did you lock up the room so she wouldn't get out?"

"I dunno. Maybe. Probably," I responded apathetically.

"Jesus, Nathan. How could you not remember something like that? Do you want it to run away? Do you care about her or me at all?"

"Yeah, of course, it's just that, you know, having a cat is a lot of responsibility. I don't know if I'm ready for it yet."

Then came the waterworks. Judy began crying giant body-heaving sobs that could be heard from neighboring area codes.

I switched into damage-control mode and tried to assure her that I loved her, I loved my new cat, and I couldn't imagine a more thoughtful present. It didn't work. For a solid hour she sobbed uncontrollably as we walked down the road and I tried to assure concerned passersby that the hysterical woman weeping openly in public was perfectly OK despite all the evidence to the contrary.

Finally Judy was all cried out, and after she angrily turned down one suggested dinner spot after another, we wearily trudged into Rocky Rococo's, a Wisconsin pizza chain whose mascot and namesake was a sunglass-sporting, white-suit-wearing, regressive Italian stereotype with extra-virgin olive oil pumping through his veins who lov-a his mama and like-a to make-a the pizza for the nice people and probably work-a for the Cosa Nostra in-a hees free time. Heading into the restaurant, I noticed a white Mercedes with vanity plates reading "Rococo" but thought nothing of it.

After glumly ordering a heart-shaped pizza that came with an even tackier heart-shaped balloon, I made a horrifying discovery: Rocky Rococo was in the building. Or rather an actor playing Rocky Rococo was strutting about the restaurant in his trademark white suit kibitzing with customers and oozing cornball old-world charm. When Judy spotted Rocky we shared a knowing smile and an unexpected moment of genuine human connection. I may have been in the doghouse but we intuitively united in our fervent desire to avoid interacting with Rocky Rococo.

Even in her raw, diminished state Judy possessed a mile-wide mean streak and razor-sharp tongue capable of reducing a Rocky Rococo impersonator to tears. Even at her nicest she was still at least moderately evil. So we collectively sent off a chilly, defensive "Leave us the fuck alone if you know what's good for you" vibe that succeeded in warding away Rocky. It did not, however, keep him from standing at the front of the restaurant and loudly announcing, "Hi, everybody! It's-a me, Rocky

Rococo, and I'm here to do the Pizza Rap! Rocky is my name and I'm here to say / Eat-a some pizza every day!" He went on like that for several agonizing minutes but I've purged the rest of his lyrics from my memory. It might seem strange that Rocky chose Valentine's Day to make an unexpected appearance at one of his stores until you realize that February 14 is also Crude Ethnic Stereotype Appreciation Day. Then it makes all the sense in the world.

Judy shot me an incredulous look that conveyed without words that we were clearly in the midst of the best/worst Valentine's Day ever. We headed home, where our fragile peace was broken when we couldn't find Maggie anywhere. We tore up our room frantically looking for her. After nearly giving up, we discovered her sleeping peacefully behind our bed. Maggie went on to teach me everything I know about dignity and grace. Despite my initial ambivalence, she's easily the greatest gift I've ever received.

Not long after Judy brought home Betty I had a hernia operation that unfortunately coincided with Betty's "paper training." The hernia doctors couldn't sew up the area they'd operated on, so I had a gaping wound that took weeks to close.

In desperation I would sometimes disobey the doctor's orders and lurch Frankenstein-style a block or two to Taco Bell, where I became obsessed with their quickly abandoned marketing gimmick the "diet" menu. Day after day I'd trudge clumsily down to Taco Bell and consume anywhere between ten and fifteen "diet tacos." Yet I inexplicably never seemed to lose any weight. On the contrary, my waist expanded rapidly.

I'd entered the co-op a sober, virginal, clean-cut, well-scrubbed young striver brimming with optimism and hope. Within months I'd devolved into a foul-smelling beast who knocked back handfuls of painkillers with cheap beer and subsisted on a diet of reduced-fat tacos, Mountain Dew, shitty weed, and greasy pizza. I'd entered the Fat Elvis stage of my development. I had officially become, in the woozy parlance of the Doors, a "large mammal."

The dispiriting endgame stage of my first real relationship stretched on for months. Endless, joyless months. Our relationship deteriorated until we became a road-show version of Richard Burton and Elizabeth Taylor in *Who's Afraid of Virginia Woolf?*, all icy glares, pointed sarcasm, and withering retorts. The words "I love you" grew colder and colder until they came to mean "I hate you." Yet we were too ferociously committed to each other's unhappiness to pull the trigger and go through the messy business of breaking up.

The beginning of the end arrived when an earnest folksinger habitually clad only in a pair of baggy overalls membershipped at our house. "I ain't too good with talking or nothing. Would it be OK if I just played a song for everybody?" he nervously inquired before his membership meeting. He was so gosh-darned cute in his folksy, aw-shucks country-bumpkin kinda way that I seriously wanted to punch him right in the fucking face.

Overall Boy immediately began sleeping with Judy's bestest friend, Kendall, a daft, likable hippie chick always up for a wake-and-bake, further misadventures in sense derangement, or an impromptu drinking binge. She was ever so much more fun than me, with my bourgeois "job" and "college career" and dreary "instinct for self-preservation."

Overall Boy's arrival coincided with both Judy's twenty-first birthday and the arrival of Overall Boy's best friend, Billy, a lanky, handsome guitar-strumming troubadour who lived on the floor above me. Judy fell helplessly in love with Billy and on a nightly basis left me in favor of a new and exciting world of bar hopping and flirting with strange men alongside Kendall, Billy, and Overall Boy.

Judy finally worked up the nerve to dump me. Being young and naïve and writhing with self-hatred, I was convinced Judy was the only human being in the world who'd ever want to be with me. One sad evening I got down on one knee and nervously proposed to Judy with a cheap, plastic skull ring I got at the video store as a promotional tie-in for *The Phantom*.

The words "Will you marry me?" tumbled uneasily out of my mouth. I'm not sure even I believed them. The only thing that scared me more than a future with Judy was a future without her.

"Jesus, Nathan. I bet you didn't even buy that ring. I bet it's just something you got at work," Judy replied uneasily. To her credit, she said no.

With Judy officially out of my life I threw myself into getting back to my dating weight through a depression-fueled regimen of diet, exercise, and gut-wrenching, appetite-destroying despair. I mustered up the courage to skip gaily past Taco Bell instead of popping in for a dozen diet tacos. Soon my slimmed-down physique attracted the attention of a pretty, green-haired, slightly spacey coworker named Rosanna. She was moving to Seattle to go law school to become one of those green-haired hippie lawyer types in a few weeks, so she had little to lose.

One magical night she came over to my apartment and we drank cheap red wine and smoked weak pot. As she perused my runty little book collection, Rosanna marveled, "Burroughs, Kerouac, Henry Miller, *A Confederacy of Dunces*. Wow! You're such a walking cliché! What, do they just give you these books at freshman orientation as your wannabe-intellectual starter kit?"

It was the single meanest thing anybody had ever said to me. It was also, not coincidentally, the truest. Rosanna saw right through me. We lay down on my leaky, foul-smelling septic tank of a waterbed—yet another horrible idea of Judy's I was saddled with—and tried to watch *Dementia 13*. Partially out of boredom and partially out of curiosity we began kissing. We were making out in Madison, just to pass the time. I suspect that Rosanna fucked me largely as a means of shutting me up. It was apparently the lesser of two evils.

Being young, free, and an exhibitionist, Rosanna strutted

bare-ass naked to the bathroom I shared with four or five house-mates. The co-op being a fertile breeding ground for gossip, news of my unlikely paramour's impromptu Lady Godiva impersonation quickly got back to Judy. The next day Judy tear-fully asked for a reconciliation. The prospect that this naked, green-haired mystery woman might bring me unimaginable heights of happiness was simply too much for Judy to bear. So we engaged again in the eternal dance of attraction and repulsion, make-ups and breakups, reconciliation and reestrangement one last time before finally calling it quits.

I didn't realize it at the time but I was probably the only thing standing between Judy and near-total self-destruction. One night early in our relationship we drunkenly proposed bottoming out together, throwing ourselves into a cesspool of drugs, drink, and bad behavior so we could emerge from the other side wiser, stronger, and imbued with the hard-won wisdom of people who'd been through hell yet survived. When you're nineteen years old and drunk and high on mushrooms, that kind of self-negation seems romantic. But only Judy pursued this bleak path to the bitter end. It was like a suicide pact only one party honors.

After we broke up and Judy got her fill of the bar scene, she hooked up with a scruffy-looking homeless teenager and his girlfriend and immersed herself in a nighttime world of hard drugs and raves. Her new soul mates were as dissimilar from me as you could possibly get.

My attitude toward Judy during this stage of her life was one of willful ignorance: I didn't want to know what she was doing or who she was doing it with, but, since I lived a mere ten feet away, her messy life couldn't help but spill over into mine.

In a rare moment of self-reflection Judy confided that she had smoked crack in front of Betty. It filled her with shame. I couldn't imagine a more horrifying juxtaposition than Judy, a woman I had once admired and adored, smoking crack in front of an adorable little puppy that gazed up at her with uncomprehending big brown eyes. Smoking crack was bad enough; doing it in front of a puppy was damn near unforgivable.

By the end of my stay at the co-op I couldn't bear to be in the same house as Judy. I went MIA from a life that had spiraled out of control. But in extricating myself from Judy and the co-op I regained my fragile sense of self.

One of Us, One of Us!

Freaks
Le Shithole

Director Tod Browning ran away from home as a young man to pursue two quintessential American rites of passage: joining the circus and heading to Hollywood to make it in the pictures. After triumphing with 1931's *Dracula*, Browning put his years working for a circus sideshow to good use in 1932's *Freaks*, a film so shocking it destroyed his career and was banned in Great Britain for decades.

What makes *Freaks* so viscerally unsettling is its verisimilitude. Browning hired genuine sideshow freaks to play the star attractions of a sleazy traveling circus that rises up in righteous vengeance when one of its own, a wealthy, good-hearted midget (Harry Earles), is seduced and betrayed by a heartless trapeze artist (Olga Baclanova) out to poison Earles and share his fortune with her strongman lover (Henry Victor). Browning's initially reviled horror melodrama combines the primal power of a nightmare with the elegant simplicity of a fable. Once seen, *Freaks* characters like Zip and Pip the Pinheads, the limbless Living Torso, Koo Koo the Bird Girl, and Half Boy can never be forgotten.

Audiences for *Frankenstein* could take comfort in the knowledge that once filming wrapped, Boris Karloff could take off his makeup, go home, put on a silk robe, putter around in the garden, and read Yeats. But when Browning yelled, "Cut," Elvira and Jenny Lee Snow were still microcephalic (or pinheads) and Johnny Eck still had no legs or lower torso. Being a freak wasn't a role they played, then discarded. It's who they were on a biological level.

Freaks marked a strange marriage between MGM, the classiest of studios (it employed F. Scott Fitzgerald at the same time it was sending paychecks Johnny Eck's way), and the freak show, that least reputable of American pastimes. As is often the case, the very qualities that made *Freaks* such a scandal upon its release—its fearless originality, nightmarish intensity, sordid subject matter, and sympathetic treatment of marginalized outsiders—ultimately made it a cult classic. Punk rock adopted the film as its own, most directly in the music and imagery of the Ramones, who transformed the freaks' joyous cry of "Gooble gobble we accept you" into an anthemic roar of "gabba gabba hey" on "Pinhead."

In my mind *Freaks* will forever be associated with my two-year stint in a castle-like co-op at the end of Madison's fraternity row that I lived in with Judy known as Le Château (or as it was more appropriately, commonly known, "Le Shithole"), and not just because two of my fellow co-opers operated a makeshift freak show whose biggest attraction involved fire breathing and pounding nails into each other's nostrils. Like the sideshow in *Freaks,* Le Château represented a tight-knit, supportive community of outsiders. At the very beginning at least; then we all turned on each other.

My fellow co-opers were the stuff of Lou Reed songs: jaundiced-looking ex-junkies with hard faces and sagging skin, brawny, half-assed transsexuals with hulking physiques; underage bisexual nudists; depressive stoners; creepy, drug-crazed drifters with homemade orgone boxes; and, for a month or two, Jamie Toulon, a burned-out sixteen-year-old and veteran of the world's youngest punk band (Old Skull).

When I first visited Le Château it struck me as dirty, drug

infested, utterly disreputable, and insane, an inmate-run asylum. In other words, it felt like home. It was like a co-ed Winchester House with ready access to drugs; alcohol; casual, sanctioned nudity; and indiscriminate sex.

White liberal guilt was the life-giving oxygen on which Madison ran. White men rule the world but Madison catered slavishly to people who deviated from the norm. Nobody exploited this dynamic more directly than a housemate who went through his early life as Glen, a burly high school soccer player. At some point in his teens, however, Glen came to the realization that he was really a big, ugly lesbian trapped in the body of a big, ugly heterosexual man. So he decided to get a sex-change operation.

I have nothing but the greatest respect for people who undergo sex changes. Anyone willing to pay doctors thousands to cut off their penis and replace it with a makeshift vagina possesses a degree of commitment and bravery I can't begin to fathom. But Glen/Glenda seemed intent on getting a very half-assed sex-change operation. The doctors said she should lose fifty pounds before going under the knife. She figured twenty pounds would suffice. The doctors suggested that she actively dilate the hole where her makeshift lady-business would be for several hours every night. She'd just stick a rod in there for an hour or so and call it a day.

There are some things in life you can be half-assed about. You can probably skip a lot of that introductory women's studies syllabus reading and walk away with an A. You can probably fudge a little on your taxes without anyone noticing. But changing your gender: there's an endeavor where you really shouldn't cut corners.

I know this is a terrible thing to say but getting a sex-change operation to become a lesbian somehow feels like cheating. It reminded me of the scene in *Private School for Girls* where Matthew Modine and his buddy dress up as women so they can sneak into the girls' dorm taken to its logical extreme. Except this time instead of merely dressing up like a girl to participate in such vaunted girls-only endeavors as naked pillow fights, wet T-shirt cookie bake-offs, and all-night lesbian make-out parties, Glen/Glenda was literally becoming a woman to gain entry into the secret world of lady folk. My suspicions were only confirmed when Glen/Glenda later moved out of Le Shithole and membershipped at Womyn's, an all-female co-op.

But before Glen could become Glenda there was an excruciating in-between phase where she was not quite a man and not quite a woman. Like many of her housemates, Glenda was an exhibitionist. So it wasn't unusual for her loosely fitting robe to "slip," thereby affording anyone within eyeshot an explicit look at the changes her personal space was undergoing. Apparently everyone in the co-op got a harrowing glimpse or two, or three, of Glenda's genitalia while still under construction. Except for me. My potent Jewish neuroses served as a force field protecting me from the potentially traumatizing images.

Glenda was smart, funny, lonely, and vulnerable yet she devoted much of her energy to pushing people away. She was an aficionado of free jazz, and while the progressive part of me understands that free jazz is a legitimate, challenging art form, I'd be lying if I said the results didn't often sound like the work of musically disinclined sadists using saxophones to simulate the hideous shrieking of cats being tortured. As a sadistic form of revenge against her housemates, Glenda regularly blasted jarring, assaultive, eardrum-puncturing free-jazz freakouts at top volume from her stereo. But it wasn't long until she figured she could lose friends, alienate people, and make a vastly more obnoxious racket by playing free jazz herself on a beat-up old saxamaphone on State Street, Madison's busiest street. Madison is such a tiny, insular, sadistically tolerant community that when the fuzz slapped Glenda with a ticket for creating a noise disturbance with her infernal saxophone bleating, she became a cause célèbre among lovers of atonal squawking and free expression.

Normally, I would empathize with plucky street musicians getting hassled by the Man. But, in this instance, I didn't think the cops went far enough: Glenda should have become the first woman sent to the gas chamber for a mere noise disturbance.

People moved into Le Château for different reasons. There were, of course, the true believers, Wiccans with hairy armpits, deodorant-averse anarchistic gutter punks, and gloomy grad school Marxists who genuinely believed they were sticking it to the Man and striking a blow for economic democracy by removing landlords from the housing equation. Then there were the budget-minded pragmatists who sniffed out co-op living as the best value on campus. For three to four hundred bucks a month a spendthrift could have their food and shelter needs taken care of.

In the co-op, "career" was a dirty word. A job was something you did to keep a roof over your head and buy cases of Blatz and nickel bags of weed, not the core of your existence or a path to self-actualization.

A good illustration of the co-op's relaxed attitude toward money and conventional morality can be found in the strange case of Jamie Toulon, the aforementioned sixteen-year-old punk rock has-been. In the late eighties Toulon and his Old Skull bandmates rode the incongruity of adorable children playing abrasive punk rock, opening for Sonic Youth, the Flaming Lips, and GWAR, recording two albums (*Get Outta School* and *CIA Drug Fest*) engineered by a future member of Garbage (Steve Marker) and appearing on MTV and *A Current Affair*.

The group even attained a strange, posthumous pop culture infamy when the utterly genius radio comedy duo of Scharpling and Wurster did a brilliant routine where Wurster played a proudly square "Izod and khakis" kind of guy who re-formed Old Skull as a seven-piece smooth-jazz outfit prone to five-hour-long jams. Words cannot do justice to the subversive genius of this routine. Run out and purchase all of Scharpling and Wurster's albums immediately. You won't regret it.

By the time Toulon was shuffled in front of us as a prospective housemate his career as a prepubescent punk rock oddity was a foggy memory. Toulon had barely entered puberty, yet his best days were behind him. He was a sweet kid, but paying rent was less important to him than getting smashed every night. He admitted as much. At his final house meeting he sheepishly conceded that he could either pay his rent or buy a case of beer every day, and having a roof over his head sure as shit wasn't going to get him drunk.

We understood. Heck, if put in the same position we would have chosen a similar route. None of us was coldhearted enough to deny a sixteen-year-old his inalienable right to risk alcohol poisoning every night. We may have been druggies and degenerates. But we weren't monsters.

Then there were lonely souls shuffling unremarkably toward middle age, for whom the co-op represented the difference between returning home to a sad, sour-smelling efficiency or returning to a giant house overflowing with vibrant young people. This group overlapped with the Pervs. The Pervs consisted largely of what Randy Newman indelibly called "froggish men, unpleasant to see" who figured that their chances of having sex with hot college girls would increase exponentially if they lived within stumbling distance of co-eds intoxicated by the freedom of being away from home for the first time, in addition to other, less abstract mood-altering substances.

The most memorable of the Pervs was Cornelius, a deeply confused man in his midthirties perpetually coated in a slick coat of flop sweat. He made his living getting fake prescriptions for drugs, then selling them on the black market. Every couple of years Cornelius would reembrace Christianity and throw out his Black Sabbath albums. Then, with deadening predictability, he'd buy back all his Black Sabbath albums just so he could get rid of them the next time Jesus hit.

Cornelius's self-censoring apparatus was perpetually on the blink. I remember hanging out in a common room when he stutteringly confessed, "I just think you should know, Nathan, that when I masturbate sometimes I think about you and Judy having sex. I don't wanna make you uncomfortable or nothing. I just thought you should know."

How do you respond to something like that? More important, how was I supposed to purge the mental image of Cornelius's meaty, sweat-encrusted arms flailing against his formidable gut as he beat off fantasizing about Judy and me? I wanted to scream, "For the love of God, man, hide your shame! Tell no one of these things. Don't even concede them to yourself."

Then, as now, I am a big believer in the power and necessity of repression. I wanted to tell him the same thing when he regaled me with the story of how he'd traveled down to Milwaukee to get serviced by a pair of sixteen-year-old prostitutes. Best two hundred bucks he ever spent.

The apogee of Cornelius's sordid criminal revelations occurred when he gingerly confessed that he was so troubled and moved by the angry sexual howling of a stray cat he'd taken in that he tried to satisfy its urges with his finger. It was as if Cornelius had a long checklist of sexual perversions he was systematically working into conversation: whoremongering, statutory rape, and bestiality, just for starters. I never looked at Cornelius the same way again. I lost respect for the cat as well. Even an alley cat in heat has to have standards.

Cornelius had a best friend named Jessica who was such a shambling, out-of-control mess that he emerged as the sane, stable one in their relationship. Cornelius once confided to me in his trademark sweaty, deeply uncomfortable way, "You know, Jessica has a real crush on you and, uh, well, she's got HIV and I'm pretty sure she's an alcoholic and she's kind of manic-depressive or bipolar or something and she's off her meds but other than that she's a really great girl."

Who could resist such a pitch? When you're writing a memoir you have a natural if regrettable tendency to reduce people to their most colorful eccentricities. It's impossible to do justice to the complexities of even a single human being in the space of an entire book, let alone in a few paragraphs or a page and a half. So now might be a good time to point out that Cornelius and many of the other strange characters in my life were, and are, fundamentally good people. Beneath all of Cornelius's perversions, drug sweats, and uncontrollable urges lay a big, big heart, possibly coated in a thick, viscous layer of gravy.

I am certainly not in a position to cast judgment on Cornelius or anyone else. It's a strange law of karma that if you look down on something in others you're destined to experience it yourself.

When I lived at Winchester House I used to look down on Edgar because his mom ate her Sunday dinner at the soup kitchen. Then a different soup kitchen became my father's home away from home. I felt sufficiently humbled. Similarly, I remember a melancholy housemate at Le Château named Paul telling me that he'd gone to the hospital to have his drinking problem assessed and was pleased as spiked punch to report that he was merely a "heavy drinker" and not an alcoholic.

The difference is more than semantic. An alcoholic needs to forgo liquor permanently and embrace a life of stone-cold sobriety and spartan self-denial. A heavy drinker, meanwhile, should probably just pass up that sixth Jägermeister shot of the night. At the time I thought Paul's actions constituted the tragic self-delusion of a drunk unwilling to face the truth about himself and his addiction. Twelve years later I comfort myself at night by imagining that I, too, am a heavy drinker and not an alcoholic. I'm terribly hypocritical that way.

Drugs were the common denominator at Le Château. The house moved to the languid, fuzzy rhythms of pot, acid, and mushrooms. When a sizable contingent of the house was on acid or mushrooms together, a quasispiritual communion seemed to take place. Then you'd sober up and realize you were just a bunch of assholes taking drugs at the same time.

The eighties might have been Morning in America for Ronald Reagan. But for me it was a dark night of the soul that lasted an entire decade. I grew up in the decade of "Just Say No," a time when parents subscribed to the notion that the best thing they could do for their children was to fill them with fear that disaster lurked around every corner.

In the sixties having sex and using drugs meant you were one seriously swinging hep cat. In the eighties having sex and using drugs meant you had an insatiable death wish. Drug dealers were ominous, parasitic creatures of the night who lurked in the shadows, sported dirty trench coats, and spent their days looking for third graders to corrupt.

But when I arrived at Le Château, my philosophy concerning drugs changed. Drug dealers were no longer shadowy villains. They were the unsung heroes of the underground economy, outlaws bravely risking life and limb so they could make their clients' lives just a little groovier. A bowl after a tough day smoothed the rough edges of a nasty, hypercompetitive world. Like masturbation, pot is one of God's great consolation gifts. Not everyone can experience non-chemically-induced happiness, but on the right night a few chocolate martinis and a couple hits from the bong can provide a more-than-passable imitation of genuine, non-chemically-induced contentment.

At Le Château I was first introduced to the peculiar rules and social codes of potheads. I learned that no self-respecting marijuana enthusiast ever buys drugs from a drug dealer. No, they know "a guy" who has "some stuff" or is "dry." If the "guy" is "dry," chances are good he knows another "guy" who might be able to hook you up. Fuzziness is a formidable weapon in a stoner's arsenal. I learned to conduct every conversation with a dealer (which is to say "a guy" who "had some stuff") as if J. Edgar Hoover were recording every syllable from beyond the grave and playing it for a hostile jury.

Veteran pot users learn to communicate what they want from dealers without ever asking for it directly. Communication between dealers and users (or rather guys with stuff and guys who want to buy and use their stuff) is cryptic and elliptical. A typical phone conversation between my dealer and me went something like this:

ME: Hey, this is Nathan.
"GUY": What's up?
ME: Should I stop by? Would that be cool?
"GUY": Sure.

Potheads live with the disquieting knowledge that their favorite pastime could get them thrown in jail at any time. So they go out of their way to make the process of purchasing illegal drugs from a drug dealer seem as casual as possible. The idea is that you're simply hanging out with a buddy who happens to deal a little weed and is willing to hook you up, not meeting with a near stranger for the sole purpose of scoring drugs. This is a surprisingly easy fiction to maintain since anybody who hooks you up with weed is by definition a friend, even if you only see them once you've run out of pot.

At Le Château pot was a great social lubricant. It was remarkable how much self-important bullshit I was willing to tolerate for a few puffs from someone else's stash. Smoking from someone else's pipe gave them implicit permission to subject you to half-baked ideas for zines or screenplays, crackpot conspiracy theories, and stoned philosophizing.

Then there was the music. My two years in co-op hell left me with a deep and abiding distaste for the music of the Dave Matthews Band, Phish, Ani DiFranco, the Grateful Dead, Sarah McLachlan, and Alanis Morissette. Why, for the love of God, did I have to be a sophomore during the infernal summer of *Jagged Little Pill*? Who did I piss off in a previous life? If I never hear *You Can't Do That on Television*'s most famous alumna bray about what is and is not like ray-yay-yayn on your wedding day or good advice that you just didn't take, it will be too soon.

The first time I ever took acid, Le Château hosted a concert by a band called Quincy Punx. As the acid took hold a wave of euphoria kicked in. Suddenly everything seemed profound. I felt connected to everyone and everything in the universe. My God, I marveled semicoherently, I'm just like all these crusty gutter punks! And they're just like me! And we're all one with the Earth Mother Goddess!

After the show one of the visiting punks had his penis pierced in our kitchen, a wildly unhygienic procedure that was video-taped 'cause, let's face it, that's something you'll totally want to show the grandkids. I was tripping with Judy, my fellow co-oper Bob, and his girlfriend Janet.

Late into the night Bob was talking to the guy with the fresh penis piercing about his bisexuality when he boasted, with boozed-up bravado, "I've fucked a hundred guys and a hundred girls and I'll fuck a hundred more before I'm through."

Janet was on the verge of tears and in my delusional haze I remember thinking, "My God, acid is allowing me to see that Janet is really hurt by what Bob's saying. This is amazing!" I shared my observation with Judy and she agreed that LSD gave us extraordinary, almost preternatural powers of perception. Then we came down and realized how stunningly banal our acid-induced "revelations" were.

Parties unleashed the bad craziness forever bubbling under the co-op's mellow surface. One damnable New Year's Eve Wayne the Blockbuster Vampire thoughtfully let me leave work five min-utes early so he wouldn't have to give me a ride home. I had a really bad strep throat, so everything was headachy and off.

After an hour of waiting in the freezing cold a cab finally came. When I arrived at Le Château the New Year's Eve party was in full swing. Pausing to gather my strength before I hiked up three flights of stairs to my room, I spied what appeared to be one of the hippie revelers in our living room groping herself unashamedly in a state of stoned erotic abandon. Like a drunk in an old comedy, I wiped my eyes to make sure I wasn't imag-ining things and looked again to see that, yes, there definitely was a whacked-out stranger masturbating while a jam band called the Blissters hammered out a tribal beat in the background. The next morning the masturbating hippie lady would be the talk of the co-op, but at the time I was far too beat to pay it much mind.

I trudged woozily on up to my room. In the corner of my bed Judy and her best friend/soul mate, Stacy, held on to each other for dear life in a two-person fetal ball.

"Ohmygod Nathan we were taking shrooms and they weren't working so we took some more, like the whole bag, an entire quarter or maybe a half, and now we can't come down and we can't deal with him," Judy muttered as I assessed the situation. Judy and Stacy had fallen prey to the psilocybin delusion: you take hallucinogenic mushrooms, get mad that they're not working, conveniently forget that they take forty-five minutes to kick in, then down the whole bag and freak out when the shrooms finally kick in. That's what was happening with Judy and Stacy. Their pupils were as big as dimes.

In a rattan chair in the corner lay a passed-out stranger whose weathered face was painted white and red. Passed-out strangers were a regular occurrence in the co-op, but Judy and Stacy's drug delirium gave the situation a nightmarish dimension. "Get him to leave, please. He looks like a monster," Judy pleaded helplessly.

I gently but persistently shook the man's shoulder until he groggily came to.

"Excuse me, sir. I'm afraid you've passed out in my bedroom. If you could find someplace else to crash that'd be really cool. I've got pneumonia or something. I just got off an eight-hour shift at a Blockbuster in Monona and I'd really love to get some sleep myself," I implored meekly. He nodded in agreement and stumbled out of our lives.

The next morning the masturbating hippie lady returned sheepishly to our co-op to retrieve a hat she'd left behind the night before. I admired her courage. If I'd put on an impromptu public sex show at a local co-op I wouldn't return to the scene of the crime even if I'd accidentally left a bag of diamonds behind. We tried our best not to snicker. It was a struggle. Masturbating hippie girl had achieved instant co-op infamy. Even if she discovered a cure for AIDS, won a Nobel Prize, and served as our first female president, she'd forever be known in the co-ops as that freak who masturbated on the dance floor during the big New Year's Eve party.

Like most Madison co-ops, Le Château was "clothing optional," but most folks had the good sense to keep their clothes on. It has been my experience that the only people who flaunt their nakedness are people you'd happily scoop your eyes out with a melon baller to avoid seeing nude. That was true of Woody and Alice, a hirsute teenage couple who lived in the co-op briefly despite being minors. They flaunted their love of swinging and threesomes and public nudity along with their flabby white bellies and jiggling pools of cellulite.

A year or two earlier the notion of living with naked swingers would have sent me into a state of dizzy erotic anticipation. But when Woody and Alice plopped down on our communal couches unencumbered by clothing, dignity, or shame, all I could think about was how hopelessly unsanitary it was. It was during moments like this that I came to realize I was at heart a hopeless prudervert. A prudervert lingers under the delusion that they're sexy, swinging, and sexually progressive until they're actually confronted with unconventional sexuality, at which point they become a hopeless prude.

At Le Château we cavalierly disregarded the rules, then incurred the scars that let us know why the rules existed in the first place. We treated each other with heartbreaking callousness. I had an alpha-male housemate who coldly dumped his girlfriend. When she started to tear up he admonished her, "Please, don't cry. I don't want to remember you as being pathetic."

It was a devastating statement, brutal in its efficiency. In a single sentence he transformed a relationship from a living, breathing, open-ended entity into a distant memory and ensured that any response other than stoic, noble silence would be interpreted as needy desperation. Of course, if I said something that evil, this book wouldn't exist because I'd still be in the process of getting slapped hard by whomever I said it to. Deservedly so.

We were a real-life Addams Family. Co-op freaks represented normality and normality was freakish. Consequently our most bizarre resident was Charlene, a perky blonde senior majoring in business who worked by night as a Hooters waitress and couldn't have been prouder of her status as a "little sister" for a campus fraternity. The only thing more insufferable than a Republican pod person who works at Hooters and serves as a fraternity's little sister yet inexplicably lives in a co-op is a Hooters waitress/little sister who is incredibly self-righteous about her association with those two unassailable cultural institutions.

On the rare instances when she graced us with her presence, Charlene nattered on and on about the wet T-shirt car washes for autism and kissing booths to raise money for knock-kneed, cross-eyed spinsters her employer and frat selflessly sponsored. She spoke of Hooters and the frat as if they were primarily philanthropic organizations that reluctantly pandered to the public appetite for cleavage, chicken wings, and keggers solely as a means of funding their invaluable outreach programs and charity drives. Charlene combined the brassy exterior of a sorority president with the smugness of a born-again Christian.

Charlene wasn't the only freak in our axis. Every Sunday a wizened, fiftysomething casualty of the sixties named Hambone would show up after dinner, smoke a bowl in our second-floor phone room, then sit in on interminable three-hour-long house meetings to make sure that we were following the antiquated bylaws of the organization that oversaw our co-op.

That's how he got his jollies: by getting high, then making sure we followed protocol. It was the sickest shit I'd ever seen. Golden showers, furries, fecal freaks, adult babies: that shit I understand. But getting your kicks by enforcing the long-forgotten dictates of our Madison Community Co-op overlords? That was just wrong. Here's the really sick part: I don't even think Hambone lived in an MCC co-op. Nor did anyone request his presence at our house meetings. He just sort of showed up every Sunday on his own accord.

At one giddy high-water mark for Le Shithole a full fourth of our membership was collecting SSI, or supplementary security income. SSI is essentially money the government gives people too crazy to hold down jobs. It's the government's way of saying, "Here's some money, fruitcake. Please stay out of the way of sane people making substantive contributions to society."

One prominent member of our co-op's SSI brigade was a character named Richard. Richard claimed that when he was six years old his father tied him to a chair and dosed him with LSD. Now, sometimes when Mommy or Daddy doesn't buy us that GI Joe we want or misses our Little League game it can *feel* like they're tying us to a chair and dosing us with LSD. But I'm pretty sure Richard wasn't waxing metaphoric.

I came to Le Château because it was a drug-crazed hellhole. But we were not immune from the all-American impulse for reinvention. So we collectively decided on a name change. All manner of proposals were bandied about. My favorite was "Masada," after the legendary Israeli siege. Did we really want to promote a mental association between our co-op and a siege where Jews chose mass suicide rather than risk an even worse fate?

We chose the blandly pretty "Meridian." Still, our bad reputation persisted. Drastic measures were necessary. In her first year at the co-op, Judy made a stunning transformation from Young Republican to super-co-oper. In her role as the de facto leader of Le Château she lobbied the MCC, the board governing Madison co-ops, for something called a "re-membershipping."

For those of you lucky enough to have never lived in a co-op, a "re-membershipping" is a Stalinist purge where co-opers who fail to exhibit the proper revolutionary zeal are asked to leave while die-hards are allowed to stay. To paraphrase Groucho Marx, most of us co-opers didn't want to live in a co-op that would have people like us as members.

There was an element of Orwellian groupthink to the co-op: we were a mere charismatic leader away from being a full-blown cult. We were essentially asking the MCC to destroy us so we could be reborn anew. Revolutions eat their own and ours was developing a powerful hunger. Considering the motley assortment of rogues, scoundrels, deviants, and ne'er-do-wells that occupied Meridian, it's not surprising that most Le Château freaks opted to move out rather then submit to a re-membership meeting where a panel from the MCC would determine whether they'd be allowed to live in the scuzziest, most drugged-out MCC co-op the next year.

As the boyfriend of the leader of the revolt, I was the reluctant Madame Mao of Meridian. I had no choice but to submit myself to the humiliating re-membershipping process.

In a perfect world joining a co-op means instantly becoming part of a community of like-minded friends united in their passion for social and economic justice, questionable stews made of brown rice and whatever doesn't smell too bad in the refrigerator, the deplorable practice of smoking marijuana, and a burning desire to stick it to the Man. For a young man who grew up feeling lonely and alienated, that promise of kinship and solidarity holds a powerful allure.

But if you're depressed, that sense of community turns into a sick joke and a community of friends devolves into an intimidating galaxy of strangers. You want desperately to shut yourself off from a world gone dreary and joyless. When you have twenty-five roommates depending on you to do your part to create a socialist housing utopia out of tofu, furniture borrowed from Dumpsters, and duct tape, that's impossible.

I couldn't convince the Madison Community Co-operative board that I was a model co-oper because I didn't believe that myself. The Woodstock phase of my infatuation with co-ops hadn't yet darkened into Altamont bleakness, but I was deeply ambivalent about spending another year at Meridian and couldn't muster the enthusiasm to pretend otherwise.

The MCC board initially turned down my bid to stay in the house. That was absolutely the right decision for the co-op and for me. Alas, I had the misfortune of winning an appeal and was allowed to stay for one more season in hell.

After Judy and I broke up, my already waning interest in the co-op disappeared. My raging inner misanthrope killed my inner hippie, who was too high, wimpy, and confused to put up much of a fight. When Judy moved to the room next to mine to afford me a front-seat view of her harrowing downward spiral into hard drugs, sex, and those hideous raver pants, I finally couldn't take it anymore. I fled Madison in order to save myself.

I was attracted to Le Château because of its free-floating madness, but in the end its insanity was too much for me to bear.

The Walking Dead Like Me

The Charm of the Highway Strip
The Chapter Where I Go AWOL from My Life

Like Sam Peckinpah's strangely simpatico 1973 revisionist masterpiece *Pat Garrett and Billy the Kid,* the Magnetic Fields' 1994 magnum opus *The Charm of the Highway Strip* occupies that strange mind state called High Lonesome, where bone-deep misery punches through the darkness en route to transcendence. Sonically Stephin Merritt's New Wave synthesizer symphonies couldn't be further removed from the slide guitar and rustic twang of Nashville, but lyrically his narratives of loneliness and restless wandering are as country as anything Johnny Cash or George Jones ever recorded.

In the summer and fall of 1997, I was very much in a country state of mind. In that miserable stretch every facet of my life went flamboyantly to hell. After leaving Blockbuster I lucked into a job at Video Inferno. I only got an interview at Madison's funkiest video store because I listed *The Onion* as my last employer, thanks to a disastrous three-week stint contributing headlines to the comedy side.

"It says here that you left *The Onion* because of 'creative differences.' What exactly were those 'creative differences'?" the manager asked me during my interview.

"Well, I suppose it boiled down to me thinking I was hilarious and should continue contributing to *The Onion* and them feeling strongly otherwise."

The manager laughed, then hired someone else. Thankfully that special someone quit after a few weeks and I swooped in to take his job. A few weeks after I was hired, I was introduced to the guy who opened the store every morning.

"Nathan, have you met Keith Phipps?" my manager inquired.

"Keith Phipps. Hey, don't you write movie reviews for *Isthmus*?"

"Yeah, but I also write for *The Onion*." So he did. The seeds for my entire professional career were planted in that introduction. Keith and I became fast friends. Meeting Keith and realizing we had so much in common was like growing up thinking you're the only Minotaur in the world only to discover another Minotaur who shares your passion for glam rock, the Smiths, and the French New Wave. I embarked on a strange film-critic apprenticeship with Keith, riding shotgun while he reviewed the dreck of Madison's cinemas for *The Onion* and *Isthmus*. We solidified our bond during nighttime screenings of long-forgotten ephemera like *Booty Call*, *Sprung*, and *The Pest*.

I loved working at Video Inferno. But as I sank further and further into suicidal despair my job performance started to suffer. And by "started to suffer" I mean "turned to shit." A video store clerk's job entails enduring the condescension and contempt of customers for six to eight hours with a strained smile and artificial good cheer. But depression fatally impaired my ability to engage in socially mandated charades.

I transformed bitter personal resentments into an exquisitely passive-aggressive political crusade. I secretly turned my cash register into a no-holds-barred arena for class warfare. If a frat boy held up a cover box of, say, *Chasing Amy* and asked if I could see if any had been returned, I would hiss, "Gosh, are there any out there on the shelf?"

When the frat boy would ask me to check the return bin to

see if any *Chasing Amy* copies had been returned, I would glare at him for a good twenty seconds and ask, "Really? You want me to get down on my hands and knees and root through the return box on the off chance that there might be a copy of *Chasing Amy* in it? That's really what you're asking me to do?"

I knew damn well that that's exactly what I was being asked to do. In happier times I'd eagerly root around in the return box in search of a popular movie. But I somehow became convinced that asking employees to root through the return box to look for movies constituted a grievous personal insult to the dignity of the working class. So I wasn't just being a raging asshole for my own sake: I was being a total fucking dick for the sake of the proletariat. Or something like that. Depression has a way of clouding your judgment and turning shades of gray pitch-black.

I waged a counterproductive war on the ruling classes on two fronts. I boldly/obnoxiously stood up to the bold/obnoxious frat boys by launching what Marxists refer to as a strategic "work slowdown" while I simultaneously railed against the store's owner by giving out free rentals indiscriminately and talking shit about the capitalist oppressor signing my paychecks.

While life at Video Inferno disintegrated, my menagerie of woebegone creatures at home expanded. Judy and I lived next to Susanne, a fetching twenty-five-year-old college graduate who made twenty-five thousand dollars a year doing something with computers or money or some such adult nonsense, an unfathomable windfall to us destitute co-opers. Susanne had a very sweet Great Dane that labored under the misconception that it was the size of a poodle.

In time-honored co-op tradition Susanne fell into a deep state of lust with a housemate named Jack, an affable nineteen-year-old stoner and dedicated jam-band aficionado whose professional accomplishments peaked with a part-time gig at a local custard stand. Susanne and Jack's relationship was like a gender-switched version of the star-crossed duo in the Stephen Malkmus song "Jenny and the Ess-Dog," with all the pathos and comedy that entails.

Jack in turn owned Bandit, the world's most disgusting cat, a greasy, foul-smelling beast so covered in dandruff it looked as spotted as a moo-cow. Jack took Bandit on the road with him when he followed the Grateful Dead and Phish. Deadheads are known for many things: their preternatural patience for the self-indulgent extended noodling of mediocre jam bands, their relaxed attitude toward personal hygiene, and their enjoyment of the mind-altering powers of THC for starters. What they're not known for is the sterling veterinary care and nutrient-rich food they provide their unwittingly migratory animal companions. Accordingly, years of subsisting exclusively on Cheetos, Mountain Dew, secondhand pot smoke, and leftover nachos had rotted away Bandit's insides to mush. She no longer meowed. Instead she'd infrequently let out a blood-curdling death rattle, an unholy croak of the damned.

Bandit eschewed the niceties of drinking from a dish in favor of the more earthy pleasures of leaping into a toilet bowl and greedily lapping up the water rushing down the sides. She similarly had little use for the litter box: when she wanted to emit a house-clearing blast of putrid mustard gas, she'd simply let loose wherever she might be, whether it was inside my laundry hamper or on the kitchen table.

Bandit was quite simply the world's most disgusting cat. When Jack and Susanne decided to move in together after several weeks of deep, meaningful fucking, it was mysteriously decided by people other than myself that I would look after this scared, crazy, greasy, obese, half-dead creature until it became fully acclimated to living with a dog the size of a Shetland pony.

Alas, Bandit never did get used to living alongside a freakishly huge canine monster. Even less surprisingly Susanne and Jack's relationship—a profound spiritual bond rooted in the deep soil of mutual intoxication and primal physical attraction—fell apart within weeks. But by that time it was decided that Bandit was now my sole responsibility.

I felt for Bandit. She was just like me: a repulsive, foul-smelling pariah living a life that was almost like suicide. We were two rotting, reviled peas in a disgusting pod. But gradually Bandit became too much for me. She was a grotesque, ghoulish, unspeakably cruel caricature of a cat, a walking ghost lurking among the living.

The end of Bandit's life and my Video Inferno career occurred on the same mixed-up, no good, very bad day. It was becoming uncomfortably clear that Bandit enjoyed zero quality of life, so I decided to take her to the Humane Society to be put down. Being a seriously broke college student, I couldn't afford a cat carrier so I stuck a horrified Bandit into a flimsy cardboard box and called a cab.

It was a hundred fucking degrees that day and as I waited for the cab and struggled to keep Bandit inside the cardboard box, tears streamed down my face. Bandit screeched madly in her patented death rattle, sensing that the end was drawing near.

Finally a cab arrived and I jumped in with my angry, croaking cardboard box.

"Yeah, if you've got a cat in that thing you're going to have to stick it in the trunk. It can't ride in here with us," the cabbie barked brusquely, oblivious to my tears. I hopped out of the cab, at which point my older sister happened upon the sad spectacle of me standing forlornly on the corner, tears streaming down my face.

"Are you OK?"

What could I say? I had seldom felt less OK.

My sister said she was running late for work but would check in with me later that evening at Video Inferno. I tearfully took a more accommodating cab to the Humane Society and had Bandit put to sleep.

Sure enough, my sister dropped by Video Inferno later that evening. When Joey, the store manager, saw me talking to her instead of dealing with a procession of indignant customers he flew into a rage. Quaking with anger, he jabbed a finger at me accusingly and yelled at the top of his lungs, "You! Go home! Now!" Forget anger. He seemed consumed by something closer to Old Testament wrath. As he screamed at me that I was fired in full view of my sister, my coworkers and friends, and a store full of horrified customers, he morphed into Moses confronting the Israelites as they worshipped their golden calf.

With his long white beard and Santa Claus–like girth, my manager even looked like a biblical prophet of doom.

Flustered and in shock, all I could offer in my defense was a meek "Can't I at least finish out my shift?" as if working an additional few hours might somehow mitigate the humiliation of being publicly fired.

"No! Go home! Now!" he repeated, his anger undiminished.

At that point Video Inferno was the epicenter of my universe. I'd even hang out there when I wasn't working a shift. Now suddenly I was persona non grata in my home away from home.

Filled with semirighteous indignation, I decided to file a lawsuit against Video Inferno for discriminating against me on the basis of depression. This was a ridiculous idea. I was, after all, a terrible employee who deserved to be fired. But I was devastated by the way I'd been fired and felt like the store should have been more understanding about my battle with Vice Admiral Phinneas Cummerbund.

The case manager I was assigned for my discrimination suit seemed to feel otherwise. During our first and only phone conversation his tone was chilly and skeptical, rightly so. For I had what civil rights professionals call "a piss-poor case." "So, let me get this straight. You are a white heterosexual male and you feel that you're being discriminated against because of your depression. Is that right?"

Feeling more than a little silly, I responded, "Yeah. Pretty much."

"Now, do you have any paperwork verifying that you were

discriminated against because of depression? Do you have any incriminating memos or anything like that?"

Did I have incriminating memos? What did he expect? That my managers would fax me duplicate copies of incriminating documents that had been signed and ratified by a notary public? Wasn't that like asking someone who'd just been mugged, "Now, I know you'd like us to solve this crime for you, but if you could just give us a videotape of the crime shot from several different angles accompanied by a signed confession from the people responsible, that'd really help us out"?

"No, I don't really have anything like that."

My caseworker sighed deeply before concluding, "Well, without paperwork verifying your discrimination, you're going to have a prohibitively difficult time winning a discrimination case." That, dear reader, marked the inauspicious beginning and end of my discrimination lawsuit.

The owner of Video Inferno didn't know that, however. He was convinced I was gunning for his fortune, his business, and his very way of life. When I filed for unemployment he fought the claim, arguing in legal documents that I was, in his immortal words, an "aggressive slacker" out to destroy an honest, folksy small business built by a humble, salt-of-the-earth former corporate executive on a sturdy foundation of hard work, old-fashioned Midwestern values, and videos with names like *Clown Fuckers* and *Bathroom Sluts 3*. A court date was set for a hearing where my quivering, twenty-one-year-old self would square off against Maurice, the owner of Video Inferno; Joey; and Roy, a superflighty manager whose last employer was the U.S. Navy, a rather perplexing career choice for a diminutive, supereffeminate homosexual. Roy had left Video Inferno but was being flown in solely so he could testify against me.

A court date loomed menacingly on the horizon, where two imposing authority figures and one very confused ex-sailor would argue passionately that I was such a pox upon my former employer that I was unworthy of even the sad little consolation prize doled out to people who get their asses fired. I had nothing against Joey. He was a sweet, gentle man and I liked his wife and lovely daughter.

Maurice was another matter. I hated the way he held himself up as a pillar of the community even as he paid his employees little more than minimum wage and ensured that no one stuck around long enough to ask for benefits.

In desperation I entered therapy with a Lutheran minister who moonlighted as a clown (a surefire warning sign), but I was kicked out of counseling after missing two sessions. I suffered a corneal ulcer and then an allergic reaction to my ulcer medication that made my blood-red eyeball swell to grotesque, horror-movie proportions. The ulcer and the allergic reaction to my medication made me hypersensitive to light, so, like the Phantom of the Opera, I recoiled from sunlight and human contact in favor of solitary darkness.

In times of despair I have historically found comfort in the welcoming arms of self-pity, that bitch goddess that forever beckons with a seductive spiel: Why even bother trying, my poor, poor hopeless dear? Here, come lie down on the couch with me, this giant bag of weed, and a twelve-pack of Stella Artois, and we'll watch *Simpsons* reruns and feel sorry for ourselves until the pain goes away.

Having most recently failed as a co-oper, boyfriend, and video store clerk, I wondered if maybe I was getting above my raisin'. Maybe I really did belong in a mental hospital or a group home. Maybe that was my destiny. Back at Winchester, the kids talked reverently about two alumni. There was this one guy, Steve, who'd beaten the odds and graduated from college. It wasn't until much later that I realized that that guy Steve was Stephen Elliott, the author of books like *My Girlfriend Comes to the City and Beats Me Up* and other autobiographical works about prostitution, stripping, sadomasochism, bondage, and Democratic politics. It breaks my heart that as long as Elliott is writing about dominatrixes, childhood sexual abuse, and Howard Dean, I'll

never be the filthiest, most perverted writer ever to emerge from
the Jewish Children's Bureau. Damn you, Stephen Elliott!

My life would go on to eerily parallel Elliott's. I went on to
write for *The Onion*. He fell in with the switchblade-toting
greasers in the *McSweeney's* gang. He became a passionate political activist. I sometimes vote. He teaches at Stanford and
exposes his demons and compulsions in visceral, stripped-down
prose. I get paid modestly to write mean things about Hilary
Duff. It's like we're the same person.

I ended up following in Elliott's footsteps but that summer I
worried that I'd end up like a less distinguished former denizen
of the group home system, Ross. Everyone liked Ross. He was
funny and smart and full of big plans. Yet he could never quite
get it together and ended up crashing at the group home every
once in a while well into his early twenties. Would I end up like
Ross, using Winchester House as a safety net when my world fell
apart?

Feeling lost, hopeless, and borderline suicidal, I did what so
many of the protagonists of *Charm of the Highway Strip* do: I
hit the open road, embarking on a Magical Misery Tour that
took me first to Keith's couch, then a hostel two blocks away
from my co-op, and then to Monroe, Michigan, to visit my aunt
and uncle before heading back down to Chicago to spend several weeks with my dad.

Dad was my salvation. To the rest of the world I was an
angry ball of hate. But my dad treated my arrival like the Second Coming. He did everything he could to rouse me out of my
funk, including taking me to see Morris Day and the Time. It
was the single sweetest, most hilariously misguided gesture of
my life. Then and now, my father's unconditional love meant
everything to me.

"You like music, right?" he effused excitedly after buying
tickets.

"Uh, yeah. I, like every other person in the world, enjoy
music," I droned suspiciously.

"Great. I got us tickets to go see Morris Day and the Time at the Park West! You love Prince, right? This'll be just like seeing him."

Only in my dad's mind would liking music automatically lead to a strong desire to see Prince protégés live a mere fifteen years past their prime. But it was so disgustingly sweet and thoughtful that I couldn't help but be touched.

At the nightclub a stand-up comedian opening for the Time launched into a routine that began, "Hey, you know how it is when you go down to Jew town and they try to Jew you down on the prices of everything . . ."

My dad began shaking his cane in anger at the opening act. "Hey! That's anti-Semitic!"

A few years later, after I had relocated permanently to Chicago, my dad called with exciting news. "Hey, you know that Jewish hip-hop rapper guy you interviewed? MC Paul Barman? He's playing a show here in Chicago. We should go! It'll be fun!"

I tried to think of a reason not to go to a hip-hop show at a punk rock club/bowling alley with my helpless crippled father but quickly relented. Why the hell not? My father and I had done crazier shit together.

Barman's opening act was a noise-punk band fronted by a singer who punctuated the jet-engine roar of his group's music with blistering free-jazz saxophone freak-outs. It was one of the loudest, most abrasive acts I'd ever seen but when I glanced over at my dad he was slumped over on one of the bowling benches, fast asleep. When my dad falls asleep he leans heavily to his right and looks disconcertingly like a corpse.

"Dude, is that guy OK? He looks kinda dead," inquired a concerned concertgoer.

"Yeah, he's fine. He just falls asleep rather easily," I assured him.

But before my father could inadvertently play possum at the Fireside Bowl, I first had to make it through my Summer of Discontent. When I hit Chicago I made an appointment with an eye doctor who asked me what eye steroid my Madison doctor had prescribed. When I told her she very gingerly enthused, "Gosh, I don't know why anyone would prescribe that medication. It always causes horrible side effects like the ones you've been experiencing!" I felt a lot better knowing that my discomfort could easily have been avoided.

By the end of the summer I had mustered up the courage to face my former employers in a court of law. One chilly late-summer afternoon I headed down to the courtroom to present my case opposite the Video Inferno brain trust.

Going into the courtroom I knew two things absolutely: I knew that I had been fired in an embarrassing and unprofessional way and I knew that I deserved to be fired. I was a horrible, horrible employee. I was constantly committing termination-worthy offenses, from bad-mouthing the boss to indiscriminately giving out freebies and favors to friends to glaring contemptuously at customers I didn't like (namely, everyone I wasn't doling out freebies and favors to).

So it seemed perverse that the brain trust over at Video Inferno lobbed all manner of baseless accusations against me instead of focusing on all the horrible shit I actually did. I was accused of hurling videotapes at customers and leaping over counters. The store manager told the court that his friends had nicknamed me "Rude Boy" due to my sour disposition, a title I added to "Angriest Man in the Mental Hospital" and "Aggressive Slacker" on my list of insulting things I'd been called that actually seem kinda cool. In their zeal to keep me from getting rich off the sixty-dollar unemployment checks I'd been receiving, the Video Inferno powerbrokers tried to use the fact that I'd talked fuzzily to coworkers about visiting England during the summer as proof that I was a wealthy con man out to finance my decadent spending sprees with the money I'd finagled from simple soft-core porn merchants.

My courtroom adversaries seemed to think they had a smoking gun in my talk of visiting another country. Surely only a well-to-do child of privilege would discuss such lavish vacation plans with coworkers, right? But I was a fucking college student. College students have a habit of talking about all the shit they plan to do without ever following through. Half of my housemates at Le Château talked about how they were gonna spend a few seasons working on a fishing boat in Alaska to save up some money. That didn't mean they needed to invest in long underwear and down jackets. If anything, a college student talking big about their ambitious plans meant they were probably never going to do any of the things they talked about.

The court ultimately ruled in my favor but it was a Pyrrhic victory: since I was going back to college and with it the sweet sustenance of regular financial aid, my unemployment checks disappeared after a week. But oh how I treasured that last sixty dollars of unemployment!

By the time class resumed I'd found personal and professional salvation as a film critic for *The Onion*. Unlike Merritt's drifters and lost souls, I had found my home, my true north. My fate and the soaring fortunes of *The Onion* were unexpectedly intertwined.

A Woefully Premature Happy Ending

8 Mile
Permanent Temporary Happiness Forever

Eminem's *8 Mile* takes a page from the pop star handbook by transforming its star's real-life ascent into a semi-autobiographical vehicle. But if *8 Mile* conforms to a template that's struck gold for everyone from Al Jolson (*The Jazz Singer*) to Prince (*Purple Rain*), it's also a risky piece of pop mythology. In a rap world where vulnerability is viewed as weakness, *8 Mile* is brave enough to depict its star as a squirmy bundle of nerves, anxiety, and self-loathing. It makes audiences earn the exhilarating catharsis of its ending with two solid hours of feel-bad miserablism.

Eminem earned his stripes on the battling circuit but *8 Mile* teases audiences with an almost Bressonian combination of unbearable tension and endlessly delayed but ultimately intoxicating release. In that respect the film echoes *Saturday Night Fever,* a film most people remember as a fun movie about John Travolta disco-dancing when it's actually an almost unbearably grim working-class drama where dancing stands out precisely because it represents such a joyous release from the monotony of Travolta's workaday existence.

Similarly, a dead-eyed Eminem spends the vast majority of *8 Mile* plodding sullenly through a bombed-out hellscape of shitty jobs, fucked-up relationships, and toxic family dynamics. *8 Mile* eloquently captures what it's like to grow up in a system that gave up on you before you were even born. The verbal blood sport of battling represents an invaluable catharsis for the revenge-hungry repressed, but Eminem's character is initially too mired in self-loathing to rise to the challenge of decimating rival MCs.

It isn't until Eminem transforms everything he hates about himself—being "white," being "a fucking bum," living in a trailer park with his mom, his fucked-up friends, getting jumped, getting cheated on by a girlfriend—into strengths that he gains the tools to rise above his hellish upbringing.

Similarly, it wasn't until I turned twenty-one and lucked into a rare opportunity with a scruffy fake newspaper called *The Onion* that I managed to turn a lifetime of losing into something suspiciously resembling success. In the mental hospital my sarcasm was viewed as a poisonous pathology. At the group home it was punished. But at *The Onion* sarcasm was a thriving business and an art form. My moony infatuation with movies over real life might have made me an academic nonentity and a social outcast, but at *The Onion* it proved the key to professional success.

I fell in love with Madison and *The Onion* simultaneously. In Madison the sixties never died and nonconformity wasn't just tolerated, it was celebrated. College is where people shed their high school identities like a second skin and try out new personas and philosophies with dilettantish fervor.

When I visited my sister at the University of Wisconsin at Madison for the first time in 1991, *The Onion* was still a crude, zany black-and-white tabloid in the *Weekly World News* mold, a far cry from the sophisticated, *USA Today*–slick social satire it would one day become.

I was enraptured all the same. It was love at first sight. I recognized in the scruffy little satirical weekly the same quality I admired in *The Catcher in the Rye; Girl, Interrupted;* and

"Brick": truth. That might seem like strange praise for a publication famous for making shit up, but *The Onion* exposed a greater, darker satirical truth than publications handcuffed by their staid reliance on "facts" and "reporters" and "coverage of stuff that actually happened."

As an impressionable young person, my beloved *Mad* magazine taught me that adults were liars, politicians were hypocrites, and advertising was an elaborate con game. If *Mad* provided me with a sturdy elemental education in righteous skepticism, *The Onion* represented a master class.

My first response to *The Onion* was "My God, who are the geniuses behind this and why aren't they all rich and famous?" followed by "How can I somehow become part of this?"

I imagined that I had a special relationship with *The Onion* long before it had any idea I existed. At Madison Area Technical College I timed down to the minute when the paper was delivered each week. I would lie in wait at the lunch table, rife with anticipation as I waited for deliverymen to wheel in thick stacks of satirical goodness fortified with humorosity, comicality, and literary tomfoolery. I imagined that *The Onion* was being delivered directly to me.

Madison and *The Onion* gave a directionless young man something to aspire to, though I was far too insecure to imagine I stood a chance of making the leap from fan to contributor.

At nineteen this is how I saw my future: I'd augment the money I made substitute-teaching by selling plasma twice a week and doing medical studies whenever possible. Visits to the plasma bank and being a freak for science were staples of my college life. I didn't see any reason why that would change once I reached my thirties.

There was something refreshingly honest about medical studies: plenty of jobs metaphorically suck your blood and treat you like a bag of meat, blood, and sinew. But at Covance, the medical research center where I did multiple tours of duty, there was nothing metaphorical about it: they were literally sucking my blood (one intense day my blood was drawn twenty-three times, on the half hour) and treating me like a human guinea pig. I came to enjoy the antiseptic, almost narcotized emptiness of the hospital floor where I was sequestered during studies. Its blankness echoed the impersonal emptiness of the mental hospital but I was there by choice and I was getting paid (anywhere from seven hundred to two thousand dollars, which seemed like a massive bounty at the time), which made all the difference.

Then I met Keith and my life changed. My horizons broadened. Keith had cracked the code: he was doing what he loved and getting paid for it. Yet he didn't seem so terribly different from me. It took a year and gentle prodding from an unlikely source before I asked Keith if I could submit a test review for the *A.V. Club.* One of the last times I hung out with Judy I mentioned how well *The Onion* was doing and she articulated something I hadn't yet had the courage to ask myself: "Jeez, why don't you just ask Keith if you could write a review for *The Onion*? That's obviously what you want to be doing."

This made sense. But asking Keith for a writing tryout would violate my policy of never asking for the things I wanted. That policy had never gotten me anywhere, so I broached the subject with Keith.

I was relieved when Keith told me he'd been discussing bringing me on board with his editor Stephen and gave me my first two assignments: the 1966 John Frankenheimer artsy drama *Seconds* and *Tromeo and Juliet,* a Tromatized Z-movie spoof of a Shakespeare classic that has stalked me throughout my life, in both its straight and mutated form. The dichotomy between art and trash found in my first two assignments would come to define my work for *The Onion.* But in the early years I toiled deep in the trenches writing about dozens of not-so-golden turkeys like *Gone Fishin'* and *Trippin'* for every one *Deconstructing Harry* or *Eyes Wide Shut.*

That suited me fine: I had no faith in myself whatsoever. So I felt safer flying way under the radar. I could walk the streets confident that nobody would slam me against a wall and hiss, "Hey, asshole. I saw your review of *Baby Geniuses*. You obviously didn't fucking understand it, but don't go flaunting your ignorance in public."

Keith and Stephen quickly became the endlessly supportive, patient older brothers I never had. Growing up, I eyed my great-aunt Becky and uncle Ted's stand-up pinball machines with openmouthed envy. That, in my mind, was the definition of success: having a stand-up arcade game or pinball machine of your very own. I imagined that the Rockefellers and Rothschilds had miles of the most awesome, eye-popping stand-up video games scattered throughout their Manhattan lairs.

It blew my mind and impressed me disproportionately that Stephen collected stand-up arcade games, at least one of which (Mr. Do) he kept in a fifth-floor *Onion* office that suggested the set of *Pee-wee's Playhouse* redesigned by Michael O'Donoghue. Creativity burst from every corner. My favorite office decoration was "Gut-Shot Bear," a teddy bear modified by comedy writer Carol Kolb to emit a horrible groaning sound whenever you touched a bloody flesh wound at its stomach. It was genius and indicative of the morbid hilarity of the *Onion* office. One of my personal contributions was a Herbert Hoover "Great Leaders of the World" doll with an incongruous kung fu grip and an even more startlingly incongruous marine-style ripped physique, complete with bulging biceps and washboard abs. If this action figure was even remotely historically accurate, Hoover must have moonlighted as a stripper.

I joined *The Onion* during a surreal epoch where anything seemed possible and the culture-wide hallucination that was the dot-com boom pointed to a future beyond even Walt Disney's imagination, where anything you ever wanted was just a click of a mouse away and making your first million before thirty seemed like a realistic goal for anyone with a little moxie or hustle.

As a twenty-one-year-old *Onion* writer a year and a half out of the group home, I was stupid and naïve enough to imagine I'd somehow done something to deserve my good fortune. For me it was natural to show up whenever I wanted for a job where I worked with my best friends in a funhouse environment festooned with stand-up video games, action figures, talking Master P dolls, and *Battlefield Earth* figurines that emitted theatrical cries of "Rat-brain!" and "Puny man-animal!" every time a button was pushed. It didn't strike me as strange that *The Onion* only published forty-six issues a year and gave us six weeks of paid vacation so our precious, precious, genius superbrains wouldn't explode from overexertion.

In my early years at *The Onion* I was fast. I was dependable. I was prolific. I was fearless. But I was nothing but rough edges and raw potential. To help offset my limitations as a writer, I specialized in goofy stunts. I introduced a quickly abandoned feature called "Critical Beatdown," where I subjected actor-turned-director Peter Berg and *Saturday Night Live*'s Jim Breuer to a withering stream of abusive questions. I created a parody of men's magazines called *A.V. Club for Men* and asked Steve Albini smutty questions "borrowed" from lesser men's magazines like *Bikini*. I engaged in prankish stunts during junkets for *Idle Hands* and *I Still Know What You Did Last Summer*.

Oh, I stumbled upon a clever line or elegant turn of phrase every once in a long while, but for the most part my writing was uglier than Dick Cheney's soul. Yet Keith and Stephen saw promise where everyone else, myself included, saw only facile ideas and tortured prose. For a solid year, I began damn near every other fucking sentence with "And while." And while this got me from one painful sentence and fuzzily conceived idea to another, it only highlighted my inexperience.

Keith and Stephen believed in me all the same. At a chain restaurant just after my twenty-second birthday, Stephen, whose mom and dad were comic book royalty who founded and edited *Comic Buyer's Guide,* uttered the words I longed to hear. "So," he began casually, clearly relishing the role of fairy godfather, "how would you feel about collecting a salary as a part-time *A.V. Club* staff writer until you finish school?" How would I feel about it? I had to restrain myself from flipping over the table and doing an ecstatic Snoopy Dance of joy. At twenty-two I was a staff writer for my favorite publication. It seemed too good to be true.

I was leading a strange double life: undistinguished comm arts student by day/professional film critic by night. I avoided English and journalism classes on the grounds that sooner or later I'd be found out as a fraud and fired. I lay awake at night fearing the day a well-dressed older gentleman would burst through the door, look anxiously at paperwork from the Bureau of Professional Writer Persons, and embarrassingly explain, "Oh goodness, it seems here that a terrible mistake has been made. The head writer position at the *A.V. Club* should actually go to a thirty-three-year-old graduate of Yale and the Iowa Writer's Workshop named Ben Kleinman. It turns out your hiring was a clerical error. I do hope you understand this means you'll have to step down immediately."

In *The Onion* I found a community of outsiders. Those early years at *The Onion* seemed like a fairy tale. *The Onion*'s rise coincided with the giddy, delirious years of the New Economy and the Internet bubble, when venture capitalists threw money at anyone with a domain name and a wildly impractical business plan rooted in wishful thinking and blind optimism.

The Onion reigned as the crown jester of the New Economy. Every week a different journalist descended upon our fifth-floor offices deep in the heart of Madison's popcorn district to conduct an anthropological survey of the noble Midwestern Slobicus Domesticus in its native habitat and discover how these tragically non–Ivy League–educated souls (some of them didn't even have college degrees!) somehow managed to make comedy that tickled the funny bones of Truly Important People from Important Cities like New York and Los Angeles. Anything seemed possible. My unassuming friend and fellow staffer Rob

Siegel was named one of *People* magazine's fifty most eligible bachelors.

I was intoxicated by the romance of putting together a paper every week. In those early days in Madison, which my memory has thoughtfully buffed into a sepia-toned paradise, the *A.V. Club* staff (all three of us) would literally cut and paste each week's issue onto boards we'd then drive over to the printers at two or three in the morning. This seems like a ridiculously old-fashioned and time-intensive way of doing things now, but I found it enormously satisfying.

By the time I was driven home in the wee small hours of Monday morning, I felt like I'd really accomplished something. I felt like a newspaperman, dammit! A real, true-to-life, honest-to-goodness newspaperman with ink in his veins and newsprint in his soul. Then I'd go home, get high, and watch *The Critic, Dr. Katz: Professional Therapist,* and *Duckman* on Comedy Central. I'm fighting back tears just thinking about it.

After twenty-two years of hating myself I came to love my life. I was part of something that was vital and important and beloved. How many people can say that their coworkers are comic geniuses or that they're part of something that brings joy to hundreds of thousands of people? There was an infectious esprit de corps during those early years at *The Onion*. We were going to conquer the world. We were going to do it together.

Some of my fondest memories of Madison revolve around the Team Onion softball team, a woeful assemblage of writers, ad people, and conscripted fellow travelers that regularly lost to a team of tie-dye-clad developmentally challenged adults from a local halfway house. I know what you're probably thinking: how sweet of them to intentionally lose to a mildly retarded team. Here's the sad part: there was nothing intentional about it. On the contrary, we wanted very badly to send our archfoes home on the short bus of humiliating defeat, but we were too comically inept to do so.

Life was good. Life was better than good. Life was golden.

But, as Ponyboy could tell you, nothing gold can stay. The *Onion* core's time in Madison was running out. We were getting too big for our humble hometown, and the glamorous metropolises of New York and Chicago were beckoning. I could only hold out for so long.

You Know Mom's Crazy, Right?

Grey Gardens
        Meeting BM

The 1975 documentary *Grey Gardens* is a haunting study of the American aristocracy gone mad from desperation and want. The Maysles' iconic cult classic centers on "Little" Edith Bouvier Beale, a first cousin of Jacqueline Kennedy Onassis who lives with her mother and a gaggle of borderline-feral cats in Grey Gardens, a twenty-nine-room mansion whose dilapidation and rot mirrors the memory-haunted psyches of its inhabitants.

Once upon a time, Beale and her mother were patricians of the highest order. But time, abandonment, and bad decisions reduced them to a state of gothic poverty. By the time the Maysles brothers showed up with cameras, the Beales were essentially half-mad squatters living in the wreckage of their abandoned dreams, endlessly shadowboxing a past that contained both their early glory and later ruin.

Though approaching sixty, Beale still behaves with the flirty brazenness, endless self-absorption, and theatricality of the gorgeous, precocious teen she once was. She seems stuck mentally at the age when the future still radiated boundless promise, before time diminished her astonishing beauty and reduced her hopes and dreams to sick jokes. Like Gatsby, Beale seems to think that by rewriting the past she can fix the present, that if she could only return to the place where everything started to go wrong, she could reclaim the orgiastic future that is every American's birthright.

Beale's homemade fashion sense made her a gay icon and her endlessly quotable sound bites beg to be coopted and recycled, whether she is dramatically describing efforts to have her home shut down as a fire hazard as "the worst thing that's ever happened to anybody in America" or describing herself, with an irresistibly strong Boston accent, as a "staunch character."

In the summer of 1999 I sought out the mother who'd abandoned me twenty-one years earlier. I was horrified and more than a little amused to learn that my mother was the Little Edie of the St. Louis ghetto.

A certain crazed melodrama seemed hardwired into my biological mother's DNA. Her father died a hero's death fighting in World War II, but not before abandoning his wife and growing family first, leaving them with little more than his surname: Stray.

In a strange way I owe my existence to the Black Power movement. It was while biding his time waiting for a meeting of the St. Louis branch of the Black United Front that my father first spied my mother. They locked eyes while riding the escalator at the mall. She was a red-haired, fair-skinned beauty who looked like a cross between Marianne Faithfull and Julianne Moore. He was a handsome recent University of Chicago graduate. He was working for the Man as a low-level government bureaucrat but his involvement with the Black United Front betrayed that his sympathies, like Melvin Van Peebles's, lay with brothers and sisters who'd had enough of the Man.

Theirs was a love that defied religion. He was a member of the tribe. She was a goy. It defied class: My father was a member of the neurotic middle class. My biological mother pledged allegiance to the working poor. It was a union that defied common sense.

He was the Jewish golden boy whose kindness was the stuff of family legend. Growing up, my old man was the kind of masochistic Good Samaritan who actually seemed to enjoy spending time with elderly relatives. She was a big-talking college dropout bitterly estranged from her family. My dad's family wasn't crazy about my biological mom. Then again, her family wasn't too keen on her either.

A few years into their marriage my dad began experiencing double vision and persistent dizzy spells. The doctor's prognosis was grim: my father either had an inoperable brain tumor that would kill him before his pregnant wife could deliver his first child, or he had a debilitating, degenerative, but not generally fatal neurological disease named multiple sclerosis that would eat away at his body and mind until he died. For two agonizing weeks my father didn't know whether death was imminent.

What can you say about a twenty-five-year-old boy who almost died? That he was beautiful and brilliant? That he loved Mozart and Bach, the Beatles and me? That even though he worked for the government he was "down" with the revolutionary struggle? That despite being a cracker-American of the honky persuasion he hated whitey just as much as his proud Nubian brothers?

You can imagine how relieved my father was to learn he had multiple sclerosis. He would live but his marriage wouldn't survive. The birth of my older sister and me did little to heal the ever-widening rifts in my parents' relationship.

After their marriage had reached a dispiriting endgame, my mother met a man who was the antithesis of my father. He was a brooding, intense Vietnam veteran named Mack who used heroin to self-medicate for manic depression and worked as an orderly at a hospital that afforded him easy access to mind-bending chemicals. Mack kept so many birds around his apartment that my father dubbed him the Birdman of Kansas City. This dark, shadowy figure ended up playing a crucial role in my destiny when he testified against my mother in court and helped my father win full custody of his children.

When I was growing up my father kept an unloaded rifle in the front closet. He claimed it was a souvenir from his National Guard days. It wasn't until I was older that I learned that he kept the gun as protection in case Mack or one of Mom's other friends decided to bust into his house and retake me by force.

I like to joke that my mother carried me in her womb for nine months, went through the agony of delivery, then called it a day. But the truth is stranger and more complicated. Once it became apparent that my father would win full custody of his children—a rare occurrence for a father in 1978, especially one with a debilitating neurological disease—my mother absconded with me and embarked on a cross-country road trip down to Texas and then west to California. It was a last hurrah for Biological Mom and her Bicentennial Baby. My father dispatched detectives to scour bus and train stations to find us, and I eventually found my way home, though my father is fuzzy on how this came to be. I can only imagine how jarring it must have been for my two-year-old self. One moment my mother was my entire world. She was my sustenance, my protector. The next moment she was gone.

My dad recently gave me a fascinating artifact from somewhere deep and dark within our shared past, a poignant time capsule from the secret history of my family. As the yellowing, frayed second half of one of countless letters his lawyers sent him during his bitter custody battle, it's little more than a fragment of a fragment. But it provides a riveting window into my parents' divorce.

The letter is shot through with the dark comedy and the hard-boiled camaraderie endemic to people forever bonded by having fought a war together. My dad missed out on Vietnam but the letter makes it clear that he and his intrepid constables were immersed in psychological warfare with a foe far more treacherous and daunting than the Vietcong: my mother and her boyfriend.

In the course of just a few paragraphs the letter oscillates wildly between vitriolic digs at my mother, gallows humor, practical information, Latin phrases, pointed misogyny, unapologetic schadenfreude, and homespun bits of philosophy, sometimes in the course of a single sentence.

The second paragraph, for example, reads:

"Everyone here also appreciates your sacrifices in paying our fees in full and we in no way minimize the suffering you have undergone to do that, but you realize of course the suffering has not been unilateral, in that we had to endure your wife and the ubiquitous Mr. N———, whom we have not heard the last from yet. Mirabile dictu [wonderful to relate] even your ex-wife has suffered. But just as in a Greek tragedy it is normally the most noble person who suffers in the highest degree."

The letter continues, "Keep in touch with us concerning all new developments as far as your bankruptcy and location of [my mother] are concerned. Our skip tracer hasn't yet informed us of where Nathan is located for certain but is still working on it, and we still have funds in that trust account to pay his fee."

The lawyer signs off with "In nomine meretricis," which he helpfully translates as "In the name of the slut." Most folks would, at the very least, be moderately surprised to receive a letter where their mother is referred to as both a sadist and a slut. Not I. The letter is augmented with handwritten notes and hastily scribbled-over typos that only add to its messy, tragicomic humanity.

It amuses me to imagine my two-year-old self as the elusive prey of a bail bondsman, a skip tracer, a bounty hunter, a professional badass. I was touched by the lawyer's offhand assertion that the most noble people are often called upon to suffer the worst indignities. My father must have endured years of torment feeling like a modern-day Job.

Growing up, I felt my mother's absence like a phantom limb.

I felt like her abandonment had marked me for life, that when I walked by, strangers equipped with psychic X-rays would mutter disapprovingly, "There goes the boy so crappy even his own mother wants nothing to do with him."

Like most abandoned children, I nursed sentimental fantasies that my lost parent pined for me behind a white picket fence and perfectly manicured lawn, that, to borrow the maudlin terminology of *Annie*, "her only mistake was giving up me."

In the darkest hours of my adolescence I'd daydream sometimes that she'd swoop in from out of the blue, express horror and indignation about the low state to which I'd fallen, and rescue me from the random cruelties of fate. My father neither encouraged nor discouraged these fantasies. My biological mother was something we simply never talked about. It was as if she never existed. She had been erased from the historical record like the victim of a Stalinist purge.

When I was four years old I received a package from my biological mother containing a stuffed kangaroo. Like all the gifts I'd receive from my mother over the years, it just made me sad. It reactivated some dormant part of me that still ached from her absence and longed for her return. It made me wonder anew why everyone else had a mother except me. It engendered equal parts hope and despair: hope because she was still alive and cognizant of my existence and whereabouts, and despair because that wasn't enough to bring her back.

When I was fourteen she had a friend call me. All I remember was freaking out and giving the phone to my dad. Despite my soft-focus daydreams about a joyous reunion, the prospect of reconnecting with my mother was more terrifying than appealing.

In the intervening years, an insatiable curiosity about my mother burned deep within me. So when I turned twenty-three I asked my dad for my mother's phone number. He acquiesced willingly. If seeking her out was something I felt I needed to do, then I had his blessing.

So, with a heavy heart and trembling stomach, I finally

worked up the nerve to call a woman whose absence from my life I had felt so keenly. During that first momentous conversation I was struck by my mother's complete lack of curiosity about me. She seemed interested in me largely, if not exclusively, as an audience. Instead of a conversation, I was treated to an epic monologue about her philosophy of life. She depicted herself as an exemplar of Emersonian self-reliance who had bought a giant mansion for twenty-five thousand dollars she paid off in a year rather than be saddled with a mortgage. She worked odd jobs, mainly in sales, just long enough to raise money to get through the rest of the year.

She spoke with the brazen self-assurance common both to people who've conquered the world and are brimming with well-earned confidence, and to the mentally ill. I had fretted beforehand that our conversation would be filled with awkward silences and unbearable tension. It was a strange relief that I didn't have to worry about holding up my end of the conversation because, well, there was no my end of the conversation. Her flowery orgies of self-aggrandizement were hypnotic in their complete disconnect from reality.

When not nattering on about her heroic nonconformity, she portrayed herself as a harried supermom burdened with three children criminally ungrateful for the sacrifices she made on their behalf. In a curious bit of psychosexual masochism she'd had two children with Mack even after he testified against her in divorce court. Her reasoning was as simple as it was warped: Mack's testimony had cost her two children, so she felt he owed her two replacements.

Her fifth child was created under similarly bizarre circumstances. At thirty-nine she was struck with a late-blooming case of baby fever and decided to have another child with a man she barely knew and had no intention of involving in their child's life. I'm not entirely sure she even told him of her desire to get pregnant one last time or informed him of the blessed event nine months later.

Somehow none of this affected her unshakable belief that she was long overdue for Mother of the Year honors. She loved her kids, God bless 'em, but they were a constant source of anguish. Her son Mario was in jail after getting busted with pot and would soon have a child of his own. Her elder daughter Beverly's boyfriend, meanwhile, had embarked on a coke-fueled crime spree and was now accessible only via visitors day at a local penitentiary. Listening to her talk about her life and her children's lives had the unreal, vicarious feeling of reading soap opera updates. It was hard to tell whether the sordid events she described happened in the real world or her imagination. During our periodic phone calls, I felt like a voyeur leering indecently into the lives of people who had emerged from the same birth canal as me yet were as foreign as the battling grotesques on daytime television.

After six to eight months of one-sided phone conversations, I finally worked up the courage to visit her. After all these years of wondering, my curiosity was about to be satiated. I was torn between anticipation and soul-shaking dread. I wasn't sure this was a door that should be opened. But I was about to barrel through it anyway.

I took the train down to St. Louis and as we approached our destination butterflies congregated angrily in my stomach. Was I doing the right thing? Was my older sister right in wanting nothing to do with our mother?

As I disembarked from the train my vision centered immediately on a squat, ruddy, red-haired woman in dirty purple sweatpants and a matching dirty purple sweatshirt accompanied by two teens with the deeply pained look of hostages in a bank robbery.

As I approached the sweatpants-clad woman my internal monologue bleated out a stubborn, persistent plea:

Please don't be my mother
Please don't be my mother
Please don't be my mother

My hopes were shattered when the purple-clad mystery woman joyously blurted out, "Nathan!" I tried and failed to adopt a facial expression that didn't transparently convey horror and revulsion. Of course the red-haired woman was my mother. I didn't expect to be greeted by the mayor but I figured if there was ever an occasion to throw on a nice blouse and some clean slacks, it was upon meeting the son you'd abandoned decades earlier.

Once we entered the car, my mother launched into one of her monologues. I had been rendered speechless, so I was just grateful I wasn't expected to add anything substantive to the conversation. The mortified teenagers were my half brother, Mario, and his much younger sister, Jennifer.

Mario and Jennifer nursed few illusions about their mother. After we dropped Biological Mother off at home and headed to the mall, Mario looked back at me and asked, with disconcerting matter-of-factness, "You know Mom's crazy, right?"

Visiting absolute strangers who happened to be part of my immediate family was an experience at once jarringly foreign yet strangely familiar. I had, after all, spent five formative years living with people I had little in common with.

At the mall that day Mario shopped extensively for Insane Clown Posse merchandise, a passion of his that seemed to settle the "nature versus nurture" debate conclusively on the side of nurture. I hadn't been so horrified by a family member's, um, *unusual* taste since I watched in horror as my father guffawed throughout the Rob Schneider vehicle *The Animal*. "It's the disease," my father offered defensively. Apparently a little-known side effect of multiple sclerosis involves finding the sight of Rob Schneider dry-humping a goat hilarious.

We eventually headed back to Mario's place, where he sacked out for an hour. I was left to contemplate the sole piece of literature in his apartment: an old copy of *High Times*. Alas, Mario couldn't indulge in the deplorable practice of smoking marijuana until his probation ended, I had learned earlier that day when we stopped by one of his friends' houses and everyone there took hits from a joint but us, including his buddy's mom. Now, I'm a big fan of marijuana but I could never understand people smoking weed with their parents. The point of using illegal drugs is to horrify parents and other authority figures, not to have them serve as a bonding activity.

Once Mario got up from his nap he called his sister Beverly, whom Biological Mother had told me in disapproving tones was spending altogether too much time "partying with the Bosnians." "Haven't those people been through enough?" she wondered aloud.

Beverly then dropped by very, very briefly to meet a long-lost half brother whose existence she apparently wasted nary a sleepless night contemplating. "You must be Nathan! Hi, I'm Beverly!" she gushed exuberantly before giving me a big hug. She bolted out the door just as abruptly and energetically as she arrived. I'm afraid the only thing I remember about my half sister is that she was wearing a see-through shirt.

Now, see-through shirts generally send a message. That message invariably is "Hey, world, get a load of my tits. They're awesome!" Usually that is a message I am receptive toward. Heck, normally that's a message I embrace. But in this context it was a little jarring.

I like to think I have impeccable working-class credentials, but visiting my secret hillbilly family made me feel as aristocratic as George Plimpton at a wine and cheese party in the Hamptons. When Biological Mother showed me her sprawling, crumbling home for the first time and proudly offered me a slice from a queasy-looking, wiggling green Jell-O mold, I demurred out of the strong if insupportable conviction that eating anything from my mom's house would result in instantaneous death. God only knows what could have been floating around in that Jell-O.

I had fallen through the looking glass and stumbled into the Valley of the Super-Goys. My biological mother and broth-

ers and sisters weren't just non-Jews: they were egregiously
non-Jewish. Just as you never realize how central being an
American is to your sense of self until you travel to a country
where Americans are held in contempt, I never understood how
important Judaism was to me until I met my big fat gentile
family.

Throughout that long, surreal weekend my mother talked
and talked and talked. She talked about her life, about her kids,
about lost loves and her philosophy. She talked about how she
finally mustered up the courage to leave Mack after he hit her
and how he recently wandered unsteadily back into their lives
after decades of drifting aimlessly. She talked about the dental
student she loved madly before meeting my dad but could never
attain.

She showed me messily photocopied college transcripts documenting her decades-long quest to secure a bachelor's degree,
beaming proudly as she pointed to A's and B's. All the while she
dispensed bite-sized nuggets of homegrown philosophy. She did
not, she announced theatrically, "believe" in abortion or drugs.
When I told her that I didn't know how to drive a car she proclaimed, "Not knowing how to drive just isn't right. It's not
owning up to adult responsibilities."

I discreetly added this lecture on the importance of accepting
the responsibilities of adulthood from a woman who had abandoned two of her children to my bitter irony collection.

She talked about everything except what mattered most to me.

I wanted desperately to ask, "Why did you abandon me?"
but couldn't. To bring up the defining question of our relationship would be to burst through the wall of self-delusion my
biological mother had built around herself to keep her demons
at bay.

So we talked—or rather she talked—around the subject, seldom venturing into tricky emotional territory. Eventually she got
around to offering what I call the "Mildred Pierce defense,"
after the classic Michael Curtiz noir melodrama where Joan

Crawford plays a saintly, Christlike mother who sacrifices all and disregards her own happiness for the sake of her hateful ingrate of a daughter. Biological Mom argued, in a casual, roundabout way, that she had selflessly given up her rights as a mother because she knew deep down that my sister and I would be better off in the care of our father.

Leaving St. Louis, I was overcome with a profound sense of gratitude. As a child I bitterly resented my mother's absence from my life. It never occurred to me that maybe I was better off that way, that maybe having a flighty, pathologically self-involved mother flitting in and out of my life would have only added additional tension, anxiety, and psychodrama to an adolescence already overflowing with those qualities.

As fucked as my life had been, it could have been far worse. Even during the darkest hours it was always assumed that I'd go to college and make something of myself. I'd grown up in a culture that revered learning and history and humor and storytelling, among a people who believed in family and community and charity. Though I seldom sully the inside of a synagogue, not a day goes by that I'm not grateful to be Jewish.

Who knows how I'd have turned out if my mother had gotten custody of me? I'd probably have ended up like Mario, who at nineteen already had a felony conviction (needless to say, it was some fucking fascist cop bullshit—that brick of weed wasn't even his, bro, he was just holding it for a buddy) and a child he couldn't afford.

Sometimes family means everything. Sometimes it means nothing. Sometimes family is the strongest spiritual and emotional bond imaginable. Sometimes it's nothing more than a mean-spirited trick of biology.

I kept in contact with my biological mother for several years after my visit to St. Louis. She didn't have long distance or an answering machine, so I was always the one to call. Her updates on the lives of her children continued to have the sordid quality of soap opera plotlines. Mario's no-good baby mama was pregnant, she brooded, though she suspected that the actual father was a sixteen-year-old the harlot in question worked with at Steak 'N Shake.

She'd talk and talk and talk, and I'd listen. Like Little Edie, my mother is a hypnotic fantasist who seems to talk as much for her own sake as anyone else's. Also like Edie, she was forever engaged in the act of rewriting the past to fit the present. At the end of each call I felt more alienated from my mother than before. A little piece of me died every time I hung up the phone.

Every once in a while my mother would send me "gifts"— giant boxes of crap seemingly chosen at random, from an outsized puffy San Francisco sweatshirt to a VHS copy of *Titanic* to a cheap little dragon statue, for once upon a time I was her dragon-baby—that invariably sent me into a melancholy funk. Instead of bringing us closer, these bizarre gifts underlined how little my biological mother knew about me.

Ideally gifts reaffirm and strengthen relationships. They say, "I understand you on a profound level and have chosen a gift perfectly suited to your idiosyncratic passions." Biological Mom's "gifts," however, sent the message "I have no fucking idea who you are, but my best guess is that you're a depressed forty-year-old secretary with a thing for Leonardo DiCaprio."

Then one day I called and an automated message informed me that my biological mother's number had been disconnected. Since she never called me, that meant the end of our curious stint as phone buddies. It perfectly symbolized our relationship: I reached out to her but she was unavailable, emotionally, figuratively, and now literally.

Every Mother's Day I'm struck with an urge to send Biological Mother a card but I've yet to find one with a message like "To a Mother Who's Disappointed Me in Every Conceivable Way."

The last time I heard from dear BM she sent me a chipper little postcard on my birthday—with no return address—that began, "Can we start over?" Like everything about my mother, the postcard broke my heart. In a million different ways, I'd love to start over. But you can't. You just can't. It's fucking impossible. Gatsby can't start over. Neither can Little Edie. Neither can my mother. Neither can I.

Fresh Kid Turned Rotten

"What's Up, Fatlip?"
Fear and Self-Loathing in Madison

Pharcyde's 1992 debut, *Bizarre Ride II the Phar-cyde*, offered its largely white collegiate fanbase an irresistible variation on pop music's shimmering promise of eternal adolescence. But by the time its 1995 follow-up, *Labcabincalifornia*, arrived, the West Coast quartet was wrestling thoughtfully with one of hip-hop's most resonant themes: what it means to be a man, an artist, and a good citizen in a culture fixated on instant gratification, the blind pursuit of wealth, and disposable pop culture.

Like Dr. Dre's *2001*, Common's *Be*, Little Brother's *The Minstrel Show*, and Kanye West's *The College Dropout*, Pharcyde's cultishly revered follow-up was a coming-of-age album about reluctantly forsaking the easy pleasures of youth in favor of the responsibilities and pressures of adulthood. Pharcyde was growing up, growing apart, and falling apart alongside its fans.

At the same time kids who grooved to *Bizarre Ride* between bong hits in their freshman dorms faced graduation, an intimidating job market, and the looming specter of mortgages, marriage, and careers, Pharcyde was abandoning the mama jokes and rowdy humor of its debut for a newfound lyrical and sonic maturity.

Then, for group member Fatlip, everything fell apart. As recounted in Spike Jonze's mesmerizing 2003 short documentary, *What's Up, Fatlip?* Fatlip was kicked out of Pharcyde when group members Imani, Booty Brown, and Slimkid Tre all showed up at his apartment and told him he should do a solo album. Incidentally, I think all bad news should begin with "We think you should do a solo album." I'd have felt better about my television show's cancellation if my producer had called me up and said, "Yeah, I just got off the phone with AMC and they really, really think you should pursue a solo album. In fact, they think we should all pursue solo albums. Immediately."

Fatlip then entered the proverbial nightmare descent into booze and drugs, but out of the wreckage of his personal and professional life came "What's Up, Fatlip?" a blackly comic single that skips past self-deprecation on the way to self-laceration.

Even more than *Labcabincalifornia,* "What's Up Fatlip?" is about the death of youth. It's about waking up every morning to the chilling realization that your best days are behind you and that the future grows smaller and more claustrophobic with each passing day.

It's a suicide note of a song about looking in the mirror and hating the person you've become. In the cruel, cruel, cruel summer of 2001, that was a sensation I was intimately familiar with.

In college towns like Madison midlife crises often begin in the midtwenties. Mine did. At twenty-five, I felt older than Methuselah. Each incoming class of freshmen seemed younger and younger. By the time I left Madison, the freshman class consisted largely of sentient fetuses who'd somehow managed to escape the womb and get good enough grades and high enough ACT scores to enroll at a respectable Big Ten university.

It all started when the *Onion* comedy writers, feeling like big-ass fish in a very small pond, moved to New York. Then my best friend, Keith, moved to Chicago.

In *The Onion* I'd finally found both a makeshift family and a sense of community. Now that family had packed up and moved away. I once again entered the Fat Elvis/OCD Howard Hughes stage of my development. Personal hygiene suddenly seemed terribly unimportant. I retreated deeper and deeper into myself. Whenever I wasn't working I was high, but the drugs didn't work. They just numbed the pain. Most of the time they didn't even do that.

Under different circumstances I might have found my upstairs neighbors—a pair of bluegrass hippie Jesus freaks forever holding raucous hoedowns for the Messiah—terribly amusing. But in my depressed state they seemed put on Earth solely to bedevil me. Even their adorable little daughter seemed satanic. I was convinced her sparkling Little Mermaid slippers concealed cloven hooves.

I longed to feel something beyond numb sadness so I invested my life savings in the stock market. I started living vicariously through my money. I may have been mired in depression but my money was having all sorts of exciting adventures. It was traveling the globe, expanding and (mostly) contracting rapidly, and embarking on all manner of thrilling new endeavors.

As a first-time investor, I blithely ignored the dictates of conventional wisdom and threw caution to the wind, investing my modest nest egg into just a few volatile stocks. For I had something no other investor possessed: vague hunches about the direction the economy might be headed. What good are fuzzy notions about sectors of society you know nothing about if you don't throw all your money behind them?

But I had something more than uninformed guesses to guide me: I had a theory about the underlying nature of late-period capitalism derived from a Beatnuts lyric and half-assed observations about the way the street life echoes big business.

So if you'll indulge me, dear reader, I'd like to spit a little game all up in your ear hole. "Either you're the pimp or the prostitute," goes a quietly profound line from the Beatnuts' "Yae Yo." That's the kind of real talk they don't teach you at Harvard Business School. I would like to expand Psycho Les and Junkyard

Juju's adroit observation by arguing that, in the grand scheme of things, you're either the pimp, the prostitute, or the john.

Let me break it down. The consumers function as johns, hapless squares who fatten the pockets of pimps by purchasing goods and services created by the workers. Workers in turn are the prostitutes of the system, as they spend their days making money for their pimps (the corporations or small businesses they work for). Corporations in turn occupy a strange dual position, as they are simultaneously pimps pocketing the money generated by their hardworking, long-suffering hos (their viciously exploited employees) and hos selflessly serving the whims of their own pimps (the stockholders).

In this system stockholders occupy a privileged position as pimps whose pimp game is so vicious that they pimp other pimps. As formidable as corporations and their top executives might appear to be, they're forever at the mercy of their share-holder pimps. For example, if the shareholder pimps decide that upper management at Disney should work a nonstop forty-eight-hour shift beginning on Christmas Eve wearing nothing but thigh-high boots, a thong, and a Wonderbra despite freezing weather, then the upper management at Disney has a solemn fiduciary responsibility to do as the shareholders say and go out and make Daddy money. And if the shareholder pimps tell the CEO of Disney to jump, he is legally and morally required to inquire, "How high?"

Needless to say, in this sadistic paradigm you want to be the pimp of pimps, not a ho or a john. As employee and consumer I was both ho and john, but through the mere act of stock own-ership I could receive a magnificent promotion to pimp of pimps.

I would learn far too late that my makeshift theory of capi-talism was, to be generous, retarded. But at the time it made a lot of sense. I vowed that I would become one of these blessed, extraordinarily powerful stockholders even if it cost me my life savings. It very nearly did.

By the end of my roller-coaster jaunt through the stock market, I was 40 percent poorer and only 3 to 5 percent wiser. But at least agonizing over my stocks gave me something to think about besides the feeling that life had passed me by.

Late in the summer of 2001 my uncle Irving died. We hadn't talked much since I'd moved to Madison but he was the closest thing I ever had to a grandfather. He was what Israelis call a "sabra," after a cactus that's prickly and hard on the outside but soft and tender on the inside. That was Uncle Irving in a nutshell: a big softie masquerading as a cantankerous old coot.

When I was growing up Uncle Irving and Aunt Ruth's Evanston condo was the closest thing I had to a home. It was a beacon of warmth and support. Now the inexorable march of time had extinguished that beacon. I was crushed.

By the time I flew to Amsterdam that summer with my girlfriend, Amy, I had lurched into a crippling depression. Frequent drug users and depressives are both highly susceptible to a condition that renders them incapable of experiencing pleasure or joy. This condition is alternately known as "anhedonia" or "Judaism."

Professional frustration, grief over my uncle's passing, and the terrible knowledge that I'd eventually have to leave both Madison and the relationship I was in combined to give me a serious case of anhedonia. So it was a special form of torment that I suddenly had access to unlimited supplies of top-quality marijuana and magic mushrooms at a time when they brought me no joy. Vacationing in Amsterdam while depressed is like going to Disney World when you're an inch too short to go on any of the rides. It's just not the same watching other kids ride Space Mountain and/or get reasonably priced hand jobs from window-front hookers.

That didn't keep me from self-medicating all the same. In an Olympian fit of bad judgment, I took an eighth of mushrooms before visiting the Anne Frank House. I cannot stress this enough: do not take powerful hallucinogens before going to a Holocaust memorial. It's really not the kind of thing you want to experience with an altered consciousness and a brain already raw from grief.

Even before I ate psilocybin for breakfast and headed to the Anne Frank House, I had a long, tortured relationship with Frank's legacy. When I was in sixth grade my saintly teacher Mr. Gutnick (shout-out to my man Mr. Gutnick!) mistook the shaky nervousness I exhibited during the *Diary of Anne Frank* auditions for brooding Method intensity and cast me as Anne Frank's father, Otto. My dad was in the midst of his second divorce at the time, so I was deep into the acting-out-to-get-attention phase of my adolescence. So I figured I'd lighten things up during rehearsals with zany improvisation and madcap riffing. Now there are lots of places where zany improvisation and madcap riffing are encouraged. A sixth-grade production of *The Diary of Anne Frank* is not one of them. I was fired just a few days into rehearsals. I felt vindicated, however, when the actor, or rather the scheming, backstabbing Judas who took over the role, failed to get a single laugh opening night. Ha!

That experience was far from my mind, however, while walking through the museum where Frank and her family hid from the Nazis. For whatever reason (the drugs? The despair? The combination of the two?) the unspeakable horror of Anne Frank's death hit me with feverish intensity. It felt like a fresh wound, like she'd died a few months ago, not over a half century earlier. It all just seemed so goddamned unfair. I started crying and was weirdly surprised and disappointed to see that Amy, my girlfriend, seemed to be holding up just fine.

The situation reminded me of a scene from *U Turn*. In it, Claire Danes's small-town ditz asks Sean Penn's cynical drifter why Patsy Cline "don't put out no more new records." When Penn tersely replies that Cline is dead, Danes earnestly inquires, "Don't that just make you sad?" Penn quips, "I've had time to get over it." Incidentally, about three years later I found myself paraphrasing these lines to John Ridley, the man who wrote them, on national TV. But we'll get to that later.

It took September 11 to rouse me out of my glum inertia. I was sitting at home, luxuriating in a comforting cocoon of infinite sadness, watching *Brenda Starr* for an *A.V. Club* feature called "Films That Time Forgot," when I got a tersely worded e-mail from Keith: "You should turn on the news." I logged on to CNN.com, where a screaming banner headline read AMERICA UNDER ATTACK.

I turned on the television to find that the rest of the country was now shrouded in a thick fog of hopelessness and despair. It can be easy to forget the incredible fragility of that cultural moment, the widespread sense that the foundations of freedom and democracy had crumbled along with the World Trade Center. In a heartbeat the unthinkable had happened. If a group of zealots with box cutters and fearsome religious convictions could strike such a forceful blow to the heart of the world's richest and most powerful country, then who could say that the worst wasn't still to come?

It is one of life's bitter ironies that the worse things are for humanity, the better they are for satirists. Consequently my generation's defining tragedy became *The Onion*'s finest hour. When I visited *The Onion*'s New York offices not long after 9/11 for my friend Rob's thirtieth birthday party, the *Onion* comedy writers were just as shell-shocked, sad, and confused as the rest of the world. They were hurting. They ached. The attacks hit them where they lived. Yet they did not retreat into apathy or hopelessness. They realized that at that uncertain time satire wasn't silly or superficial, it was goddamned essential.

While the rest of pop culture walked on eggshells, the *Onion* comedy writers turned out an issue about nothing but 9/11. They were walking a tricky tonal tightrope. Even a single miscalculation could get them crucified in the press as callous provocateurs exploiting a national tragedy. The 9/11 issue pretty much had to be perfect or it would be an outright disaster. And it was perfect.

There was nothing at all glib or aloof about the 9/11 issue. It provided a raw, cathartic, dangerous healing laughter that implicitly said, "Yeah, this is horrible and scary and unprecedented and we're all grieving and spooked but we're going to get through this and we're going to get through it together. We won't survive by cutting ourselves off from laughter and joy; we'll survive by retaining our sense of humor and humanity. We'll survive because we're strong and resilient and brave even when we feel weak and powerless and lost."

It was a goddamned wonder to behold. I never felt prouder to be a part of *The Onion* than when I read the 9/11 issue for the first time. I feel like I can say that in good conscience since my contributions to that issue were even more marginal than usual. That *Brenda Starr* "Films That Time Forgot" I wrote on 9/11 wasn't going to inspire anyone to do anything other than wonder why the hell *The Onion* kept a hack like me on the payroll.

If my friends and coworkers, that slouching, dysfunctional gang of insomniacs, depressives, and dropouts, could do something as important and vital as the 9/11 issue, then surely I could muster up the courage to escape my grim little hell in Madison and move to the glistening metropolis where I was certain my future lay.

To save myself I had to leave Madison, but sometimes survival trumps all else. That's the thing about depression: it feels like it'll never end, but as long as you don't give in to it, it always does. When the demon is at your door in the morning it won't be there no more. Any major dude will tell you the same.

Living Like a Gypsy Queen in a Fairy Tale

"My Old School"
Twin Trips to the Whorehouse

Steely Dan songs are like musical Rorschach blots. People get out of them what they put into them. To fans Walter Becker and Donald Fagen are subversive, sophisticated pranksters who Trojan horse all manner of arty weirdness and boho perversion into infectious pop singles. That's the genius of the Dan. Under the placid, highly polished surfaces lies seriously fucked-up shit.

To people who despise Steely Dan—there seems to be no middle ground—they're geriatric yuppies making glorified elevator music for middle-aged, BMW-driving assholes with combovers, graying ponytails, and trophy wives with fake tits.

In songs like "My Old School," the boys lay out a series of cryptic, provocative clues and details, then leave it to the listener to figure out what everything means. The song begins on a bittersweet note of nostalgia with the protagonist remembering "thirty-five sweet good-byes" he received before being put on a train to Annandale-on-Hudson, where Steely Dan's Donald Fagen attended Bard College. It then veers into darker territory, as the singer recounts a father's surprise at learning that his daughter was now with the "working girls" at the county jail. I suppose the "working girls" line suggested a *Belle du Jour*–like world of upscale bourgeoisie prostitution, a fuzzy contention supported by at least some of the song's lyrics, like when the protagonist bemoans the obscure object of his desire for "living like a gypsy queen in a fairy tale" and warns that he tried to tell her about mysterious figures named Chino and Daddy Gee.

It's never quite clear who exactly Chino and Daddy Gee are, but they're clearly up to no good, just like the antiheroes of so many Steely Dan songs.

I willingly concede that my interpretation of "My Old School" is fuzzy and undoubtedly off, but the juxtaposition of cryptic references to prostitution and collegiate nostalgia make it the perfect theme song for my shadowy descent into low-rent whoremongering in the fall of 2001.

At some point during that cruel, cruel, cruel fall I stopped thinking of myself as the plucky, lovable hero of my life story and began to view myself as more of a weird supporting player with dark desires and inscrutable motives. I was living with a wonderful woman and a weird, dainty little old lady of an Australian shepherd who looked down her noble snout at me like disreputable household help to be tolerated at best. Yet I felt utterly, agonizingly alone. It was as if there was a sheet of glass between me and the rest of the world that kept me from experiencing anything beyond numb pain.

In my desperation to feel something, anything, I had thrown my entire life savings into the glorified casino that is the stock market. After breaking up with a girlfriend I loved deeply, I became unhealthily obsessed with a run-down establishment on the east side of Madison called Hello, My Concubine. It was an open secret around Madison that Hello, My Concubine was what old-timey individuals call a house of ill repute, a den of sin, vice, iniquity, and loose morals. Also, there was prostitution.

I desperately wanted to explore Hello, My Concubine but nerves, anxiety, and inhibitions held me back. For days I would loiter around it, trying futilely to muster up the courage to enter its door. Then one day my curiosity and desperation overcame my oft-slippery moral compass and I entered Hello, My Concubine to find a wood-paneled dump rife with the stench of stale air, shattered dreams, and cheap perfume. Five or six women ambled about in ugly lingerie trying and failing to look casual.

Finally a woman broke the awkward silence by cheerily asking, "Have you been here before?"

"No," I gulped anxiously.

"Here's how it works. You choose the girl you'd like to give you a massage. Then you go to a room, shower, and get your massage. It's eighty dollars for the massage plus an eighty-dollar tip for the girl. Any questions?"

"Uh, no. Thank you." I then surveyed the selection and chose a perky blonde with big fake tits. God, I am such a fucking cliché. Sometimes I hate myself. I really do.

"Hi, I'm Barbie," the woman offered gingerly. Of course you are. And I'm Thor, Nordic Warrior of a Barbarian Land. She took me to a room and "suggested" I take a shower.

"I've never done anything like this before," I mumbled anxiously. I meant, of course, that I'd never paid a stranger for a hand job before. But I was such a quivering, shaking puddle of anxiety that I suspect my paid paramour assumed I was a virgin, a misunderstanding that would go a long way toward explaining the unexpected tenderness of our encounter.

"What's your name?" the fetching, mostly-naked stranger in the baby-blue thong asked offhandedly. There was something strangely innocent about Barbie. In another life she may have been a kindergarten teacher. In this one she gave strangers hand jobs for money.

Fuck, fuck, fuck! "Um, John. John Smith," I responded unsteadily, immediately feeling ashamed of myself. What kind of writer can't come up with a better fake name than John Smith? I might as well have told her my name was Crumplesnatch T. Steeplebottom.

"What do you do?"

"I'm a writer." Fuck. I was even worse at this anonymity

business than she was. "A technical writer." Ooh, good save, genius.

"What kind of stuff do you write?"

"Oh, you know: manuals, instructions, things like that. Nothing too exciting."

"Would you like to touch my breasts?" Barbie asked. Our conversation was suddenly taking an interesting, if not unexpected, turn.

"Uh, sure," I squeaked anxiously. I started fixating on the music wafting into our sordid room like musty air freshener. It was Peter Cetera's "Glory of Love," a song I'd sung in chorus as a fourteen-year-old at New Trier. As Cetera overemoted, a strange sadness came over me. Giving hand jobs to strangers for money was one thing. Giving hand jobs to strangers against a smooth-rock backdrop of the mellowest hits of the seventies, eighties, and today was another entirely. I imagine that when Barbie was a little girl she didn't dream of someday giving hand jobs to strangers while listening halfheartedly to elevator music, just as I couldn't have anticipated that when I belted out "Glory of Love" during an undistinguished stint with the New Trier chorus twelve years earlier, I'd be reintroduced to Cetera's love theme from *Karate Kid II* during my initiation into the world of paid sex.

The song took on a sad symbolic significance. When I was eight years old I genuinely felt that Chicago's "You're the Inspiration" was the single most powerful love song ever written. I'd stare out the window of my classroom at the Milwaukee Jewish Day School and daydream about the moment I'd fall in love and finally live out the lyrics to that most profound of love songs. Like most children, I was unable to differentiate between sentimental sap and epic romantic prose, between real love songs that brood and bleed and live and the cheap synthetic substitutes found on Top 40 radio. Now Cetera's irony-free bleating mocked the sad mess of a life I'd made for myself.

When I sang "Glory of Love" in the New Trier choir I was a

scared, lost, lonely boy terrified of what the future might bring and uncomfortable in my own skin. But when I got a hand job at a low-rent whorehouse to "Glory of Love" at twenty-five, everything was different. The context had radically changed. I was now a scared, lost, lonely *man* terrified of what the future might bring and uncomfortable in my own skin.

After a minute or so of indifferently massaging my legs and chest, Barbie poured some lotion on my cock and within twenty or thirty seconds of diligent kneading I ejaculated all over my legs. My "massage" couldn't have lasted more than five minutes.

While I looked down at the mess I'd made, literally and figuratively, Barbie completely disarmed me by very sweetly asking, "Would you like a hug?"

"Yes. Yes, I would." I was so inexplicably touched by her gesture I felt like crying. Somehow that hug felt far more intimate than any sex act.

Everything about Barbie was fake: her tits, her bleached blonde hair, her narcotized smile, her feigned enthusiasm, even her name. But when I hugged her, our connection felt genuine. Maybe all I really wanted all along was someone to hug me, to hold me close and tell me everything would be all right, that the pain would end and I'd return inevitably to the world of the living, bruised and battered but gloriously, wonderfully, unmistakably alive. Well, that and a hand job.

My fixation on Hello, My Concubine should have ended there. But I couldn't leave well enough alone. A week later I returned. I was no lost babe in the woods this time around and the woman I chose had a hard, unyielding face and none of the ingratiating fake softness of Barbie.

She nevertheless felt the need to make small talk—maybe that's an occupational hazard—and it gradually came out that we'd both graduated from the University of Wisconsin at Madison in 1999. And now here she was, straining to bring me to orgasm, the stern expression on her face betraying nothing—not fake happiness, not discomfort, just the stern determination of someone doing a job no matter how distasteful they find it. I yearned for the sweetness and odd vulnerability—however feigned—that characterized my first encounter at Hello, My Concubine. Two years earlier we might have been classmates. Now I was paying her for something that barely constituted sex. I was tempted to feel sorry for her. She very well could have felt sorry for me. After all, my fellow Badger left our sordid encounter a hundred and sixty dollars richer while I left with a much lighter wallet and a pervasive sense of shame.

I Enjoy Talking to Famous People

Don't Look Back
Tales Beyond the Transcript

D. A. Pennebaker's seminal 1967 cinema verité masterpiece, *Don't Look Back,* is both a quintessential rock and roll movie and a penetrating examination of the complex, contradictory, and sometimes antagonistic relationship between artists and journalists. While touring Great Britain with his way-cool gypsy caravan, Bob Dylan wages a war of aggression on a battalion of clueless reporters designed to undermine the very foundation of journalism itself, or at least its coke-whore bastard child, entertainment journalism.

Ideally, artists and journalists enjoy a symbiotic, mutually beneficial relationship. The reporter helps publicize and promote the artist. The artist in turn provides journalists with snappy quotes and knockout features. But in *Don't Look Back* angel-headed quipster Dylan and the hopelessly square journalists he antagonizes are operating at cross-purposes. Dylan's goal as an enigmatic poet-troubadour is to preserve the aura of mystery endemic to his persona, while the journalists' job is to explain Dylan to their clueless readers.

Dylan and his hapless interrogators don't even seem to be speaking the same language, let alone sharing the same wavelength. Dylan speaks an abstract language of poetry and obfuscation while the L7 scribblers who follow him around traffic in the reductive vernacular of sound bites, pull quotes, and screaming headlines. The bullied and overmatched scribes in *Don't Look Back* can't unlock the complicated truth of Dylan by asking him maddeningly literal questions about his "message" and audience any more than they could decipher the mysteries of nature by asking clouds or flowers about their position on soybean subsidies.

Dylan's free-floating contempt for journalists and the mainstream press transforms a pair of would-be Q&As into angry attacks on the legitimacy of journalism as a construct and caustic referendums on the writers' existence. Dylan is so unrelentingly, imaginatively hostile toward a particularly pathetic science student/would-be reporter that it's not hard to imagine the hapless scribe heading home after the interview, making himself a cup of tea, then hanging himself out of shame. Assuming the man didn't kill himself, I imagine he suffers Pavlovian anxiety attacks every time a Dylan song comes on the radio.

Then there's the *Time* writer with tragically British teeth Dylan dresses down for being part of an organization and a trade that spews forth endless lies. When the *Time* reporter guilelessly asks what kind of journalistic truth Dylan would condone, he responds, as only a twenty-three-year-old convinced of his own genius can, a "photo of a tramp vomiting into a sewer." Dylan must have missed *Time*'s controversial 1965 cover story HOBO PUKES IN GUTTER.

Dylan's snappy answers to stupid questions remind me of a Q&A I attended in Madison with David Lynch, another enigmatic genius none too keen on deconstructing his own oeuvre. A particularly shameless fanboy asked Lynch a question along the lines of "Excuse me, Mr. Lynch sir, but if you freeze-frame three minutes into the second episode of *Twin Peaks,* you can clearly see a midget doing a cartwheel in the bottom of the frame. How does this relate to Jung's theories concerning the universal subconscious?"

After pausing for a while Lynch responded, in that faux-naïf Gumpian Midwestern drawl of his, something to the effect of "I done made a teevee show called *Twin Peaks*. People seemed to like it. They don't show it on the teevee no more. Also, I enjoy eating pie."

What Lynch was suggesting and what Dylan outright argues throughout *Don't Look Back* is that the best way to process art is to enjoy it without trying to dissect or analyze it, at least not with the artist directly. There's a great deal of truth to that argument, but then my entire career is predicated on the antithetical notion that analyzing art can help people appreciate it on a deeper level.

When I read Pauline Kael and Greil Marcus for the first time, their ideas changed the way I viewed not just the art, movies, and music they were discussing but life itself. Nevertheless, as an interviewer, critic, and member of the media (boo! hiss!), I understand that film critics and journalists lag just shy of baby-seal clubbers and professional nun killers in the respect they inspire among the general public.

Anyone who conducts interviews regularly has suffered through *Don't Look Back*–style interviews so assaultive and dispiriting they're forced to take a cold, hard look at themselves in the mirror afterward and wonder if maybe they really *are* an evil parasite.

The most punishing interview I've ever conducted was with Ghostface Killah. At the risk of sounding heretical, I think that with the possible exceptions of habitual shape-shifters Madlib and MF Doom, and maybe Aesop Rock, Ghostface is the closest thing hip-hop has to Bob Dylan. They're both perpetual comeback kids with a genius for abstraction and vivid, surrealistic imagery. And they both have little use for interviewers.

You know you're in for a long interview when even lazy softballs over the plate get treated like Nolan Ryan fastballs to the face. When I asked Ghostface to tell me about his new album (*Fishscale*), he answered, "What do you want to know about it?" but the edge in his voice said, "What's that, Officer? I don't know nothing 'bout no new album. You can't connect me to no new album. I demand to speak to my lawyer!"

From there he just barely humored me with terse one-word answers, nonanswers, and unexpected blasts of inexplicable vitriol. In response to a seemingly innocuous question about his prefame existence, Ghostface ended the interview by vowing to return to robbing, shooting, and knocking motherfuckers out should his career go south. My interview with Dick Cavett closed the same way.

As Chuck Klosterman has written, you don't really "meet" the people you interview. Though plenty of my colleagues would like to imagine otherwise, you're not two old friends having an intimate, deeply spiritual conversation that, in a funny, seemingly random twist, is later transcribed and used to help sell magazines, advertisements, and movies. Incidentally, if you ever encounter someone who refers to the celebrities they've interviewed by their first names, you officially have my permission to punch them hard in the face. It's for their own good.

So it is delusional to ever imagine that you're anything more than a hack with a story to file and an entertainer with a product to peddle conducting a publicist-stage-managed, wildly artificial, hopefully mutually beneficial transaction designed to help put more money in the coffers of our corporate masters (luvya corporate masters, I write non-passive-aggressively!).

When I do an interview with Joe or Jane Productoshill I never get a deep, penetrating insight into the core of their being. At best I get a quick little snapshot that, if taken in just the right light and from just the right angle, reveals something funny or surprising or poignant about who they are and how they see the world. I'm only getting fleeting images indelibly rooted in a time, a place, and a highly specific cultural context, but sometimes snapshots can be enormously revealing. Also, like most raging egomaniacs, I wrestle with low self-esteem. I worry that unless I lard this memoir with gratuitous celebrity anecdotes, I'll have a hard time selling copies to people outside my immediate sphere of friends and family.

You never quite know what you're in for when you sit down to conduct an interview. Alan Arkin seemed confused and mildly angered that I was asking him questions about his life, career, and latest movie (*Little Miss Sunshine*).

I called up eccentric Wu-Tang mastermind RZA literally forty or so times at our predetermined interview time, only to receive a voice mail message saying, "You've reached Digi." After the thirtieth call I started to feel like a character in a bad cyberpunk novel: "I've gotta talk to Digi on his cell about ODB and GZA and the Clan!" When I e-mailed his publicist about my frustrations, she diplomatically insisted that RZA wasn't "into" listening to his voice mail messages. But when I finally reached RZA several days later, he was an absolute delight, funny, loose, uninhibited, and unpredictable. Who knew he was such a big Jerry Lewis buff?

When I interviewed Rick James he was keen to play up the respected-veteran-musician aspect of his career and downplay the unfortunate business with burning imprisoned sex slaves with crack pipes. My favorite part of the interview was when, with a blissful absence of self-consciousness, he talked about how in the eighties he and James Brown decided they weren't going to let their music be sampled by rappers unless they cut it out with their potty-mouthed filth and disrespectful comments about bitches and hos. In case the contradictions in James's puritanical critique of rap profanity weren't glaring enough, his exact condemnation went, "It's like you motherfucking can't do a record without using profanity and motherfucking demeaning your own race."

My ultimate "why the hell not" interview was Gene Simmons of Kiss/Gene Simmons Toyota fame. I have no respect for Simmons as a musician or human being. But it's hard not to respect the sprawling business empire he created out of a half-assed bar band in silly makeup.

Ten times out of ten a publicist sets up a concrete interview time acceptable to the interviewer and interviewee. That is how reasonable human beings do things. That is not how leather-skinned rock god and legendary pussy-wolfer Simmons does things.

When I tried to nail down a time for our interview, I learned that Mr. Simmons couldn't be nailed down to a time or date. It cramped his style, man. I was told that Simmons would call me, or not, possibly within the next few weeks or possibly on his deathbed. I was apparently expected to linger by my phone indefinitely on the off chance that a creepy old Jewish man and thoroughly detestable human being might decide to call me.

The first time Simmons tried to call me was on New Year's Eve, long after I'd gone home from the office. He was probably in a Jacuzzi full of hundred-dollar bills and a dozen naked groupies, getting ready to get his Dick Clark on, when he thought, "You know what would really make this moment complete? Talking to a twenty-three-year-old in Wisconsin."

I'd given up on interviewing Simmons when I got an unexpected call one Wednesday afternoon. "Is this Nathan?" it inquired impatiently, annoyed and aggravated before the interview even began.

"Yeah."

"This is Gene."

"Oh shit, I've been waiting to talk to you for a while," I blurted while I scampered off to round up a tape recorder and my list of questions.

"Oh yeah, well I've been waiting to talk to you forever too," he hissed accusingly, a statement that made up for what it lacked in graciousness or logic with sheer douchebaggery.

Then the interview began.

"So, you were born in Haifa, Israel, eh?"

"Yes. If you ask me yes or no questions, those are the only answers you're going to get. Yes. Or. No," he bitched.

About a minute into the interview, Simmons groused, "You

know you have this habit of saying [affects slack-jawed hillbilly voice], 'Uh-huh, uh-huh,' after everything I say. Did you know that?" Simmons sneered. Gosh, I sure did. But nobody's ever been a huge enough dick to make a big deal out of it. I say things like "uh-huh" during phone interviews for a very specific reason: to show whoever I'm talking to that I'm listening to them and immersed in the conversation in lieu of eye contact or other non-verbal cues. Phone interviews rely heavily on rhythm and chemistry. So silence is deadly. A good way to avoid the conversational black hole of silence is by repeatedly assuring your subject that you're paying attention to them.

The interview grew much less contentious after that. I enacted a stealthy form of passive-aggressive revenge, however, when Simmons's interview appeared in the *A.V. Club* interview collection *Tenacity of the Cockroach* and the glowering rock demon was represented by a photo of the official Gene Simmons Kiss Beanie Baby.

Like many ragingly heterosexual men/hip-hop critics, I spent the summer of 1999 listening to Belle and Sebastian's *If You're Feeling Sinister* on my Walkman while aimlessly riding my bike in the wee small hours of the morning. While I weaved up and down East Washington Street, luxuriating in the album's exquisite melancholy, I imagined that if Belle and Sebastian front man Stuart Murdoch and I ever met, we'd instantly become soul mates and while away lazy Sundays prancing through meadows, picking wildflowers, reciting poetry to each other, and sharing intimate secrets under the moonlight. But not in a gay way. No homo.

Belle and Sebastian encouraged such fantasies by hiding from the press and parceling out live gigs sparingly early in their career. Since there was no such thing as a public Belle and Sebastian, fans were free to project their innermost fantasies onto the band. They could imagine that Murdoch was singing directly to them in a secret language only they understood. Nothing Murdoch could say in interviews or live gigs could compete with the fantasy figure that existed in fans' imaginations. Belle and Sebastian created an aura of mystery that added immeasurably to the heartbreaking poignancy of its music.

Just about everyone has harbored the delusion that their favorite artist would reciprocate their affection if given a chance. Great artists offer the illusion of intimacy while maintaining a tantalizing distance. Celebrities become, to borrow the title of a Bill Zehme profile collection, intimate strangers. We know them yet they somehow remain aloof, mysterious, unreachable, hidden behind locked gates and vast swarms of bodyguards. They exist in a rarefied realm yet willingly expose themselves through their art. It's a pop culture striptease.

So it was with profoundly mixed emotions that I volunteered to interview Murdoch when he tentatively began reaching out to the press. I worried that the real Murdoch couldn't possibly compete with the Murdoch in my head.

My fears were, as always, well founded. I could barely hear him through the crackle and distortion of the phone line, and what I could hear was damn near indecipherable due to his thick Scottish burr. I somehow managed to get a usable interview out of it but in my head this is how the interview went:

ME: Could you talk a little bit about the college recording project that led to Belle and Sebastian's first album?
STUART MURDOCH: [Crackle, crackle, static, impenetrable Scottish whispering; awkward silence that could mean the end of an answer, a pregnant pause, or that our connection has conked out completely; crackle, crackle, crackle, the sound of my hopes and dreams dying.]

No, no, no. It wasn't supposed to be like this! We were supposed to forge an instantaneous bond, not stumble our way awkwardly through thirty minutes of mumbly, nervously asked questions and sputtering, awkward-silence-infused half answers.

During times like this I begin to feel like Rupert Pupkin. Is it really asking too much for my creative heroes to live up to the impossible ideal I've created for them in my head? It looked like I would have to find someone else to while away lazy Sundays prancing through meadows, picking wildflowers, reciting poetry, and sharing intimate secrets under the moonlight with. Maybe my close personal friend Gene Simmons would be up for the job.

When I first started at the *A.V. Club* we indulged periodically in a sordid little racket called "junkets." Junkets are a noxious subsection of the Hollywood hype machine whereby cash-rich studios fly "journalists" out to Los Angeles; put them up at the Four Seasons; give them gaudy per diems to waste on steak dinners, bottles of champagne, and forty-dollar room service tips; show them a craptastic new movie, possibly after first pumping them full of free, judgment-impairing alcohol; then have them "interview" actors and filmmakers at roundtables where actors pretend not to be filled with rage by having to answer the same asinine question ("What was it like working with ___?") for the four hundredth time that day. Sounds sweet, huh? It's not. Junkets give entertainment reporters the illusion of Hollywood glamour and importance while controlling their every move.

Like so much of our world, junkets are rooted in mutually beneficial deceptions. Studios pretend that Joe Nobody from the *Pawtucket Democrat-Ledger-Herald Tribune* is a big-shot tastemaker worthy of being bribed with tacky little gifts. In return Joe Nobody from the *Pawtucket Democrat-Ledger-Herald Tribune* pretends that the deep thoughts of, say, the producer of *Senseless* are somehow of interest to anyone other than Mr. *Senseless* Producer's immediate family. Even that's a stretch.

Junkets exact a high psychic cost for the tawdry blasts of glamour they afford. That hundred-dollar-a-day per diem might seem impossibly generous for someone making fifteen grand a year, but that's an awfully cheap price for even a hack's soul. Satan would have a field day at junkets. He could probably walk away with dozens of trophies just by offering the weak-willed a satin *Legally Blonde 2* crew jacket in exchange for their eternal soul.

I attended junkets just long enough to realize I despised them. When I attended the *Girl, Interrupted* junket I was so agonizingly bored I found myself tuning out of a group chat with Angelina Jolie, a huge star both in film and in my masturbatory fantasies. It was apparent to everyone that *Girl, Interrupted* was going to be a star-making film for her, so one of my colleagues asked her, "So, what are you going to buy with all your money? Are you gonna splurge on something really exotic or extravagant?"

I was only partially paying attention, however, and my mind began to wander to rich eccentrics past. I started thinking about Michael Jackson and his famous love of primate-Americans. Unbeknownst to me, someone elaborated on the money question by asking if she'd be buying a home, a villa, a bat cave, someplace fun to live in.

Having ignored the follow-up and still contemplating Michael Jackson, I chimed in with, "Yeah, you know, like a chimpanzee?" I had my mind on some Bubbles and some Bubbles on my mind.

"What? Are you asking me if I want to live inside of a chimpanzee? Like in *Being John Malkovich*? Boy, you're weird. I like you. You're cool," Jolie answered as everyone laughed uproariously at my miscue.

When I interview someone I'm looking to make a connection with them, however fleeting or brief or insubstantial. But there are always going to be Dylanesque interview subjects who don't know you but already hate you and act as if they're being interviewed at gunpoint against their will. At least I have the consolation of writing for a paper that, unlike the *Time* magazines of the world, actually tells the truth. Though even we won't run headlines like TRAMP VOMITS INTO SEWER. Unless, of course, it's a really slow news week.

When I interview someone for the *A. V. Club* I'm protected by the clearly defined roles of interviewer and interviewee. It's intimidating staring down Robert Duvall with nothing but a tape recorder and a list of questions but at the end of the day I have a job to do and so does he.

The same can't be said of celebrities encountered in the wild. My strangest celebrity encounter would have to be the time Topher Grace totally vomited in front of me at the tail end of a flight from LAX to O'Hare. If I can fast-forward here, this was deep into the second season of *Movie Club,* the poorly rated, mildly disreputable basic-cable movie-review panel show I appeared on from December 2004 to June 2005. The Sunday night flight back to Chicago that week began on a forgettable note. *Because of Winn-Dixie,* the in-flight movie, failed to pique my interest (Dave Matthews + Dog That Teaches Life Lessons = No Thanks). The Frank Sinatra biography I was reading for work sucked the proverbial giant donkey dick, which is good for the giant donkey but bad for everyone else. And the dude sitting next to me spent the entire first half of the flight with his head on his food tray. Then about halfway through the flight he got up, went to the bathroom, and announced, "I feel much, much better now," the implication being that he had just done his best impression of Linda Blair in *The Exorcist* in the airplane bathroom.

His voice and face seemed familiar. Even with his sickly ghost-white pallor he was strikingly handsome. With his elegantly faded jeans, ironic lemon-yellow "Squirt" T-shirt, and old-school Adidas, he looked like he'd just emerged from a *Details* cover shoot. Even his hint of manly Don Johnson stubble was attractive in a heroin-chic kind of way.

He was a sexy motherfucker. But where did I know him from? Or did all twentysomethings in L.A. look like movie stars? I found myself looking over the shoulder of the handsome stranger next to me so I could peruse his copy of *Entertainment Weekly.* Reading over someone's shoulder is obnoxious enough. But I made it worse by staring deep and hard at the guy next to me in a futile attempt to ascertain why he seemed so familiar. He, meanwhile, shot me a look out of the corner of his eye that said, "Hey, you, annoying homosexual. Please stop checking me out and reading over my shoulder."

Then two thoughts hit me simultaneously. They were, in order:

1. My God, I'm seated next to Topher Grace!

and

2. My God, I think I might be gay!

I had been impressed by his performance in *P.S.* a few weeks earlier and now here I was annoying him *in person*! But why would Topher Grace be flying coach to Chicago? It didn't make sense. Surely a hot young movie star could afford first class. But couldn't the same be said of a charismatic young senator who'd captured the imagination of the American people with his dashing good looks, stirring oratory, and goofy name?

If I can rewind a little, here's what happened the week before: I was waiting to board my flight when I heard a disembodied voice compliment someone on a speech they'd given. Since that constituted atypical airport banter, I swiveled around to see the distinguished visage of Barack Obama and his lovely wife waiting for my flight. I was faced with the question of whether to go up and profess my respect for Obama or to let him and his wife travel in peace.

My first instinct was to let him be, but then I reckoned that as his constituent I had a God-given constitutional right to tell him exactly how great he was. You know, really give him a piece of my mind. I know these fat cats in Washington hate it when you tell them you think they're God's gift to politics but I wasn't about to let that stop me from really giving Obama my two cents' worth about his awesomeness.

So I walked over to the dashing stranger and very meekly asked, "Excuse me, sir, but are you Barack Obama?" He replied affirmatively, and like a tongue-tied schoolgirl, I inarticulately stammered, "I just, uh, wanted to say how proud we all are of you and how much your speeches mean to all of us." I don't remember specifically but I may very well have thrown in an "and stuff" for good measure.

Obama handled the situation with extraordinary grace, shaking my hand firmly and thanking me for my kind words. In hindsight, I regret not giving him a terrorist fist jab or the Islamist secret handshake. I hear he's quite adept at those. It was almost as if dealing with gushing strangers telling you how great you are constitutes a regular component of a famous politician's everyday existence.

I felt a little weird not saying anything to Obama's wife and briefly pondered telling her, "You seem great too!" but thought better of it. One gushing display of fanboy worship was enough for the evening. There was no need to make myself look even more ridiculous by spraying adoration in the direction of everyone in sight.

I felt silly. Who exactly was this "we" I professed to speak for? Me and my friends? The city of Chicago? The state of Illinois? God's own United States? Mankind as a whole? Then again, all my friends really *were* proud of Obama, for he is that rarest of anomalies in our grim political landscape: an elected official who can talk eloquently about hope and optimism without coming across as just another pandering phony telling people what they want to hear.

You never think of the right things to say until long after the time to say them has passed. So it wasn't until much later that I realized what I really wanted to say to Obama was that he was a life-affirming ray of hope in the black hole of the 2004 election. I wanted to tell him that I was literally moved to tears by his acceptance speech upon being elected senator and that the hopes, dreams, and aspirations of every right-thinking American rested squarely on his sturdy shoulders. I wanted to tell him that we were counting on him to be the savior of the Democratic

Party, if not politics and the nation as a whole. So don't fuck up! And don't let the pressure get to you!

Having just taped a gimmick-heavy *Star Wars*–themed episode of *Movie Club* where we were encouraged to bring as many film-related tchotchkes as possible, I still had a *Win a Date with Tad Hamilton!* autograph book in my luggage and for a brief moment pondered what a coup it would be to have Obama sign it. I ultimately decided it was beneath the dignity of the office for a senator to sign a girlish pink autograph book promoting a frothy Topher Grace movie no one saw.

I didn't want Obama to think of me, should he think of me at all, as the weird dude who tried to get him to sign a pink autograph book in an airport.

News of Obama's presence on the plane spread quickly. We civilians were disproportionately impressed to see that not only was Obama flying on a commercial flight like the rest of us but that he wasn't even sitting in first class. Obama's decision to mix with the ignorant rabble (aka "his constituents") was deemed even more heroic once rumors spread that he'd been in Los Angeles for Oprah's fabulous party for the rich, beautiful, and wealthy. Obama could undoubtedly have borrowed one of Oprah's private planes, possibly with John Travolta as his pilot, yet here he was flying with us. Truly Obama is a man of the people. It should be noted, however, that he was flying in economy plus and subsequently enjoying the decadent five extra inches of legroom United tries to get suckers to pony up thirty-four extra dollars for. Fucking politicians.

All right, enough backtracking. Let's get back to the lecture at hand: I started to rattle off the reasons why the guy seated next to me couldn't be Topher Grace. For starters, Topher Grace is tall and lanky and this guy was, well, fuck, he was just as tall as me (I'm six-two) and twenty-five pounds lighter to boot.

Maybe I was seated next to Topher Grace. Maybe we weren't so different after all. By that point we were both TV personalities in our late twenties. I had spent eight years growing up just outside Milwaukee before moving to Chicago at eleven; he spent an equivalent amount of time pretending to grow up in Milwaukee on *That '70s Show.* Syndication and a thriving film career undoubtedly had made him a multimillionaire. I was (just barely) a multithousandaire. He made out with Laura Linney in *P.S.*—I masturbated watching Laura Linney in *P.S.* He was a thinking dame's sex symbol. I was no longer a virgin. It's like we were twins!

As we neared our landing I pondered whether to make my move. Once we reached our gate and the plane stopped moving, I very nervously asked the green-hued man sitting beside me, "Hey, has anyone ever told you you look just like Topher Grace?"

"That's because I *am* Topher Grace," Pukey McGee deadpanned.

"You're probably not going to believe this then, but I actually have a *Win a Date with Tad Hamilton!* autograph book in my carry-on luggage," I sputtered. Great, now Grace probably thought I was an obsessive *Win a Date with Tad Hamilton!* fan in addition to being an obnoxious homosexual.

"Are you press or something?" he asked, perhaps because the alternative—that I was a deranged stalker pursuing him cross-country in a crazed bid to get him to sign a *Win a Date with Tad Hamilton!* autograph book—was too horrifying to face.

"Yeah, I'm actually the head entertainment writer for *The Onion.*"

"Wow, I'd totally shake your hand if I wasn't so sick."

"Hey, you were great in *P.S.* That was a really fantastic film."

"Yeah, I'm really proud of that one."

"So, what are you in Chicago for?"

"I'm meeting with a director about a film."

Jesus, small talk is just as excruciating when you're talking to a celebrity. "Which one?"

"Harold Ramis."

That certainly explained why he was flying to Chicago. Ramis was such a Chicago guy that he filmed his movies in Illinois and avoided Hollywood as much as possible. He was powerful enough that he could literally make the movie industry come to him.

"It's funny, I was actually in L.A. shooting a movie-review show Harold Ramis was supposed to be the original host for."

See? Twins.

"Huh."

"You know, it's funny, last week I was flying back to Chicago and Barack Obama was flying back on my flight. It was really weird. He was flying in coach and everything."

"Yeah, he's great. That dude's a rock star," Mr. Grace retorted woozily, which struck me as a terribly young-movie-star thing to say. He's right, though. Dude is a rock star.

"Say, I wouldn't ask if I wasn't so sick but I think I dropped my lucky hat and I can't really bend down to pick it up, so if you wouldn't mind, could you look around for it? It should be somewhere around here," Tophy ('cause by that time I felt entitled to refer to him as "Tophy") asked apologetically.

This was getting weird. Was Topher Grace really asking me to crawl around on my hands and knees within spitting distance of his man-junk? Moreover, was I secretly excited about this prospect?

"Sure," I responded, and then got down on my knees and began to search for Grace's beloved chapeau. Sure enough, I found the hat under the row of seats just in front of us. I waited a few seconds before I retrieved it. During that time—which seemed to simultaneously slow down and speed up—I contemplated quickly shoving the hat in my pocket and telling Tophy that I had looked everywhere but couldn't find it.

Then I'd cackle maniacally to myself, giddy with the furtive knowledge that I had pilfered Topher Grace's lucky hat. What a secret that would be! I could just imagine people complimenting me on my awesome new hat. I'd just chuckle a deep, self-satisfied laugh before blowing their minds with the revelation that I had stolen it from Topher Grace.

During those pivotal few seconds, during which I considered

hat thievery most foul, I fantasized that by stealing Grace's hat I'd steal his professional and personal mojo as well, that I'd rob him of some vital life essence. I'd usurp his position in the Hollywood hierarchy. He'd be down and out, reduced to appearing on a cheesy basic-cable movie-review panel show, while I'd be pursued by starlets, offered plum roles, and treated like a minor deity.

But I couldn't bring myself to steal Topher Grace's hat. He was standing just inches away, all sick and vomity and vulnerable, counting on me to facilitate a joyous reunion between him and his headwear of choice. So I came up and handed him his lucky hat.

"Thanks," he said sincerely, "I feel even worse about this now but I'm totally going to throw up."

Topher Grace, teen heartthrob, rising movie star, and one of the most promising actors of his generation, then enthusiastically blew chunks into an airsickness bag maybe ten inches away from me. Here's the really sick part: I was jazzed. "Wow," I thought, "this is great. Topher Grace is totally vomiting in front of me!" It was so much cooler and more intimate than a handshake or small talk!

Here's the extra-special sad part: even after Mr. Grace unloaded the contents of his gastrointestinal system into an air-sickness bag, I still held out hope that he'd sign my *Win a Date with Tad Hamilton!* autograph book. What a coup that would be! Maybe he'd even personalize the autograph with references to our time together—you know, something like

> *To Nathan: I am forever in your debt,*
> *Sorry 'bout all the puking,*
> *Yer Bestest TV pal,*
>
> Tophy
> XOXOXOXOXO

P.S. The next time you're in town we totally gotta hang out at Planet Hollywood!

Part of me felt like having a *Win a Date with Tad Hamilton!* autograph book with Topher Grace's and Barack Obama's signatures might have been worth the loss of self-respect engendered in attaining them. The part of my psyche that views dignity as an unnecessary luxury did a cost-benefit analysis of the whole peculiar situation and ascertained that I should give it one last go. So I waited just outside the plane after we got to Chicago, bright pink autograph book in hand.

But Tophy foiled my fiendish plot by racing to the bathroom at the front of the plane, from which the following telltale sounds, familiar to all *Mad* magazine readers, could be heard: "Blech," "Bloo-arrggg," and especially "Retcch!!!!!!!!" Nevertheless I stood outside the plane for a good two minutes, deeply ashamed of myself yet eager for Topher to emerge and scribble down words that would memorialize our brief, strange relationship for posterity before finally giving up and trudging home.

Clearly, Mr. Grace was interested in doing exactly two things at that particular moment: vomiting his lungs out and going to sleep. I wasn't about to keep him from doing either. 'Tis truly a blessing and a curse to be intimately familiar with the depths of your desperation. But the moment I gave up on securing Grace's signature for my pink promotional autograph book, I became cognizant of the limits of my desperation as well. Dylan would have admired my restraint.

Yesterday I Was a Sun God

The Bad and the Beautiful
Head Producer Guy

In Vincente Minnelli's impossibly opulent 1952 melodrama, *The Bad and the Beautiful*, Kirk Douglas plays Jonathan Shields, an unscrupulous movie producer who is magnetic and destructive, charismatic and duplicitous, utterly amoral yet strangely irresistible. He's a star maker, backstabber, hero, villain, and antihero all wrapped up in one larger-than-life package. He's Hollywood personified, the glamour and danger and mystery and madness of show business with a cleft chin.

The film unfolds in flashback *Citizen Kane* style as a wry, cynical, pipe-smoking writer-professor (Dick Powell), not quite worldly enough to realize that when you sell a project to Hollywood they expect you to throw in your soul for free; an ambitious director (Fred Amiel); and a boozy, heartbreakingly fragile movie star (Lana Turner) recount the pivotal role Shields played in launching their careers before he bitterly betrayed them. Powell's, Amiel's, and Turner's characters all have ample reason to despise Shields. But when they're asked to bail Shields out of a professional jam, they're all clearly tempted to help him just the same. He may do horrible things but he does them with style. In Hollywood that counts for an awful lot: if you can't do right, at least do wrong with pizzazz.

Guys like Shields are easy to like but hard to trust. When I was twenty-six I met my very own Jonathan Shields. I was introduced to a gentleman I will heretofore refer to as Head Producer Guy by JMac, a nouveau riche businessman who'd made a mint in sports merchandising and wanted to break into television by launching a Head Producer Guy–engineered *Siskel & Ebert*–style movie review show starring the film critics of the *A.V. Club*.

In true Jonathan Shields fashion, Head Producer Guy commandeered JMac's idea and quickly elbowed him off the project. When *The Onion* rejected handing over its name to a pair of disreputable characters, Head Producer Guy launched a nationwide search for photogenic young people who were either critics or willing to play one on television.

Every few months Head Producer Guy would call and inquire, "Ya got a minute?" as if concerned he might be pulling me away from the final stages of finding a cure for cancer, and update me on what crazy new shape his movie-review show was taking.

When Head Producer Guy told me he had sold American Movie Classics on funding a pilot, I was delighted.

"That's great!" I enthused. "Where's it going to be taped?"

"We're not sure."

"OK, so who's going to be on the show?"

"We haven't finalized that yet either. We're narrowing people down."

"What about the host?"

"That hasn't been decided either."

In an impressive display of chutzpah, Head Producer Guy sold AMC on funding a pilot that would be taped in a city to be named later, that would or would not feature various people, and that would probably be hosted by some person, maybe. I had to admire Head Producer Guy's hustle in getting AMC to pony up cash for such a vague venture.

A few months later I got another call from Head Producer

Guy. He began with his obligatory "Ya got a minute?" Then he told me the good news. The show he'd taken to calling *Movie Club* was a definite go. It was going to be filmed in Chicago with two local critics (Peter Sobczynski and Jae-Ha Kim), myself, and a host to be named later.

Being an incorrigible optimist, Head Producer Guy seldom hedged his spiels with "ifs" or "maybes." Being an equally incorrigible pessimist, I mentally inserted them into each of his sentences. If Head Producer Guy said, "The show's definitely a go in Chicago with you, Peter, and Jae," I would interpret his statement to mean "If we somehow manage to get a show on the air then you, Jae-Ha Kim, and Peter might appear on it. Possibly. And it might be filmed in Chicago. Or not."

Head Producer Guy cautioned me not to tell my fellow *A.V. Club*bers about my imminent television debut on the grounds that it would drive them mad with jealousy. I refrained from telling my colleagues about what Head Producer Guy had told me for a more practical reason: I didn't want to look like an idiot if, or when, the show never materialized.

That turned out to be a wise move. Two months later I got another call from Head Producer Guy. He'd found his host.

"Hey, Nathan, do you know who Harold Ramis is?"

Know who Harold Ramis is? Cunt-fucking Christ on a crucicracker, the man is an icon, a legend, a comic genius, a man who'd acted, directed, and/or starred in some of the best, most beloved and successful comedies of the past fifty years. His credits read like a list of the top-grossing laughers of all time: *Animal House, Caddyshack, Stripes, Ghostbusters* and *Ghostbusters II, Groundhog Day, Back to School,* and *Analyze This.* That's not even mentioning his seminal role as a writer and performer on *SCTV.*

"Yeah, of course I know who Harold Ramis is. The guy's a legend."

"Yeah, he is, and he's eager to get back into the spotlight. He misses performing, so he's going to host *Movie Club.*"

My first response to this news was "Wow!" followed by "Why?" Why would a player of Ramis's magnitude, who could live comfortably off the residuals for *Ghostbusters* for the rest of his life, want to do a cheesy movie-review panel show on basic cable? Beyond the allure of wearing makeup in public, what could a show like ours possibly offer a man of his stature?

Ramis hosting a basic-cable movie-review panel show was like J. D. Salinger returning to the public sphere by penning an episode of *CSI: Miami*: it was a little beneath him. Nevertheless, if Head Producer Guy insisted that Harold Ramis was going to host a basic-cable movie-review panel show, then I was willing to concede that there was a remote, outside, perhaps one-in-twenty chance that it might happen.

My cynicism served me well. It wasn't long before Ramis dropped out. Head Producer Guy said Ramis was worried about scheduling conflicts if he directed a movie while the show was still in production. But I suspect that he simply looked in the mirror one day and said, "I'm Harold 'Ghost-Bustin'-Ass *Groundhog Day*' Ramis! Why would I want to host a basic-cable movie-review show when I can smoke a giant bag of weed, roll around in a pile of hundred-dollar bills, and hire high-priced call girls to act out the complete works of George S. Kaufman while dressed in French maid costumes instead?"

Every month after that I got a call from Head Producer Guy updating me on the show's status, which seemed to change hourly. I feared one day I'd get a call from Head Producer Guy and after the ubiquitous "Ya got a minute?" he'd explain that for reasons far too convoluted to go into, *Movie Club* was now going to be a triweekly three-and-a-half-hour variety show/minstrel show revue filmed in the jungles of Guatemala starring me, the USC marching band, Joey Heatherton, and possibly Jae-Ha Kim.

In early 2004 Head Producer Guy hit me with another jarring twist in his movie-review show's strange evolution. For financial and practical reasons the show was going to be filmed in Los Angeles rather than Chicago. That was the bad news. The good news was that I was still in the running for it. After looking at a reported eighty critics—though Head Producer Guy's definition of a film critic was flexible enough to include anyone who'd ever seen a movie—nationwide, AMC and Head Producer Guy had narrowed the field down to eight contenders for the four critic slots. Now it needed a host.

Ramis was out, obviously. Head Producer Guy told me he was considering such heavyweights as John Landis and Peter Bogdanovich for the hosting duties slot and had taken a lunch with the estimable Andy Richter, formerly of *Late Night with Conan O'Brien.*

In Head Producer Guy's telling, Richter was eager to do the show.

"'It should be a breeze,'" Head Producer Guy quoted him as saying. "'I can just pop into the studio, tape for an hour or so, and then duck out.'"

If I were running the show, literally and figuratively, I'd have allowed Andy Richter to host it in his bathrobe and pajamas by remote from a beanbag in his living room if so inclined. But Head Producer Guy was willing to draw a line in the sand. Any host of *Movie Club,* he proclaimed dramatically, would be required to see every movie discussed on the show. It would be an absolute prerequisite for the gig. Or not. Head Producer Guy's fierce convictions had a way of evaporating at the first sign of resistance.

What kind of a bizarro alternate universe had I stumbled into where Andy Richter, Peter Bogdanovich, and John Landis were somehow deemed unworthy of doing *Movie Club* while I was still being considered for the show? It was flattering and insane and still felt terribly unreal.

Though the show still lacked a host, Head Producer Guy nevertheless planned to hold auditions for *Movie Club* in late summer 2004. The audition setup was simple. He'd fly three outside film critics into Los Angeles the day before the auditions to try out with five local "critics." We'd meet the mystery host and do a practice run that Saturday evening. Then the next morning we'd divide up into two groups of four. In the morning one group of four would do a practice show/final audition. In the afternoon a second group would do a practice show/audition. Then the AMC executives, Head Producer Guy, and his loyal right-hand woman, R.L., would look at the tapes and send home four of the eight critics. The remaining four would then film a pilot for the show on the spot.

Before I flew down to Los Angeles, Head Producer Guy and AMC settled on a host: John Ridley, a handsome, charismatic, insanely prolific and wildly enigmatic pulp novelist, producer, director, NPR commentator, comic book scribe, graphic novel author, webtoon guru, screenwriter, big-league provocateur, and playwright best known for penning the story for David O. Russell's masterful *Three Kings* (and having a bitter falling-out with the director), the source novel and screenplay for Oliver Stone's *U Turn* (and having a bitter falling-out with the director), and the story and original script for Malcolm Lee's *Undercover Brother* (you can probably guess what happened with Ridley and the director on that one).

Head Producer Guy finally narrowed down the candidates for the show's four critic slots to eight and had the three outside critics fly to Los Angeles for a high-stakes critical royal rumble to determine who'd make the pilot and who'd go home with nothing but an undying hatred of Head Producer Guy. The final candidates pitted a genuinely respected heavyweight critic (*The Boston Globe*'s Wesley Morris) against a bunch of telegenic lookers whose critical credentials were pretty much irrelevant.

Thanks to jet lag, a serious dearth of sleep, and zero television experience, I bombed during the first night's rehearsal. As I left the set Head Producer Guy warned me gravely, "You're really gonna have to step it up if you're gonna make the pilot, Nathan. You're gonna need to really kick up the energy and the volume. You can't just sit there not saying anything. AMC's not going to go for that."

Head Producer Guy wasn't telling me anything I hadn't beaten myself up about already. As I sat down in the food court of the Beverly Center in front of lukewarm fish tacos that night, I felt dispirited. I had come to L.A. for one reason only: to land a slot on the pilot. I felt farther away from that goal than ever before.

Then I started thinking about the professional wrestling matches I watched as a kid. How much fun would it have been if the good guy had beaten the living shit out of the villain right out of the gate? Not much fun at all. No, in order for the match to work dramatically—and what is wrestling if not a sweat-stained, trailer-park-friendly form of theater practiced by large, hirsute men in spandex?—the hero first needs to endure such a vicious beating that his humiliating defeat seems certain.

Bruised, bloodied, and seemingly down for the count, the hero must then make a miraculous recovery at the last minute and avenge his earlier humiliation with a stunning come-from-behind victory. The crowd goes nuts. The announcers go hoarse expressing disbelief at such a shocking, unprecedented turn of events, and the delicate balance of good and evil is maintained. Everyone goes home happy.

Applying this structure to my own struggle, I figured I'd already nailed the whole bit about enduring a beating so vicious that my humiliation seemed certain. Now all I needed to do was to execute the stunning come-from-behind-victory thing. I took some relief in the knowledge that redemption lay firmly within my grasp, that a knockout audition would magically erase the grim comedy of errors that had constituted the day's events.

After two years of dead ends and false starts I went to sleep that night cognizant that my day of reckoning was at hand. I hoped that I was up to the task.

With a little unintentional help from Michael Medved's

creepy brother Harry, a drop-dead gorgeous Ann Coulter wannabe named Govindini Murtry intent on dissecting the Marxist connotations of *Dodgeball: A True Underdog Story*, and potentially lethal quantities of Mountain Dew, I ended up landing the *Movie Club* pilot alongside Anderson Jones, a homosexual black critic whose specialty was ferreting out the gay subtext in every film ever made; Josh Kun, a smart, bespectacled Jewish college professor whose self-deprecating shtick so eerily echoed my own that I came to think of him as my evil doppelgänger; and a skinny blonde entertainment reporter with blindingly white teeth named Zorianna Kit, who would become my professional archnemesis and the subject of the next chapter.

Despite low scores among focus groups who hypothesized that all the male critics on *Movie Club* were gay and that the show as a whole was "too gay," AMC nevertheless seemed keen on *Movie Club*. A few weeks after we'd filmed the pilot, Head Producer Guy called and said that AMC was "over the moon" about it, that they couldn't be happier, that an epidemic of exuberant touchdown dances had broken out throughout AMC's executive suites after they watched our once-in-a-lifetime masterpiece of the televisual arts. Accounting for Head Producer Guy's penchant for exaggeration, I took that to mean that AMC thought the pilot was anywhere from "not bad" to "all right."

A few weeks later Head Producer Guy called with two important bits of news, one exceedingly good, the other, not so much. AMC had picked up *Movie Club* for ten episodes, three of which would be "practice" episodes that we'd tape but wouldn't air. Roger Ebert had years to win the hearts, minds, and loyalty of a television audience. Excluding commercials, we had about two and a half hours to do the same.

Then came the not-so-good news: "Of course you'll be the regular guest critic since you live in Chicago. We'll try and get you on the show as often as possible, maybe five or six times in the initial run, and then Zorianna, Anderson, and Josh will of course be the regular regulars," Head Producer Guy said nonchalantly as my mood darkened.

He delivered the news with disconcerting matter-of-factness, as if we'd all agreed eons ago that I wouldn't be a regular. "Oh, OK," I muttered weakly, trying not to sound disappointed. I'd seen this coming since I'd been introduced as a guest critic on the pilot.

I could understand the uncharacteristically sane logic behind Head Producer Guy's decision. Josh was better looking than me, more experienced, and more natural in front of a camera, which he treated like the kind of old friend you don't have to impress anymore. He also happened to live twenty minutes from HDTV Studios, where we'd be taping, not two time zones away.

Head Producer Guy's decision to go with Josh over me wasn't just reasonable; it was a no-brainer. I would have made the same decision myself. I tried to convince myself that maybe it was a good thing that I wouldn't be a *Movie Club* regular, that I wouldn't have been able to handle the pressure of traveling every weekend and performing in a new, high-profile medium.

At Winchester House we had a depressing if eminently reasonable saying: know your limits. Other families or institutions have aphorisms designed to trick children into believing in themselves and following their dreams. In my family and at the group home we had sayings specifically designed to prevent us from believing in ourselves or following our dreams. I suspected that flying to and from Los Angeles to tape *Movie Club* every week would push me beyond my limits. That made me feel better about coming in fourth in the mad scramble to secure a slot on *Movie Club*.

After a few weeks I'd just about convinced myself that I actually preferred being a guest when Head Producer Guy called.

"So, Nathan, it looks like Josh isn't going to be able to fit four or five shows into his schedule. So it looks like he'll be the guest critic and you'll be a regular after all."

For an evil doppelgänger, Josh was shockingly noncompetitive, a real mensch. My pessimism was lifting. Maybe life wasn't about knowing your limits. Maybe it was about realizing that you're capable of more than you ever dreamed possible.

The night before we taped our first show that would actually air, Head Producer Guy and R.L. took me to dinner at one of the many restaurants and bars in Los Angeles where everyone knew his name.

Throughout our meal Head Producer Guy and R.L. looked at me with a gaze that seemed somehow rapacious, even predatory. It was a look that gave me a distinct feeling of déjà vu. I'd seen it somewhere before. But as much as I wracked my brain, I couldn't remember where.

"You know, Nathan, to me, you, Ridley, and Josh are the core of the show. You guys are Tiffany. Anderson and Zorianna were more sort of forced on me by the network," Head Producer Guy confided conspiratorially without ever taking his gaze off me.

"Thank you. That's very kind of you to say," I stammered self-consciously.

"You know, Nathan, you're probably going to start getting recognized now that you're going to be on TV. Some people can't handle that. [*Sneak Previews'*] Neal Gabler couldn't deal with it. He thought it was just terrible that people would stop him in the street, that it was some big inconvenience. How do you think you're going to handle it?"

Around this time Ludacris had a single called "Get Back" where he responds to unwanted attention by growling, "Get back, motherfucker, you don't know me like that!"

I thought briefly about answering that if I were approached by a theoretical *Movie Club* fan, I'd probably push them away while shouting, "Get back, motherfucker! You don't know me like that!" but thought better of it. I wasn't entirely sure Head

Producer Guy didn't consider hip-hop a passing fad, like Pet Rocks or voting rights for women.

"I don't think I'd have a problem with that," I replied in a colossal bit of understatement. The truth was that I felt like there was a giant spiritual vacuum at the core of my being that could only be filled with fame, money, drugs, liquor, sex, and mindless adulation. Or Scientology. Or Jesus. I doubted I'd be recognized regularly, if at all, and my highly attuned pessimism had seldom steered me wrong. It's hope that invariably bites you in the ass, not hopelessness. Hopelessness is your friend.

R.L. interjected, "Now, you're probably also going to be getting a lot of offers from various places. All we ask is that you let us know about them."

I doubted I'd be deluged with offers. But I was flattered by the dazzling future my producers laid out ahead of me. Again, I replied that I couldn't see it being a problem. I tried my damnedest to maintain a healthy level of pessimism but it was hard not to get caught up in the excitement. I was torn between my bone-deep pessimism and the infectious optimism of my bosses.

I laughed long and hard when it finally hit me, back at my hotel room at the Sportsmen's Lodge, where I'd seen Head Producer Guy and R.L.'s predatory gaze before. It was the look Burt Reynolds and Julianne Moore give Mark Wahlberg just after discovering the fantastical secret Wahlberg keeps hidden in his trousers early in *Boogie Nights*. It was the unnervingly satisfied look of the cat that swallowed the canary, a look that says, "I'm not entirely sure, but I suspect that I can make money off you."

I'm not saying that possessing the ability to discourse in a glibly amusing fashion about popular culture is the same thing as packing a thirteen-inch monster cock. If it were, this book would probably sell a lot more copies. But they are both, in this sick and sad and strange and beautiful world, commodities, superficial gifts that can be converted by the right person into filthy lucre.

• • •

There are moments that define a generation. V-J Day. The Kennedy assassination. The day the *Challenger* exploded. For me, the defining moment of my generation was not September 11 but rather the day Ol' Dirty Bastard died. Forget what Don McLean sang: when ODB cast off this mortal coil and raced into the loving arms of his Lord and Savior, it was truly the day the music died. Forget December 7, 1941. To me November 13, 2004, is the real day that will live in infamy.

Ol' Dirty Bastard was the John F. Kennedy of his era: a powerful incubator/disseminator of venereal disease and a wildly charismatic, sex-crazed drug addict whose stirring oratory captured the hopes and aspirations of an entire generation. JFK famously thundered, "Ask not what your country can do for you. Ask what you can do for your country." ODB had that song where he talked about getting "burnt by gonorrhea two times." I'll leave it up to you, dear reader, to determine which is the more timeless and enduring piece of rhetoric.

Nobody ever forgets where they were when they learned that ODB had died. I, for example, was eating lunch during a break while taping the non-airing second episode of *Movie Club with John Ridley*. The news hit me with devastating force. With the death of its beloved jester, America had truly lost its innocence. Granted, it could be argued that a nation built on the twin pillars of slavery and the genocide of Native Americans never possessed a fundamental innocence to begin with. But that hasn't kept cultural commentators from insisting that our nation has lost its innocence anew any time disaster strikes. Apparently America's innocence is an endlessly renewable commodity. You know, like oil.

I was infinitely more shaken by the news of ODB's death than my colleagues, none of whom seemed to grasp the magnitude of the event. I wondered whether I'd even be able to crack wise before the cameras in the wake of such tragic news. But Big Baby Jesus represented nothing so much as the importance of a strong

Judeo-Christian work ethic, so I soldiered on. Call me a hero if you must. No, seriously. Call me a hero. You must.

Our resident wacky DVD reviewer Regan Burn's film that day was the nouveau blaxploitation joint *Soul Plane,* so when he sat next to me I was able to empathize with his ordeal. "Hey, Regan, I suffered through *Soul Plane* as well, so I just wanted to say how sorry I am that you—"

Before I could continue, Head Producer Guy shot me an icy glare and interrupted with "Hey, Nathan, you know that Zorianna's husband wrote *Soul Plane,* don't you?" This all transpired within earshot of Zorianna.

Trying to weasel my way out of a corner, I continued, "Right. So what I was going to say is that I'm sorry that you didn't get to see the unrated director's cut of *Soul Plane,* 'cause that was even more hilarious than the theatrical version! Good times! Good times!"

I then lowered my head and focused intently on the food in front of me.

"It's OK if you don't like *Soul Plane,* Nathan," Head Producer Guy assured me. "I mean, I made sure it was OK with Zorianna to do it as Regan's video pick and she was totally fine with it. Besides, I thought *Soul Plane* was great. I thought it was the funniest movie of the year."

The sad part is that I don't think Head Producer Guy was being facetious. Nor do I think he was merely claiming to love *Soul Plane* to curry Zorianna and her potentially powerful husband's favor.

As I would come to learn over the course of my misadventures in L.A., people within the industry like Head Producer Guy view movies differently than critics or audiences. You or I might look at a movie like *Soul Plane* and see a crude, random assemblage of scatological gags filled with offensive racial stereotypes that was eviscerated by critics and *The Boondocks,* condemned by civil rights leaders, and a box-office flop. Whereas Head Producer Guy would look at *Soul Plane* and see a film that first and foremost got made—a triumph in itself—and ultimately turned a tidy profit on DVD, where standards are lower and audiences tend to be more forgiving (and stoned).

The bottom line for guys like Head Producer Guy could be gleaned from the cold, hard calculus of dollars and cents, profits and losses, budgets and grosses, not abstract, ineffable concepts like artistic or cultural merit.

Besides, Head Producer Guy seemed to take a perverse pride in his cultural illiteracy, seeing as few films as possible in the theater, especially once the show started. Like many people in Hollywood, he seemed to view sitting through even a big fluffy popcorn movie as a grueling endurance test, not one of life's great pleasures. So his contention that *Soul Plane* represents the cream of 2004's cinematic crop makes a lot more sense if you factor in that he probably only saw a handful of new movies that year.

Nevertheless, the atmosphere at *Movie Club* as we began our unheralded run reminded me of my heady early days at *The Onion*. There was an infectious spirit of camaraderie, a giddy excitement in getting a shimmering new enterprise off the ground. *The Onion* had long since evolved into a streamlined, smoothly run organization but *Movie Club* still felt like an unruly pirate ship of an enterprise, a motley collection of rogues, boozehounds, scoundrels, pill-poppers, inveterate liars, con men, and ne'er-do-wells sailing blindly into uncharted territory. And if the captain was a little drunk and a little crazy, and there was something ineffably off about the whole enterprise, well, that was part of its ramshackle charm.

After having stumbled into an important position with a newspaper of considerable quality, prestige, and respectability, I was strangely relieved to once again be throwing my lot in with a gang of sketchy, disreputable characters.

From the very beginning, *Movie Club* suffered from an identity crisis. It was half NPR thoughtfulness, half ditsy E! gossipfest.

This split identity was personified in the conflict between Josh and me, with our fancy-pants college words and highfalutin "ideas," and Anderson and Zo, who began each episode with a big theatrical kiss and tended to talk about movie stars' private lives as much as the films we were ostensibly reviewing.

The culture divide between the clashing sensibilities of Josh and me and Zorianna and Anderson was apparent early on, though it'd grow more pronounced as the series progressed. Anderson and Zo approached films from a similar place. Zorianna talked about movies in terms of actors and performances. To her the art of film *was* the art of film acting. If a film succeeded, it was because the actors were amazing and had great chemistry. If it failed, it was because the actors were lousy and had terrible chemistry.

Anderson and Zorianna talked about movies in primarily emotional and personal terms. I liked to joke that each of Anderson's or Zorianna's reviews began with an hour-long personal anecdote only tangentially related to the film at hand. So Zo might begin a review with, "Now, in 1874, when my nana back in the old country . . ."

Josh and I tended to view films from more of an academic or political perspective. Josh liked talking about the political ramifications of ostensibly apolitical fare like *The Longest Yard*, much to the aggravation of Head Producer Guy.

Head Producer Guy and Zorianna shared a love for gossip that led to one of my more memorably bizarre *Movie Club* moments. One Sunday on the *Movie Club* set rumors began circulating that Geoffrey Rush, who had appeared in one of the films we'd reviewed (*Swimming Upstream*), had dissed *Movie Club*. We were all outraged, not to mention confused and strangely flattered that Rush even knew *Movie Club* existed.

How dare anyone claim that our poorly rated, mildly disreputable basic-cable movie-review panel show was anything other than highly rated and reputable? The rumor traveled so fast and gained so much inexplicable currency that Ridley even threw a "fuck Geoffrey Rush" into his first run-through of his show-opening spiel.

This confused Head Producer Guy. "Hey, Ridley, what's with the 'fuck Geoffrey Rush' talk?" he asked bewilderedly. When we explained that we were merely avenging what we imagined was Rush's horrific slur against our beloved *Movie Club*, Head Producer Guy burst out laughing. It seems *Movie Club* was dissed not by Oscar winner Geoffrey Rush but by film critic Jeffrey Lyons, the father of future *At the Movies* cohost Ben Lyons. Jeffrey, who worked with Head Producer Guy on *Sneak Previews*, had sent him an exquisitely passive-aggressive note that began by congratulating Head Producer Guy on *Movie Club*'s pickup before questioning our credentials and insisting he'd never heard of any of us. In that respect he was like 99 percent of the American public.

It was like the popular children's game Chinese Whispers, where moppets line up and pass a secret down the line that has a funny way of subtly changing with each telling. For example, a child at the front of the line might begin with a rumor like "Susie's got cooties," which by the time it reaches the child in the back has somehow morphed into "The assistant principal is complicit in the genocide of Muslims in his native Bosnia."

After every episode Head Producer Guy, a smattering of crew people, and I would adjourn to Residuals, a local bar, for a boozy post-mortem on that week's show. Head Producer Guy had a way of sucking you into his fantasies, of making you feel like his aspirations and goals were your own. In a tinny black-and-white world he had the audacity to dream in CinemaScope and Technicolor.

Head Producer Guy was a consummate hustler. Every week he had a new scheme to sell the show to a new audience. One week he breathlessly reported that NPR, which has a serious hard-on for Ridley, was interested in doing an audio version of the show. The next week Head Producer Guy was eager to sell the show in Great Britain. When someone pointed out that movies are often released in England months or even years before or after their stateside run, he replied that maybe the limey *Movie Club* would just focus more on DVDs. Nothing fatigued Head Producer Guy's indefatigable optimism. Like Gatsby, he had a genius for hope, just as I had an equivalent gift for hopelessness.

R.L. and Head Producer Guy tried to counsel me on how to handle fame and recognition, but what I really needed was help coping with the utter lack of fame and recognition that came with appearing on *Movie Club*. Fame may be a bitch. It's nothing compared to anonymity.

This was reinforced when I attended the opening of John Ridley's play about kamikaze pilots in World War II, *Ten Thousand Years,* and the very pretty Asian woman handling admittance couldn't find my name on the guest list and asked me if I was friends with the playwright.

"Oh yeah, I'm actually a regular on his show," I answered with altogether too much pride.

"That's great. Do you play a bad guy or something?" she inquired obliviously (Ridley was executive-producing, head-writing, and show-running Showtime's adaptation of *Barbershop* at the same time).

"Yeah, I get shot and killed in the third episode. It's really quite sad. For me and my agent at least," I retorted grumpily.

Movie Club was flying well beneath the pop culture radar and I was making little more than union scale, but it was exhilarating to fly to Los Angeles every weekend to tape a national television show, however humble.

Head Producer Guy's modus operandi in matters of renewals was to promise the maximum, then act overjoyed with the minimum. That's how it was with *Movie Club*'s pickup. He fearlessly predicted an order of twenty or thirty episodes, then acted delighted when we got picked up for eight more episodes, to be taped after a punishing, seemingly inexplicable, perhaps show-destroying three-and-a-half-month-long hiatus. It was written into Head Producer Guy's contract that if AMC picked up *Movie Club*, it would have to increase its order size. Since three shows never aired, our eight-episode renewal was literally the fewest shows AMC could order while still honoring Head Producer Guy's contract.

Like many relationships, the bond between film critics and their audience relies heavily on reliability, dependability, and consistency. The reader or viewer needs their favorite film critic to be there for them week in and week out, acting as a fearless Sherpa of the multiplex, leading them away from the dreck and toward the light.

To extend my critic-moviegoer relationship analogy to its breaking point, if you had a boyfriend who disappeared for three and a half months without warning or explanation, then reappeared begging for a quickie, you'd probably tell him to go fuck himself, literally and figuratively. So it was perhaps deluded for AMC to imagine that *Movie Club* could disappear for an entire season without warning or explanation, then return and somehow retain a devoted cult willing to follow it through yet another long, unexplained absence from the airwaves.

In addition to ordering eight more episodes, AMC promised an ad blitz to refamiliarize audiences with our spunky little Rip van Winkle of a television show. To help with that ad blitz, AMC flew me out to Los Angeles for a day of shooting promotional photos. Flying to L.A. on business was nothing new. But I'd always flown to L.A. for concrete work purposes. I was just doing my job. Now for the first time I was flying to Los Angeles solely for the purpose of standing around and letting a professional photographer take pictures. It felt terribly decadent.

After the photo shoot Head Producer Guy took me to a bar for a few drinks before my flight back to Chicago. I'd spent lots of time with Head Producer Guy during the show, and after the show at Residuals. But we seldom conversed on a one-on-one level, so this sit-down was special.

Not long after we sat down and starting pounding back

Bombay Sapphire martinis and vodka cranberries, Head Producer Guy told me something I'd been waiting to hear all my life.

"You know, Nathan," he told me in a near-whisper, "I think you've got more than just one show in you. I don't even know if it'd be a movie show necessarily. Maybe it'd be a movie show, maybe it'd be something different, but I'd very much be interested in developing another show with you."

Yes! Finally the words I'd longed to hear: You're a star, baby! One television show's just the beginning! You're a one-man media empire in the making, you sexy, sexy bitch! Dazzle me with your million-dollar ideas, you crazy diamond! It was the opportunity I'd been waiting for. You better believe I did not rise to the occasion. My mind swam with ideas I'd nurtured for years. For starters there were all my book ideas, nearly all of which could be transformed into television show ideas. Which one should I bring up first? The one where I'd go undercover as the world's oldest frat boy? The documentary miniseries documenting the fascinating, little-explored, and complex relationship between hip-hop and film? The pilot idea where I'd travel around the country, immersing myself in colorful subcultures? There were so many ideas to choose from. Should I let them all out in one big rush or dole them out separately, carefully sizing up Head Producer Guy's interest in each one?

Somehow all this mental deliberation resulted in me answering with a meek, "Uh, thanks. Yeah. Huh. Let me think about it." By the time those words dribbled lamely out of my mouth, that golden, precious, irreplaceable moment in which Head Producer Guy and I would plant the seeds of our future business empire together had evaporated. And once Head Producer Guy moves on to the next topic, he completely loses interest in whatever it is he's just said. He is a man forever living in the present and future tense.

Head Producer Guy and I are both shameless emotional exhibitionists. So our increasingly boozy talk quickly devolved into a race to see who could confess the most in the smallest amount of time. There are few people in the world who can out-talk me, or are foolish enough to try, but Head Producer Guy is definitely one of them. Talking to Head Producer Guy always reminded me of John Gielgud's wonderful line in *The Loved One* about how people in Hollywood "talk entirely for their own pleasure and they never expect you to listen."

Alas, I was knocking back vodka a little too vigorously, for at one point Head Producer Guy turned to me with paternal concern and said, "Hey, Nathan, you're pounding them back pretty quickly there. Are you sure you can handle it?"

"Oh yeah. I am a big, strapping lad and I can handle my liquor," I slurred confidently. This was true, but in the back of my mind I envisioned Head Producer Guy telling crew people, "Yeah, Nathan seems like a really cool, together guy, but man, does he pound 'em back! A real drinker! And cheap as the day is long too! He squeezes each penny so tight I bet he's got a change drawer full of copper wire at home!"

In a strange way I'd almost be offended if Head Producer Guy *didn't* say horrible things about me behind my back. It'd seem terribly out of character. Head Producer Guy depicted himself in anecdote after anecdote as the lucid, responsible, even-tempered voice of reason constantly called upon to put out fires and calm the frazzled nerves of temperamental, hard-drinking creative types.

As I sat there at the bar, pounding back vodka and worrying about whether I'd miss my flight at seven thirty, I wondered if Head Producer Guy ever experienced a strange surge of happiness upon realizing that a horrific personal trauma could be alchemized into an amazing anecdote. I wondered if he found himself thinking, "God, this is horrible. But it'll make for a great story!"

You never knew where Head Producer Guy was coming from, if he was going to be the strangely paternal dispenser of life lessons and unsolicited but sometimes sound advice and shepherd of our strange little *Movie Club* flock, or the slippery, horndog barfly whose word was worthless.

Movie Club's greatest strengths had always been the chemistry of the cast and the vibrant personalities of the host and panelists. When the show was cooking it didn't matter that we were talking about movies. We could have been discussing television or music or popular culture and the show would have probably been just as entertaining. The weakest, most static moments of *Movie Club* were those explicitly rooted in movies and movie reviews.

We all noticed that the web-exclusive content for *Movie Club* was looser than the show itself due to the comedic free-for-all aspect of our banter. Head Producer Guy was eager to inject the spontaneity of our web content into the show itself, to recapture the free-form loosey-goosey vibe of our unscripted quips. Head Producer Guy thought *Movie Club* would be an even sweller bit of popcorn escapism if he could only wean his movie-review panel show off its debilitating need to review movies. So as we prepared to film our second set of shows, Head Producer Guy made a modest proposal. What if, he insouciantly proposed, we fight poverty, overpopulation, and starvation by eating the babies of the poor?

No, wait, that's Jonathan Swift's modest proposal. Head Producer Guy's proposal was even more radical and somehow involved even more baby eating. What if we did away with scripted reviews altogether? What if Ridley simply set up a movie, the critic talked about it in general, unscripted terms, we showed clips, and then we threw it to the panel? Then we could all head over to Residuals to eat babies.

The show worked best when we deviated from our scripts. So why have a script in the first place? Removing scripted reviews from a movie-review show seemed downright revolutionary. But was it revolutionary in a *Jazz Singer* way or a *Cop Rock* way? Would it be a great leap forward or a regrettable dead end?

AMC sent an executive in from New York to oversee *Movie Club* tapings during our first set of ten episodes. The executives were a delight and seemed to have little feedback beyond "Keep up the good work." In our second season, however, AMC stopped sending executives to oversee the show but began making lots of demands.

AMC wanted stars, we were told. Big, big guest stars who'd drive up ratings and generate publicity. They wanted guests in the critic slots as well. Lots of guests! New faces everywhere! A steady stream of foxy dames conversing about the biggest films of the day! And gimmicks, oh boy, did AMC want a whole lot of gimmicks! Why not experiment with a different terrible new idea every show! And big movies! AMC was no longer willing to settle for shows about *Swimming Upstream*. No, they wanted big sexy movies discussed by big sexy guest stars and big sexy guest critics.

As I geared up for the show to start shooting again, I felt as if my life had attained a pleasing velocity. But a big question mark loomed in my future. Would the next eight episodes of *Movie Club* and the accompanying ad blitz make or break me? As it turned out, it'd do a little of both.

Los Angeles is where people go to lose themselves and find themselves. In that respect it's like college for subliterates. I came to L.A. a bemused outsider wryly taking in the whole gaudy spectacle. But I returned to L.A. with a fierce hunger to make it, to follow in the footsteps of previous generations of scruffy urban Jews who made their fortunes in Hollywood and sometimes even managed to avoid losing their souls.

Was I in danger of losing my soul? Would going to Hollywood every weekend inevitably result in the lamentable existential condition known as having "gone Hollywood"? I began to feel terribly conflicted. When I saw *Star Wars III: Revenge of the Sith*, I felt like Anakin Skywalker, and not just because I envy his fetching rattail. Over one shoulder I had Keith, my very own Yoda, counseling me, "Unglamorous, modestly compen-

sated, yet creatively satisfying the life of a serious film critic is."
Over the other shoulder I had Head Producer Guy, my answer
to Senator Palpatine, cooing, "Three-Bombay-Sapphire-martini
lunches! Erotic Asian masseuses who look like models! Two
hundred grand a year and national fame for an hour's work a
week!"

Given my internal conflicts and the very Maureen Dowd
manner in which I processed them (oh, popular culture: is there
any better lens through which to filter the world?), it seems
appropriate that *Revenge of the Sith* was one of the films we
reviewed for the first show back. When 7-Eleven started selling
coffee mugs shaped like Yoda's head, it gave me an idea. What,
I asked R.L. in a fit of crazed hackdom, if I were to decry the
overcommercialization of *Star Wars* and the oppressive ubiquity
of its merchandise and then very discreetly reach down and
drink daintily from my Yoda coffee mug? Wouldn't that be terribly amusing? Or mildly amusing? If you're high, maybe?

"Oh, don't worry about it. We've got something similar
where John will ask if maybe *Star Wars* is overcommercialized
and then you'll all bring out *Star Wars* merchandise. Josh will
act all disgusted but then we'll call him on his cell phone and it'll
have a *Star Wars* ringtone, you know, the theme song or whatever, and then he'll make plans to go see *Star Wars III* with the
person on the other end of the line."

"Oh, OK," I told R.L. as I backed slowly away from my
hacky little proposal. As ads for *Movie Club* conveyed, Josh Kun
was indeed the "smart one with glasses," so it made sense that
he'd be the one to take a bold stand against overt commercial-
ism, if only for the sake of a labored gag.

Alas, the casting of Josh as the sole voice of taste and
restraint in a gaudy wasteland of cheesy ideas turned out to be
a little too dead-on. Josh was quite adamant about not wanting
to do the *Star Wars* overcommercialization gag.

R.L. told me to bring as much *Star Wars* crap as possible to
the taping for the gag. I decided to bring my *Win a Date with*

Tad Hamilton! promotional autograph book along with me as well. After all, you never know when a promotional *Win a Date with Tad Hamilton!* autograph book will come in handy (see previous chapter).

The *Star Wars* overcommercialization bit epitomized Head Producer Guy's sense of humor. Head Producer Guy was a very funny guy and *Movie Club* could be quite chuckle inducing. But Head Producer Guy's comic sensibility ran toward broad humor, racial stereotypes, raunchy sex jokes, and over-the-top shtick.

Head Producer Guy was a man who thought *Soul Plane* was the funniest movie of the year and considered Martin Lawrence a comic genius. But the truest embodiment of Head Producer Guy's comic sensibility is a program called *The Rerun Show.*

Television cancellations are invariably tragedies to the people involved and dark comedies to everyone else. To Head Producer Guy the premature cancellation of *The Rerun Show* was the defining trauma of his career.

For those who missed *The Rerun Show* during its 2002 run, its premise was simple. Improv performers would mug their way through real scripts from Nick at Nite favorites like *Diff'rent Strokes* and *The Partridge Family,* augmenting the retro hijinks with leering double entendres and winking sexual asides.

Years after *The Rerun Show* was canceled, its premature demise still haunted Head Producer Guy. If only NBC had believed in *The Rerun Show* the way he believed in it, Head Producer Guy seemed convinced, then it'd still be on the air. That's the heartbreak of television. It can take a show years to make it onto the air only to die an unwatched death in months. Or weeks.

I was not alone in worrying that if left to his own devices, Head Producer Guy would transform *Movie Club* into a *Rerun Show*–like aggregation of over-the-top gags and snickering sex jokes, or rather into *even more* of an aggregation of over-the-top gags and snickering sex jokes.

For the first run of ten episodes Head Producer Guy seemed

to follow my old boss Stephen Thompson's dictum to hire good people, then let them do their job. Even when we screwed up, he allowed us the time and space to figure things out for ourselves. A laissez-faire attitude reigned over the set and the mood was generally loose and relaxed.

That all changed once we began taping again. The mood around the set was electric with tension and anxiety. For the first time since the premiere, there was a sense that people might actually watch the show. It was as if the first seven airing episodes were only practice shows, ways to work out the kinks before the show was given a real shot at finding an audience.

There was a strange vibe on the set that first episode back. When the cameras started rolling, everyone seemed a little nervous. We were all rusty due to the hiatus. The sheer volume of new ideas, segments, and gimmicks AMC had ordered us to experiment with only ratcheted up the anxiety.

In case the review-free show proved unusable, we did a take using review scripts. Josh was a consummate pro at delivering copy in a relaxed, conversational manner, so he led off the show with his review of *Star Wars III: Revenge of the Sith*. When Josh started talking about the film's politics, Head Producer Guy stopped the take and walked onto the set.

"Hey, Josh, I'm only telling you this for your own good, but you're going to want to cut the political stuff out of your review. It's not that relevant to the movie and people at home are going to find it pretentious. I'm sorry. That's just the way it is. Believe me, I'm only saying this to protect you because I don't want you to come off as pretentious," Head Producer Guy told Josh while we all looked on in horror.

To his credit, Josh fought Head Producer Guy pretty hard. He could afford to. He'd always been the most reluctant *Movie Club*ber. As with Ridley, *Movie Club* represented to Josh only one small aspect of an eclectic, prolific career spanning multiple mediums, not the entirety of his professional future. He could take it or leave it.

Josh kept his cool but as I sat there waiting for the storm to pass I could see Josh's enthusiasm for *Movie Club* diminish before my eyes. Josh clearly only wanted to do a movie-review show if he could do it on his own terms. The tawdry glamour of being on television didn't hold much allure for him.

Considering the unnecessary psychodrama that sprang up around Josh's *Star Wars* review, it shouldn't come as a surprise that the *Star Wars* bit was botched on every level. Josh's lack of enthusiasm shone through in his delivery, though I had fun putting on a Darth Vader mask and waving around a light saber. I seemed to regress mentally at least a decade every time the cameras started rolling.

The bad vibes didn't end after we stopped taping. When Josh grumbled something about the show being a disaster, a consulting producer I call Graying Ponytail Guy displayed a genius for saying the exact wrong thing by telling Josh, "What are you talking about? You totally had your big moment with that *Star Wars* bit!"

Considering Head Producer Guy's populist sensibility, it shouldn't come as a surprise that a line about the gender politics of *Monster-in-Law* being reprehensible, like Josh's discussion of the politics of *Star Wars*, never made it onto the air.

Just before I took my usual shuttle back to LAX, Head Producer Guy pulled me aside and warned me about the possible ramifications of my contempt for movies like *Monster-in-Law*. "You know, Nathan," he informed me gravely, "we're not going to get anywhere saying that we hate movies. Not with studios. Not with anyone."

"Well, you know, my dad always taught me that 'hate' is a really powerful word that should be saved for stuff that really merits it. You know: You hate the Nazis. You hate the guy who killed a family member. You hate the guy who raped your wife," I sincerely told Head Producer Guy, playing up the good-Jewish-son angle.

"Good. You should bring that up on the show," Head Pro-

ducer Guy told me approvingly. He was always keen on inject-
ing our personalities and personal histories into *Movie Club*. He
relished the opportunity to show that we were just ordinary
folks with dads, mortgages, and spouses (just like the rubes in
the audience!), and, in Ridley and Zo's case, nannies, multiple
houses, and/or personal assistants, rather than disembodied
Cartesian brains floating somewhere high up in the ether, discussing weighty ideas.

I paused for emphasis before I spat out, "And I fucking hate
Monster-in-Law."

After the first taping back, I got a call from Head Producer Guy.
After the usual "Ya got a minute?" he launched directly into the
purpose of his call. "So, Nathan, you've seen *The Longest Yard*,
right?"

"Um-hmm. I caught the Chicago press screening."

"Whaddya think?"

"It was OK. It's pretty much what I expected. As I said in my
Onion review, it's just good enough not to completely suck."

"Would you say you liked it then?" Head Producer Guy
asked impatiently. There was clearly an ulterior motive behind
his questions.

"I wouldn't say I *disliked* it necessarily. For what it is, it's
alright. Adam Sandler's fans will enjoy it."

"So it sounds like you liked it."

"Like I said, I didn't dislike it necessarily. It's not really my
thing."

"Well, Nathan"—Head Producer Guy inhaled deeply—"it
would really help with the studios if I could tell them that you
really liked *The Longest Yard*. Paramount already hates Zorianna because of what she said about Brad Grey [see next chap-
ter], so they're not going to do anything to help us. So it'd be
really great if I could tell them that you're crazy about the film
and that you're gonna do the review on the show."

I strongly suspected that Head Producer Guy had already

told Paramount that I liked *The Longest Yard,* which made our conversation both moot and ridiculous. Head Producer Guy wasn't at all shy about bending the truth when it suited his purposes. To him the end invariably justified the means, so there was no use sweating minor details like professional ethics.

The atmosphere on the set when we taped our second show back was nearly as toxic as it had been the week before. The feeling of déjà vu was only heightened when Josh used his *Longest Yard* one-liner to argue that the film trivialized the out-of-control expansion of the prison-industrial complex. In a veritable replay of the *Star Wars* incident, Head Producer Guy once again bounded onto the set to tell Josh that for his own sake he should change his one-liner to something less pretentious.

I shared Josh's desire to use *Movie Club* as a springboard to talk about the larger ramifications of movies and their relationship to the world beyond popular culture. I wanted *Movie Club* to be a place where people could discourse intelligently about *The Longest Yard* in sociopolitical terms. I shared his concern about the exponential growth of the prison-industrial system.

It's terrifying how much of the United States populace is currently behind bars. Seriously. Look at the person to your left. Now look at the person to your right. Now be honest with yourself. Both those motherfuckers are in prison, aren't they? And so are you! Unless the chump-ass public defender the state saddled you with gets off his lazy ass and files an appeal, you ain't goin' nowhere either!

If I could see Josh's enthusiasm for the show wane before my eyes during the *Star Wars* segment, I saw it fizzle and die when Head Producer Guy shot down his *Longest Yard* one-liner and he grudgingly replaced it with something apolitical.

After taping one week, Head Producer Guy decided to forgo our usual trip to Residuals in favor of a fancier establishment high up in the hills. As Head Producer Guy, R.L., and I took in the exquisite view and knocked back drinks, a palpable feeling of accomplishment swept over us. After a rocky start and plenty of bumps along the way, the show seemed to be coming together nicely, despite the bad craziness behind the scenes. It felt like good things loomed tantalizingly in our future.

Somehow the conversation turned toward how much we made.

"Hey, Nathan, how much do you make per episode?" Head Producer Guy asked unashamedly. Though he was obsessed with money, he delegated financial duties to other members of the crew.

"I make about six hundred dollars an episode, which works out to about four hundred and sixty dollars after taxes."

Head Producer Guy shot me an empathetic look and said, "That's terrible. I mean, there are weeks when you have to see *three* or even *four* movies for the show."

Head Producer Guy uttered the words as if he could barely fathom the commitment that would lead an otherwise sane man to spend four to six hours a week in an air-conditioned screening room watching movies. "Yes," I thought glumly to myself, "that's why I deserve more money."

I deserved a big raise because I somehow mustered up the superhuman strength to watch flickering images on a movie screen three or four times a week. *That* was what impressed Head Producer Guy.

So he decided to give my fellow *Movie Club*bers and me an automatic 25 percent raise to seven hundred and fifty dollars a week. It was as easy as that. Sitting high in the hills, basking equally in the camaraderie of my coworkers and the breathtaking view, and warmly contemplating the glorious future ahead felt unmistakably like a high-water mark. I'd reached the pinnacle.

When I was a kid my father succinctly summarized the random, cruel machinations of fate in the following homemade aphorism: The Big Bird Shits on Everyone. Now, superficially my father's existential wisdom might appear indistinguishable from the random nonsense paranoid schizophrenics scream at passersby. But there's a method to his madness. Life does have a strange way of defecating on everyone, metaphorically speaking, especially when they're puffed full of a false sense of accomplishment. Feeling smug and overconfident is like putting a big invisible sign on your back that reads, KICK ME, FATE. KICK ME LONG AND HARD AND KEEP KICKING UNTIL BLOOD GUSHES DOWN MY BACK.

When the great celeb watchers of the distant future look back at the summer of 2005, it will be remembered as a time when the legendary "Brangelina" controversy transfixed the nation. The pop history books shall also relate that a great movie star known as Tom Cruise lost his goddamned mind. For years Cruise's craziness was kept in check by publicist Pat Kingsley, a woman whose personal manner and mastery of the PR game earned her frequent admiring comparisons to Joseph Goebbels.

Kingsley is a legend in the field of show-business PR. She's the first publicist to demand the soul of a journalist's firstborn child in exchange for an exclusive interview. Now that's common practice. But she pioneered the concept.

But then, in what was to become an increasingly common fit of bad judgment, Cruise fired Kingsley. Even less advisedly, he replaced Kingsley with his sister, a woman whose primary advice seemed to be to crazy it up and really play up the Scientology thing. Soon Cruise was jumping on the couches of prominent talk show hostesses, his arms flailing wildly, a crazy-man gleam in his eyes while he flamboyantly professed his "love" for a terrified young starlet named Katie Dawson. Dawson responded to Cruise's public displays of affection with the kind of mortified body language and embarrassed smile people generally reserve for doddering relatives talking about "the Jews" or "the Blacks" or "the Gays."

What does any of this have to do with our humble narrative? Well, it seems that when Cruise transformed himself into a raging tsunami of bad press, he threatened to take *War of the*

Worlds, the movie he was ostensibly promoting, down with him. What had long seemed like the closest thing there is in Hollywood to a commercial sure thing had suddenly become a two-hundred-million-dollar question mark.

In damage control mode the studio refused to screen the movie for almost every major critic in the country until a day and a half before its official release, thereby rendering timely reviews impossible.

War of the Worlds opened on a Wednesday and screened in L.A. and Chicago Monday night at seven thirty. So our only chance of getting into a preview for a timely review was scoring an invitation to a junket screening in New York exactly one week before the big Chicago and L.A. previews. Zorianna and Josh couldn't fly to New York for the screening. So the producers decided that Anderson and I would fly to New York, where I'd connect with a New York critic to be named later, who'd fly in to do the show the next weekend.

The producers were fuzzy on the specifics of the trip. At various times, I was told that I might or might not have to pretend that I was part of the junket. "Don't worry," R.L. assured me, "Anderson will take care of everything."

As Monday approached I experienced a chilling sense of foreboding. To allay my fears I sent Anderson the following e-mail:

Hey Anderson,

I just wanted to email to say I'm "psyched" about going to New York and seeing War of the Worlds *with you but I'm worried I might have some difficulty getting into the screening (it's a junket screening, eh? That's a weird X factor). So if you could reassure me that you're working your schmoozing magic and that everything will go A.O.K. that would mean a lot to me. I know I shouldn't be neurotic but it sure seems like most movie publicists these days are twenty-six-year-old tyrants in short skirts who derive an almost sexual pleasure out of exercising their*

power in the most arbitrary, draconian fashion imaginable.
Anyway, it'd be great if you and me and the mystery dude
from Time Out New York *[David Fear] could hook up*
beforehand and go on in together. Present a United Front
and all. Incidentally, what's your cell phone number and
where exactly is the War of the Worlds *screening? That's*
the kind of info it'd probably be helpful to know.

Nathan

On Monday I flew to New York to attend a junket screening whose location remained a mystery. I was worried but didn't think the show would fly me to New York unless they were absolutely certain they could get me into a screening.

Upon touching down, I called David Fear, who very nicely informed me he wasn't able to get into that evening's screening and didn't know where it was. Alarmed, I called R.L., who told me I'd really have to "work my magic" that evening.

The first theater R.L. sent me to assured me that they weren't even showing *War of the Worlds* after its official release, let alone hosting a preview screening. I was, however, invited to attend a preview screening of *Herbie: Fully Loaded.* I respectfully declined. I called up R.L. and she gave me another address along with another disturbing admonition to "work my magic." Apparently, over the course of the past week I'd somehow morphed from critic to magician, from Anthony Lane to David Blaine.

As the acid in my stomach churned violently, oblivious to regular helpings of Tums, I took a taxi to the other theater, where two publicists sat behind a table in front of a big *War of the Worlds* poster. At last! This must be the place! I nervously introduced myself to the publicists and was told that the head publicist for the junket would be down to see me imminently. That had to be good, right?

The head publicist was a beefy thirtysomething with a linebacker physique and an edgy, aggressive manner. He stuck out a meaty paw for me to shake and nervously inquired, "You're Nathan, right?"

I answered affirmatively. With a look of profound irritation he told me, "Yeah, here's the thing. There is no way in hell you're getting into that screening. I called up Anderson last night at ten o'clock and told him specifically not to fly to New York because he wouldn't be getting into the screening. You guys never had permission to attend the screening. Somebody should have told you that."

I wearily told him that I didn't know anything about his interactions with the producers or Anderson and just wanted to be able to see the movie so I could do my job.

"Yeah, here's the thing," he told me agitatedly again. "My bosses are up there checking IDs personally and you and Anderson are specifically barred from this screening. If you go up there you will be physically ejected from the theater and I'll probably be fired."

Feeling the hopelessness of the situation deepen by the moment, I told him I could empathize with his predicament but that I had a job to do and would feel terrible about flying to New York just so I could not get into a screening.

"You know, in a weird way, them sending you all the way here is the final nail in your coffin," he told me, his body language tense and coiled, as if he might be forced to spring into action at any moment, chasing me if I made a mad dash for the screening. "'Cause if they thought I'd have to let you in just 'cause you traveled all this way, they were wrong."

Then he added, "And this kills me 'cause I love *The Onion*. I'm a huge fan. I started reading it back in—Where'd you guys start out, Champaign?"

"Madison," I answered joylessly.

"Yeah, I had a buddy up in college and he'd send me them and I'd show them to everyone in my dorm. I even got a subscription. This was way, way back, like '95, before *Our Dumb*

Century or the 9/11 issue or anything. Don't get me wrong. You seem like a nice guy and all and I'd love to be able to help out *The Onion* any way I can, but my bosses have specifically told me not to let you in."

Head Producer Guy had admonished me to drop power broker Sandy Wernick's name in case of an emergency. Running out of cards to play, I duly mentioned to *Onion* Fanboy that our show was executive-produced by Wernick.

Movie Bouncer grudgingly, obliviously informed me, "I know, I know. I know who Sandy Wernick is. I know she's a very powerful—"

"Actually, Wernick's a man," I informed him without relish. Apparently he/she wasn't powerful enough. Just when I thought the conversation couldn't get any more dispiriting, *Onion* Fanboy told me that when he considered the show's request to be included in the junket screening, he talked to other people in marketing and none of them had even heard of *Movie Club with John Ridley*. By that point even I began to wonder if *Movie Club* genuinely existed or if it was just a fevered, possibly alcohol-induced hallucination the cast and crew shared.

I called Head Producer Guy, who seemed disappointed but not terribly surprised. It was almost as if he knew damn well I wouldn't be allowed into the screening but sent me there anyway on the off chance I'd be able to finagle my way in. "Are you sure there's no way you could kind of sneak in?" he asked hopefully.

He was semiseriously asking me if I could magically transform into Houdini, another nice Jewish boy from the upper Midwest, and sneak into a screening more heavily guarded than most presidential inaugurations.

But Head Producer Guy seemed strangely Zen about the whole situation, which put me at ease. When I told Head Producer Guy that Paramount's movie-bouncer guy told me he had specifically told Anderson not to fly to Los Angeles, Head Producer Guy unexpectedly turned paternalistic and defensive.

He began painting a tragicomic portrait of Anderson as a hapless man-child who needed the show to buy him a computer, install a phone line, and chauffeur him around just so that he'd be able to do his job. Moreover, Anderson had recently had his wallet stolen and the IRS was taking back taxes out of his *Movie Club* checks. Head Producer Guy stopped just short of telling me that he had to drive over to Anderson's every day, wake him up, tie his shoes, and pick out his outfit.

There was something strangely touching about Head Producer Guy's protectiveness toward Anderson. Anderson was clearly the flamboyant gay black son he never had. As Head Producer Guy painted an increasingly pathetic portrait of Anderson's life and career, my anger abated.

All that mattered really was that I had come to New York solely to see *War of the Worlds* and was turned away. A strange feeling of calm swept over me. I had feared that I wouldn't be let into the screening. That's exactly what transpired. Yet the world had not ended.

I trudged across Manhattan at twilight, taking in the sights. It was beautiful and melancholy and as I made my lonesome way back to my hotel, I spied a huge contingent of cop cars traveling together, as if they weren't hunks of metal and machinery but a strange herd of wild animals. It was surreal. I wondered if all those cop cars were traveling to the world's largest donut shop.

I ducked into a giant mall with massive white couches overlooking huge windows on every floor and settled in as the sun began to set, casting a pink rosy glow over the Manhattan skyline as it sank deeper and deeper and then disappeared altogether. It was a wonder to behold. The trip was a failure but it was an extraordinarily colorful failure. Besides, if you've gotta be stranded somewhere, you could do worse than downtown Manhattan. It all seemed terribly cinematic. As I walked back to my hotel, a mournful horn played as my own personal soundtrack, something slow and bittersweet.

Head Producer Guy asked me to make sure that Anderson had made his flight and checked into our hotel. But it turned out that Anderson had gotten confused, missed his flight, and ended up sleeping at the airport. In Los Angeles. "Anderson will take care of everything" indeed.

By that point another X factor entered the equation: Billy Bob Thornton's special guest appearance. Since the show's taping had to be scheduled around both a Monday night L.A. screening of *War of the Worlds* and Thornton's availability, it was determined that the show would tape in two parts. Zorianna would lead a Ridley-free discussion with Thornton on Monday morning, after which we'd close up shop, go see *War of the Worlds* together, and head back to the studio for a taping that would begin around ten or eleven o'clock. I hoped to then hop on a red-eye back to Chicago that evening, but that proved impossible. So a show that normally required no more than two days suddenly promised to take up six, four of them *Onion* workdays.

The Saturday afternoon after I arrived in L.A. for the big, amorphous weekend, I drove around in Head Producer Guy's convertible with the top down. As the wind raced through my hair and the sun beamed down on my pallid Midwestern skin, I felt like a real Angeleno for the first and last time. After we dropped off an outtake reel at FedEx, Head Producer Guy pointed to an establishment he heartily recommended if I was ever in the mood for a hand job. This was no ordinary house o' hand jobs, he excitedly explained. No, the women who worked there were all model-quality Asian knockouts and the talent pool was constantly replenished from Hollywood's ever-growing ranks of failed actresses and women merely aspiring to become failed actresses.

I don't know what horrified me more: that Head Producer Guy pegged me as a guy who'd happily pay a stranger to jerk him off or that he wasn't wrong.

That evening we sojourned at Head Producer Guy's house on a hill, which was cozy, tastefully decorated, and surprisingly unassuming. Ever the show-runner, Head Producer Guy quickly took charge, giving the associate producer and myself grill duty. After dinner we sat around and talked and drank, and the Guy from Brooklyn Who Laughs Too Loudly at All My Jokes mentioned that he used to co-own a cigar shop in Brentwood that O. J. Simpson frequented. Even after the whole unpleasantness involving his ex-wife, the Juice still managed to sleep with all the store's cigar girls, who ostensibly figured a celebrity infamous for (allegedly) brutally murdering his ex-wife and her friend still qualified as a celebrity and therefore was overqualified for a one-night stand. This prompted Head Producer Guy to share an anecdote about being sent a "demo reel" for an actress to consider for future projects that turned out to be a clip of Ronald Goldman's sister breaking down and sobbing during press appearances. Hollywood!

As the evening progressed and the drinks kept flowing, the associate producer volunteered to drive me back to my hotel. The associate producer had always been a rock of stability amidst the glittery madness of the show. That night, however, something was different about him. I've never done coke, so my only conception of coked-up behavior comes from movies and *Late Night with Conan O'Brien*'s Coked-Up Werewolf. Nevertheless I was alarmed when the associate producer's conversation began racing a hundred miles a minute, rambling from topic to topic with manic intensity. He had a weird gleam in his eyes as he agitatedly insisted that the 1991 remake of *Father of the Bride* was one of his all-time favorite movies and claimed that "everyone can agree that *When Harry Met Sally* is one of the five greatest romantic comedies of all time."

This was worrisome. I was terrified both by the possibility that I was being driven home by a guy who was drunk or high, and that I had put my life in the hands of someone who counts Nora Ephron among the all-time greats. In the backseat R.L. smiled placidly, unconcerned about her imminent demise. In my imagination a headline screamed: OBSCURE FILM CRITIC PER-

ISHES IN L.A. CAR CRASH: UNREMARKABLE LIFE RECALLED DIMLY BY FEW, AUTHORITIES DESCRIBE THE DECEASED AS "UNLIKELY TO BE MISSED."

This would be followed by "Colleague Keith Phipps says it's fitting Rabin died the way he lived: expressing shock and horror that anyone enjoys the work of Nora Ephron or Charles and Nancy Meyers."

"I don't wanna die this way," I thought. Thankfully, I made it home in one piece and was so grateful, I slept in the next morning till nearly three in the afternoon, squeezing nearly two days' worth of sleep into one marathon orgy of Zs.

The actual taping of what I didn't realize at the time was my last episode of *Movie Club* went relatively smoothly, all things considered, but the following week I learned that my reward for flying to New York at *Movie Club*'s request solely to be rejected from a screening was getting unceremoniously bumped from the last show of the season.

About two months after the last episode of *Movie Club*'s second season aired, I got the following voice mail message from Head Producer Guy: "Hey, Nathan, it's [Head Producer Guy]. I just wanted to let you know the series got a pickup for the fall. A minimum of thirteen episodes, perhaps as many as fifteen. So when you're on [live, local PBS show] *Chicago Tonight* you can announce, 'Oh, no, we're coming back in the fall starting in November, December, January, February, all the way through March and the Oscars.' I just wanted to make sure you had something to announce on the *Chicago Tonight* show. Congratulations! I'm pretty happy. They had to make the decision because Ridley's appearing at the Television Critics Association this coming Sunday at eight A.M. and I pointed out to them, 'What's he announcing, guys, anything?' So they had to pick us up early. Bye!"

I held off deleting the message for months. I should have been delighted by news of our renewal but there was something wavering and unsteady in Head Producer Guy's voice, something strangely unconvincing in his tone. Was the news legit or was it more in the vein of "Anderson will take care of everything": wishful thinking taken to its deluded extreme?

I got an answer soon enough but it sure wasn't the one I was hoping for. I was walking to therapy one lazy Thursday afternoon and decided to check my cell phone messages, something I did as infrequently as possible at the time. The only message immediately sent shock waves of panic rippling through me: "This is [Head Producer Guy] traveling on Tuesday. I have important news and I need to talk to you about it today."

Oh, fuck. This couldn't be good. I called Head Producer Guy back and steeled myself for the worst. After exchanging pleasantries, Head Producer Guy exhaled deeply and softly said, "If I'd reached you on Tuesday I'd have had some really bad news." After a dramatic pause he continued, "Which would be that we're canceled." In his mind it was an ambiguous cancellation (a contradiction in terms?), when to everyone else it was as final as death.

Canceled? Holy motherfucking shit. The mind reeled. Canceled after being picked up for thirteen to fifteen episodes? Canceled after scoring the best press of our entire run, a glowing feature in *Chicago Tribune Magazine*, complete with an ego-flattering photo of R.L., Head Producer Guy, and me, aka "the Chicago Connection"? Canceled after I'd promised thirteen more episodes of *Movie Club* on *Chicago Tonight*?

As I struggled to regain my composure, Head Producer Guy spelled out the big picture. Turner Classic Movies had long been at war with American Movie Classics and felt that it alone reserved the right to use terms like "classic" and "movie" merely because it still shows "movies" that can reasonably be considered "classics." Time Warner Cable sued to have AMC taken off its cable system, arguing that AMC had betrayed its name and mission statement by no longer showing anything that even vaguely resembled classics, unless *Braddock: Missing in Action III* and *Two Weeks Notice* rank high in your personal pantheon. AMC saw the move as a transparent bid to hamper competition and sent Lionel Hutz–level hacks to represent them. AMC lost and was instantly dropped by eleven million subscribers. To make up for lost revenue AMC decided to cut one and a half million dollars from every department.

When AMC saw that *Movie Club with John Ridley* nonfortuitously cost 1.5 million dollars to produce for thirteen more episodes, they canceled it, despite Ridley and myself publicly trumpeting the show's renewal. AMC's sad little website similarly admonished weary souls to watch for *Movie Club*'s return in the fall of 2005 over a year after its cancellation. *Movie Club* lived in obscurity. It died in obscurity as well.

"But didn't you tell us we'd been renewed for thirteen to fifteen episodes? What happened to that?"

"AMC told us orally that they'd pick us up for thirteen episodes but that doesn't mean anything. The only pickup that counts is the contract they send to my management office. And that never arrived," Head Producer Guy announced gloomily.

"Yesterday I was a sun god. Today I'm a man without a show," Head Producer Guy declaimed theatrically, referencing his favorite movie, *Network,* with the grim black chuckle a condemned man might muster on his way to the guillotine.

After returning home I checked my answering machine and morbidly listened one last time to my saved message of Head Producer Guy announcing that the show had been renewed.

AMC had sold its soul for ratings, advertising dollars, and the opportunity to run *The Omen IV* on a never-ending loop. The chickens had come home to roost. AMC paid a terrible price for losing its integrity. In yet another bitter irony, AMC later attained its greatest creative and commercial success when it decided to forgo the whole "movie" thing altogether by picking up *Mad Men,* a brilliant show about hard-drinking ad men in the early sixties that's as uncompromising and pure as *Movie Club* was compromised and muddled. It did not escape my attention that *Mad Men* and another AMC cult favorite, *Break-*

ing Bad, have fuck-all to do with movies, classic or otherwise. Apparently abandoning classic movies was both the worst *and* best decision AMC ever made.

Head Producer Guy would call me every once in a while with updates on the show's status. First he proposed slashing the show's budget by a third, then half, and taping two shows at a time to cut down on costs. He was full of ways to slash the show's budget. Regan and his gaudy seven-hundred-and-fifty-dollar-a-week salary were history, he triumphantly announced. "We'll replace him with celebrities who'll work for free!" he declared happily. Of course! Why pay someone a little over AFTRA scale when Tom Hanks was dying to head down to Ventura Boulevard to appear on a poorly rated, mildly disreputable, ambiguously canceled movie-review panel show?

AMC passed on that as well but Head Producer Guy steadfastly refused to accept the show's passing in a dignified manner. It was as if he'd just watched his wife miscarry and, insane with grief, tried to collect together the messy remains and shove it madly back into the womb.

So he conceived wild plots and harebrained schemes to keep the show on the air at any cost. His tactics bordered on surreal, if not downright criminal. Cable television was inundated with niche programming, right? It's chockablock with stations devoted to women or gay men or left-handed librarians or narcoleptic chefs who sleep with their mothers. So Head Producer Guy devised a version of the show to fit any possible demographic. He excitedly tried to sell a guest critic I'd become friendly with named Kimberly Ann Morgan on this desperate new tactic. Why, he could do a women's show for Oxygen with her and Zorianna and guest critic Govindini Murty! Or a black show for an African-American station, possibly with Zorianna, Josh, and me in blackface!

But my favorite of Head Producer Guy's crackpot schemes for keeping the show on the air involved trying to sell it as a gay movie-review show to a channel like Logo. To Head Producer Guy it wasn't as comically implausible an idea as it might have seemed. Hadn't more than one focus group respondent advanced the unsolicited notion that all the male critics on *Movie Club* were "gay" and that the show as a whole was "too gay"? The mad genius of Head Producer Guy's idea was that it transformed a potential disadvantage into a tricolored rainbow of delusional hope. He was merely embodying the old aphorism that when life gives you fake-gay lemons, turn them into fake-gay lemonade.

Head Producer Guy despaired that he'd never be able to rope Ridley into hosting a fake gay movie-review show. Thankfully, Head Producer Guy confided in Kim Morgan, the rest of us all "read gay." Besides, "Gay people love Josh! They think he's adorable!" It was the single most retarded idea I'd ever heard. I loved it.

Head Producer Guy's mad, manic, hustling energy had made the show happen in the first place, had created my whole unlikely TV career, however modest or brief. He was the disreputable but beloved father figure who transformed a bunch of misfits into a dysfunctional TV family. But now it appeared that his live-wire 24/7 hustle was turning on itself. The idea that he'd try to turn *Movie Club* into a gay movie-review show I found at once hilarious and deeply sad.

"Appreciate this while you can, Nathan. It's never going to be this fun or easy or free ever again," a more dignified Head Producer Guy had said of *Movie Club* more than once early in our run. It wasn't until the show had been canceled and desperation set in that I truly understood what he'd meant.

Head Producer Guy warned me early on that we'd have to put up with an eternity of being treated like upstart nobodies before anyone took *Movie Club* seriously, that we'd have to wander in the wilderness for ages before making it to the promised land. Now it was clear that we'd never make it. My grandmother used to talk acidically about people who "started on the ground floor and stayed there." That was *Movie Club*. We started on the fringes and died there. There would be no happy ending for *Movie Club,* just a bitter, unmourned death.

That pretty much spelled the end of my professional relationship with Head Producer Guy, though there were both amusing and tragic postscripts to our television misadventures. About a year after *Movie Club*'s cancellation Head Producer Guy tried to get me to use my nonexistent clout for a DVD show we were thinking about pitching together.

"Hey, Nathan, who's that actor friend of yours?" inquired Head Producer Guy impatiently.

"Actor? I'm not really friends with any actors."

"You know, that guy you rode on a plane with."

"Topher Grace? I wouldn't say we're friends necessarily. We're more like people who once sat next to each other on a plane."

"Yeah. Him. What did he do again?"

"He was on *That '70s Show* and did a bunch of movies."

"Yeah, do you think he'd do a show with you? 'Cause the folks over at IFC are real star-fuckers. They tried to get me to produce a show for—who's that jazz guy who was in that movie by that guy who made the movie with Roberto Benigni and the pumpkin?"

"John Lurie?"

"Yeah, they wanted me to produce a talk show where they'd film it all from twenty feet above the set. I said, 'No, thank you.' That's what they're all about at IFC. Stars and gimmicks. I'm sure the only way they'd pick up *Movie Club* would be if you all wore space suits and floated around in zero-gravity."

"So you're asking if Topher Grace would be in a show with me?"

"Yeah."

"He's kind of a big star. He's the bad guy in the new *Spider-Man* movie, so I think he probably wouldn't be into doing a basic-cable show. He'd probably consider it beneath him."

"Yeah, but weren't you obsessed with that movie he did?"

"What movie?"

"Do a Thing with Todd Something or Other."

"*Win a Date with Tad Hamilton!*?"

"Yeah. Don't you love that movie?"

"I've never actually seen it. I saw part of it on TV once but I've never seen the whole thing. I had a promotional *Win a Date with Tad Hamilton!* autograph book. Maybe that's what you're thinking about."

"Oh."

Of course, it's possible that I was mistaken and that Topher Grace left *That '70s Show* not to pursue a thriving film career but rather so that he'd be available on the off chance that I asked him to be my sidekick on a DVD show for IFC. If that is, in fact, the case, please contact me, Mr. Grace. We have important matters to discuss, as well as some unfinished business involving a certain notorious pink autograph book and a signature egregiously missing from it.

All I ever wanted from my *Movie Club* experience was to have all the money in the world and be worshipped as a god. Now it looked like I wouldn't even achieve that.

Fast-forward to two years after *Movie Club*'s cancellation. I got a message on my answering machine from Head Producer Guy. Anderson was dead. In yet another bitter irony, Anderson had died of a heart attack while attending a preview screening of *A Mighty Heart*. He was thirty-eight years old, something I learned only by reading his obituary. Like the diva he was, Anderson zealously hid his age.

Following *Movie Club*'s cancellation I never worried about Ridley or Josh. They both had thriving careers in multiple mediums. They were rich. I never worried about Zo. There will always be a place on television for perky, skinny blondes with perfect teeth and mad teleprompter skillz. Zo was made for television and television was made for Zo. I suspect that when the doctor delivering Zo saw her shiny hair and blinding smile he proudly enthused, "Congratulations! It's a television personality!" Zo turned out to be too big for the small screen. In the summer of 2008 alone she appeared in three movies: *Iron Man,* *The Longshots,* and *Lakeview Terrace.*

But I worried about Anderson. He was never more than a few short steps away from oblivion when he had a national television show. I could only imagine the desperation he must have felt when *Movie Club* failed. He lived his entire life at the tricky intersection of comedy and tragedy. He was funny. He was vibrant. He had the kind of phosphorescent personality that fills up a room. Now he was gone.

As *Movie Club* barreled inexorably toward cancellation I got to see a whole lot of Head Producer Guy's bad side, but Anderson's death brought out the best in him. He was once again the wobbly but proud shepherd of a wayward flock, the loopy father figure to a dysfunctional showbiz family.

After he attended Anderson's funeral, Head Producer Guy sent out an e-mail titled "ANDERSON DIED RICH." Being literal-minded and dopey, I immediately thought, "Anderson came from money? Wow. Who knew?" but, of course, the e-mail meant that Anderson died with a wealth of friends, precious memories, valuable life experiences, and other assorted sentimental horseshit. It was sweet and sappy and it reminded me that behind all the opportunistic craziness, Head Producer Guy was a big softie with a special place in his heart for the bedraggled little orphan that was *Movie Club,* and for Anderson in particular. Even more than Head Producer Guy, Anderson was *Movie Club*'s boozy, bleary, funny, sad, self-destructive, wonderful, poignant, ridiculous soul.

Looking back, two memories of Anderson stand out. Early in *Movie Club*'s run I was riding in a car with Anderson and he remarked sadly, "You know, you're never going to get anywhere in this business unless you have people working with you who really love you." It was an uncharacteristically sober, melancholy statement from a man who lustily embraced the stereotype of the ebullient queen at a steep price. I think Head Producer Guy and R.L. both loved Anderson. You had to. Only people who genuinely loved Anderson and saw the smart, serious man underneath the glittery exterior were willing to put up with his bullshit. I think Head Producer Guy and R.L. also loved me. In my own strange way I loved them back.

My second memory of Anderson also comes from *Movie Club*'s infancy. I was being driven to the airport and I asked Anderson if he liked living in Los Angeles.

"Not really. But if you want to work in the business you have to live here. You don't really have a choice."

"I can see that. I must say, however, that I like being able to fly back to Chicago every Sunday. Things seem a lot more sane there."

"Yeah. You'll end up living in Los Angeles, though. You will," Anderson said with disconcerting certainty, as if it wasn't a hunch or a prediction but a simple statement of fact. It felt like a gypsy curse, as if I had no choice in the matter and the pagan gods of Hollywood would have their way with me no matter how hard I tried to remain a good Midwestern boy on his own.

I can imagine Head Producer Guy reading this book, or at least skimming the relevant sections, and, with highly theatrical self-pity, wondering aloud, "Gosh, Nathan, was it really so terrible, flying you to Los Angeles and putting you up in a hotel and giving you free clothes and food and putting you on TV every week? Was it really so awful that you had to write those things about me?"

To answer this phantom Head Producer Guy's unasked question, no, it wasn't terrible. It wasn't terrible at all. It was pretty fucking wonderful most of the time. I'll always be grateful to Head Producer Guy for giving me an opportunity to do something most people can only dream about. But the parts I will always cherish haven't blinded me to the dark side of the whole experience. Besides, Head Producer Guy is above all else an entertainer, and I did my damnedest to put on a good show.

The Bad and the Beautiful's ending invites the question: if Head Producer Guy were to call tomorrow and ask me to fly out to Hollywood to work on another project, would I? The answer is an unqualified yes. I'd jump back on that roller coaster in a heartbeat no matter the ultimate outcome.

Confessions of a Moderately Likeable Gay Everyman

"Homer's Enemy"
Zorianna Kit

"Homer's Enemy" is perhaps the darkest non–Treehouse of Horror *Simpsons* episode, and one of the best. It's a singular attempt to inject realism into *The Simpsons'* cartoon universe by showing how an outsider might respond to Homer Simpson. The show centers on a satirical truth other episodes largely ignore: for a bumbling, dimwitted everyman, Homer Simpson has enjoyed a remarkably blessed life. He's been to outer space, toured with Lollapalooza, scored a hit record, won a Grammy, befriended Gerald Ford, owns his own home, and has a beautiful, endlessly understanding wife and at least one exceptional, well-behaved child.

Homer's charmed life throws into even sharper relief the cursed existence of Frank Grimes, who is introduced in a news segment outlining the Dickensian misery of his upbringing: He was abandoned by his parents at four and forced to take a job delivering presents to more fortunate children. At eighteen he was "blown up in a silo explosion" but painstakingly recuperates enough to both "feel pain" and earn a degree in nuclear physics "with a minor in determination."

His pluck impresses Mr. Burns and earns him a job at the

Springfield nuclear plant, where he's horrified by how easily
Homer coasts through life. Homer tries to ingratiate himself
with "Grimey," as he affectionately/irritatingly rechristens him,
much to Grimes's annoyance, but Grimes rebuffs his advances
and denounces Homer as his enemy. He tries to shame Homer
by tricking him into entering a contest designed for children, but
the blithely unself-conscious Homer proves immune to ridicule.
In a fit of rage Grimes fatally electrocutes himself. In a bitter final
irony, Homer upstages Grimes one last time by falling asleep at
the funeral and deliriously shouting, "Change the channel,
Marge," cracking up the gathered mourners.

Like so many *Simpsons* characters, Grimes transcended the
dingy confines of network television to become a pop culture
archetype. He represents every hard-luck case who ever scrimped
and saved and struggled just to keep his head above water only
to watch lazy dopes coast their way to the good life. When I was
a kid I identified strongly with cursed sad sacks like Grimes. As a
child I believed in God; someone powerful had to be conspiring
against me.

After *The Onion* and *Movie Club,* however, I finally began
to feel like bad luck and bum breaks were a thing of the past. Yet
in late 2004, I made a professional enemy who unleashed my
inner Frank Grimes. She was a skinny, blonde Canadian-born
mother and wife named Zorianna Kit, who seemed to stumble
obliviously into everything I worked hard all my life to achieve.
Of course it's entirely possible that Zorianna has struggled just
as hard as me but she certainly seems to live a charmed life.

If *Movie Club* were high school, Zorianna Kit would be the
head cheerleader: the tall, skinny, perpetually grinning blonde
girl all the jocks want to date and all the frumpy girls develop
eating disorders trying to look like. And Anderson, her staunch
Movie Club ally and coconspirator, would be the popular, brainy
black queen everyone thinks is a gas and a half but who cries
himself to sleep nightly clutching a bottle of Jack Daniel's
because he fears no one will ever love him.

Zorianna was an entertainment journalist by trade, a job title I feel is something of an oxymoron. Let's face it: if your beat involves discovering the identity of Mandy Moore's super-fave-rave out-of-the-way Mexican restaurant, then it's probably delusional to consider yourself the heir to Walter Cronkite and Edward R. Murrow. Kit had toiled in the Tinseltown trenches for *The Hollywood Reporter* and *People* magazine in addition to working as an entertainment reporter for KTLA, Los Angeles's former WB affiliate.

Now, I'm not saying Kit didn't tackle heavy topics for KTLA, but I have bookmarked a website with photographs memorializing a trip Kit made to one "Image by Kimarie" hair salon to tackle the explosive subject of what is euphemistically known as "hair enhancement." Ever the intrepid New Journalist, Kit threw herself on the front line by playing the human guinea pig and getting custom-made, complimentary hair extensions. And while I am not privy to the masterpiece of investigative journalism that ensued, judging by the photographs of the blessed event I can only conclude that Kit deemed hair extensions to be totally awesome, if not the hottest new follicular trend sweeping the greater Los Angeles area.

Though Canadian by birth, Kit was unmistakably a creature of the industry. She lives in Ozzie and Harriet Nelson's supposedly haunted old house, which doubles as Jeremy Piven's home in *Entourage*. She's married to an actor, writer, and producer named Bo Zenga, best known for cowriting *Soul Plane* and losing a famously acrimonious lawsuit over *Scary Movie* profits against Brad Grey of Brillstein-Grey Entertainment, the much-feared Hollywood power broker who would go on to head up Paramount.

While still a struggling actor, Zenga befriended another would-be thespian, Billy Bob Thornton, and cowrote, codirected, and appeared in *Original Material from Hell,* the piece where Thornton introduced the character he'd go on to play in *Sling Blade.*

I first met Zorianna during the rehearsal the night before the final *Movie Club* audition. It was apparent even then that Anderson and Zorianna had formed a strategic partnership rooted in their shared love of populist Hollywood pap, mutual self-interest, and the strange, intuitive bond shared by skinny straight women and sassy gay men.

Head Producer Guy's philosophy regarding the role of cosmetics in broadcasting can be summarized thusly: "When in doubt, slather on the whore makeup." Surprisingly, this went for both men and women. As a result, Zorianna looked a little like a blonde Raggedy Ann doll on the pilot thanks to a trolley-car-red slash of lipstick; apple-red, heavily rouged cheeks; and pale skin. I, meanwhile, look like a dizzy old queen with my thin dusting of pancake makeup, ghostly complexion, and seventies-style white flowered shirt with a butterfly collar.

The queeny vibe I give off in the pilot reached its apex/nadir when Zorianna and I both sang along to "Afternoon Delight" and did a gay little chair dance while an *Anchorman* clip played on-screen. It was a precious, silly, wholly embarrassing bit of narcissistic business I was mortified to see make it onto the pilot via a split screen that stuck me and Zo into the bottom-left and upper-right corners of the frame, respectively, alongside Will Ferrell and pals. What kind of a heterosexual man sings along to "Afternoon Delight" while doing a little dance? I'll tell you what kind of heterosexual man: an extremely gay heterosexual man.

An early indication that Zorianna wasn't a hard-core cinephile came when she confessed in the *Movie Club* pilot that one of the movies tested her patience so thoroughly that she ducked out twenty minutes early. What esoteric avant-garde provocation could have inspired such a hostile response? *Spider-Man 2*.

Zorianna landed the show all the same but her *Spider-Man 2* lapse hurt her with that sinister entity known as the focus group, a noxious showbiz institution wherein the ill-informed opinions of the unwashed rabble are compiled and relayed in a detached, quasiscientific, analytical fashion and distributed to relevant parties. The input of these cantankerous subliterates then helps Ivy League graduates determine how shows and movies get made, edited, and marketed.

At the beginning of our run we were each e-mailed copies of the focus group report along with a strongly worded warning not to take the contents of the focus group testing personally. We love you, the producers assured us and our fragile egos, even if the focus groups do not. The producers stressed that the report merely represents the "feelings of some of the public," not their own.

Judging from the focus group results alone, *Movie Club* never should have made it onto the air. I find the results of the report fascinating more for what they say about focus group testing than what they say about *Movie Club,* so I'm going to discuss them in detail here.

The report begins by dryly outlining its parameters and methods. It notes, for example, that testing was done in Atlanta and Oak Park, Illinois, among twenty-five-to-forty-nine-year-olds who were AMC subscribers, regular moviegoers, or DVD enthusiasts. They moreover had to possess "at least some interest" in programs reviewing or previewing movies and also "programs that consist of comedic free-for-all discussions."

So if these aforementioned statistical abstractions love movies, dig watching television, and groove especially hard on programs that consist of "comedic free-for-all discussions," then they've gotta love the televised, movie-loving comedic free-for-all that is *Movie Club,* right? Not exactly. While focus group testers were initially excited about *Movie Club* and the report notes that "very few objected in principle to the roundtable format," the testers felt that *Movie Club* just didn't measure up to the high standards for the roundtable established by *Politically Correct* and *The Best Damn Sports Show Period.* Furthermore, the report grimly stated, "In contrast to *Movie Club,* those two shows were noted to have a diverse group of commentators, from conservative to liberal, distinct 'personalities' that come across as 'real, true people.'"

Here I'd lumbered through life under the delusion that I was a "real, true" person when in fact I wasn't even a distinct "personality." Considering how fractious the show would become, it's ironic that one of the main criticisms we received was that we lacked diversity. Testers found us "too similar," "all young," "from a large metropolitan area," "same style," "hipster jokes," and "straight out of MTV." "There was no difference of opinion. They're from the same cloth." "They had a closed mindset." The report goes on to note, "Nathan and Josh seemed particularly similar to some viewers, in age, tone, and humor."

They considered us all "artsy-fartsy type people," hypothesized that we "all went to film school" (none of us did), were "all under 30" (I was the only one under thirty), and said that we "all seem[ed] to be from the same place, drink coffee in the same shop," before finally concluding that we were "too very much the same, too much of the same humor."

Over the course of the show Zorianna and I barely seemed to inhabit the same universe, let alone share the same mind-set. So it's curious that much of the focus group criticism criticizes us for being carbon copies of each other.

The testers liked *Movie Club*'s format but disliked us. Some of the focus group's criticisms were legitimate, like their belief that it was glaringly unprofessional to walk out of a movie you're supposed to review, even if it's *Spider-Man 2*. "If you're a reviewer you have a responsibility to see the entire movie," wrote one anonymous tester in a frothing fit of utter reasonableness. It was hard not to agree with the focus group's assertions that the pilot feels at once frenetic and over-rehearsed, glib and overstuffed.

An interesting variable in the pilot was the always-loaded presence of *The Passion of the Christ*. It didn't bode well for the pilot's chances with focus groups in the South that it featured two dirty, effete showbiz Jews running roughshod over a film considered sacred to much of its Christian audience. The report adorably pretends that *Movie Club*'s virulent criticism of Mel Gibson's gruesome passion play didn't prejudice respondents against the show's multiracial aggregation of godless, Jesus-hating sodomites. But it did note that respondents were mortified that we'd mocked sacred cows like *The Passion of the Christ* and *Middlebrow Mountain* but gushed over *Anchorman: The Legend of Ron Burgundy,* a movie focus group respondents deemed "totally stupid."

But it was easy to disregard the few nuggets of legitimate constructive criticism in light of some of the report's more surreal, inexplicable claims. Under the questionable heading of "SEXIST" the report dryly notes, for example, "A few panelists actually voiced the opinion that all the male critics were gay, and that the show was generally too gay."

Sweet cunt-fucking Christ on a crucicracker, what can you make of a statement like that? I'm guessing the testers' vehement assertion about the sexual preference of all the male critics was unsolicited. I doubt that there were boxes you could fill out to indicate which critics you thought were gay or that the show as a whole was "too gay." My bemusement over the damning focus group results was strengthened by the happy accident that I tested highest of all the critics.

Ridley tested higher than all of us, rightly so, but he was deemed a separate entity. Zorianna tested the poorest, with respondents taking her to task for bailing out of *Spider-Man 2* (everyone hates skinny blonde women except for the sizable contingent of the population, largely but not exclusively male, that worships them). They were even harder on poor Anderson. Though some praised him for being "ebullient" (gay), "animated" (supergay), and "expressive" (pursuing an alternative lifestyle), the report dourly concludes, "Many found his gushing over Jude Law irrelevant to a movie review, and a few, with different euphemisms, deemed him too 'swish' for their tastes."

The last part of that statement I find fascinating. When the decidedly anachronistic "swish" is being employed as a euphemism to cover up far uglier sentiments, it's hard to imagine what those nastier epithets might be.

Given my history, it's a little ironic that the focus group specifically praised me for being more "average" and "less trendy" than the other critics. So there you have it, folks. AMC paid a focus group company good money to determine what kind of a man I was. Their answer was fuzzy but discernible: I am a moderately likable gay everyman. That certainly wasn't how I saw myself. But the people had spoken. Who am I to deny their collective wisdom?

It's hard to overstate the importance of chemistry and casting for a show like *Movie Club*. Whether you're making *Siskel & Ebert* or *Moonlighting*, you want audiences to wonder if the stars of a show either hate each other, are fucking, or hate each other *and* are engaging in dirty, thrilling hate-sex. Nobody thought I was giving Zorianna the old Hong Kong Handshake or Shanghai Surprise, but plenty of people asked me if I bitterly despised her.

What I told them is what I will tell you, dear reader. I like Zorianna as a person but felt like our violently clashing ideas about film, popular culture, and the universe as a whole were a big part of what made the show work.

In a *Chicago Magazine* piece on Roger Ebert, the writer reports that in July of 2000, "Ebert volunteered that he was partial to selecting a man [as a cohost] because he would not feel comfortable beating up on a woman on the air." I could relate but I was able to separate the professional demands of a job that required me to be aggressive and adversarial from my intense personal aversion to conflict.

One of the defining moments of *Movie Club* came halfway through the third airing episode. After Josh raved about Michael Radford's leaden, misguided adaptation of *The Merchant of Venice*, Zorianna very angrily declared that *Venice* wasn't a "date movie" or a "family movie" before insisting that "if you can only see one movie over the weekend, it's not going to be *Shakespeare*."

Zorianna spat out the word "Shakespeare" with palpable contempt. She seemed to view it as a personal affront that anyone would have the nerve to adapt some boring old dead guy like Shakespeare when their talents would better be deployed making the next *Shrek* sequel or Meg Ryan rom-com.

I was flabbergasted that Zorianna didn't see the point of Shakespeare. Defending Shakespeare to Zorianna was like doing a music show and having your cohost confess early on that they thought the Beatles were nothing special, felt they peaked with "Love Me Do," and paled in comparison to their more talented counterparts the Monkees.

"You could not be more wrong," I all but screamed at Zorianna about Shakespeare's ostensible irrelevance, to which she angrily retorted, "And you could not be more out of touch!"

In that exhilaratingly tense moment the battle lines were drawn and the gauntlet thrown down. It was art versus entertainment, intellectualism against populist pandering, wry outsiders against schmoozing, air-kissing creatures of the industry, people who thought Shakespeare was an irrelevant white dude versus people who considered such thinking intellectual heresy. I'd found my perfect professional archenemy. She was a skinny striver with teeth so big and blindingly white I sometimes wondered if she wasn't the secret love child of James Coburn.

After taping that day Head Producer Guy sided with Zorianna in the debate over Shakespeare's supposed irrelevance. "Zorianna, I thought you were right on with your comments about *Merchant of Venice*. When I was in England I saw these huge subway ads for *Merchant of Venice* and thought, 'Who on Earth would want to see this movie? Who do they think the audience for it is?'" Head Producer Guy insisted. The irony is that I didn't even like *The Merchant of Venice*. But I couldn't let the idea that Shakespeare was irrelevant go unchallenged and still respect myself in the morning.

By the *Merchant of Venice* show we'd worked out many of the kinks but a few remained. The editing remained choppy and jarring. It wasn't unusual for Ridley to refer to comments that ended up on the cutting room floor. My line about *A Love Song for Bobby Long* being "bad even for a John Travolta movie," for example, was cut but not, for some inexplicable reason, Ridley's response: "Wow, bad even for a John Travolta movie. That's the hyperbole of the week." In its contempt for continuity and cohesion, our editing bordered on avant-garde.

Another strange *Movie Club* ritual was solidified the first time Ridley mocked Zorianna for her mild enjoyment of *A Love Song for Bobby Long*: the deathless inside joke that flies way over the heads of 98 percent of our audience. Ridley never stopped teasing Zorianna about *A Love Song for Bobby Long,* which must have confused *Movie Club* viewers who probably didn't even remember *Bobby Long,* let alone recall Zorianna's measured praise for John Travolta's scenery-chewing performance in it. Ridley enjoyed teasing Zorianna just as much as I did. The difference was that he could get away with it. He was the star of the show—it wasn't called *Movie Club with Zorianna Kit*—so she had to suffer silently while he embarked on an indefatigable campaign of gentle ridicule, much of which circled back, naturally enough, to *A Love Song for Bobby Long.*

Everyone gently ribbed Zorianna, even Anderson, her closest ally. Zorianna proved an excellent foil, not just for me but for Ridley, Josh, and Anderson. At one point Ridley referred to what we were doing to Zorianna as gaslighting, after the 1944 classic where Charles Boyer wages a subtle, persistent campaign to drive Ingrid Bergman insane. We weren't trying to drive Zo insane but she did eventually crack during the seventh and final airing show of our first season, a raucous, unwieldy affair where the resentment and bitterness that had been bubbling under the surface of *Movie Club* all season exploded. It was an episode so memorable and memorably insane that Head Producer Guy cut two separate versions of it, one for airing and the other for our own private edification. The show's premise was essentially borrowed (i.e., stolen) from an old *Sneak Previews* staple where Siskel and Ebert revealed who they'd give Oscars to if they ran the awards.

When it was my turn to give out my faux-Oscar for Best Actor, I chose Paul Giamatti for *Sideways*, a choice that greatly offended Zorianna's aesthetic sensibilities.

"Of course all you critics love Paul Giamatti in *Sideways*! That's because you all look and act just like him," Zo enthused bitterly. Zo's comment echoed *New York Times* critic A. O. Scott's observation that film critics championed Giamatti's performance in *Sideways* because his bitter, underpaid, cantankerous boozer of a loser was a film critic by personality and disposition, if not by trade.

Accordingly, the screening room in Chicago where films are shown to critics before their release is filled with doughy, middle-aged men who can only daydream about possessing the raw sexual magnetism of a Paul Giamatti. When moviegoers looked at Giamatti's chinless, depressed, overeducated, and underemployed *Sideways* protagonist, they saw an unattractive, unsympathetic, whiny loser. When film critics across the country looked at Giamatti's chinless, depressed, overeducated, and underemployed *Sideways* protagonist, they saw themselves.

I found it telling that in the great film critic/public divide over *Sideways* I fell on the film critic side while everyone else sided with the *Sideways*-phobic public. If Giamatti's character is a film critic by personality and disposition, if not by trade, then my fellow *Movie Club* panelists, with the exception of Anderson, were all film critics by trade but not by personality or disposition. Even Anderson, a broke, boozy, middle-aged California writer stumbling drunkenly through a midlife crisis, couldn't relate to Alexander Payne's sharp-witted yet sympathetic portrait of a broke, boozy, middle-aged California writer stumbling drunkenly through a midlife crisis.

I like to think of film criticism as a sacred calling and a way of life. But to Josh and Zorianna film criticism was nothing more than a temporary gig too sweet to pass up. Film criticism was something they did for a while, not who they are.

The atmosphere at *Movie Club* was lively, loose, and spontaneous, but without any scripted reviews to memorize and a huge break looming in the near future, the vibe around the set during the last show of the season was even more raucous than usual.

There were times when Zorianna seemed on the verge of attaining a strange spiritual and professional communion with the teleprompter, a kind of Vulcan mind meld. But when the teleprompter went too fast or she lost her place, a look of stark existential panic would dance across the otherwise placid surface of her face.

The teleprompter betrayed Zorianna more than once that final show of the season, but that didn't affect her half as much as Ridley's teasing. Ridley and Zo had a mocking, playful chemistry that was fun to watch, but on this show he was riding her hard and it was clearly getting to Zo.

When we were discussing our choice for Best Supporting Actor, Ridley asked her if she had any thoughts on the matter. She brusquely snapped, "I have not a single thought in my blonde head. Why don't you move on straight to Anderson. Pass me over! Not a thought!"

When it was time for Zorianna to give her pick for Best Director, Ridley pretended to cut her off immediately after she gave her answer, which further fueled her rage. Explaining her selection of Clint Eastwood for *Million-Dollar Baby,* Zo turned to the camera and began her spiel but soon lost her train of thought due to us giggling and talking amongst ourselves. It got so bad that Zorianna turned to Anderson and snapped, "Anderson, I'm speaking!" Finally she regained her composure and argued, "Who can direct actors better than another actor?"

Ridley turned to the camera and interrupted with a deadpan, "A director?" which cracked us up all over again.

I did little to defuse the situation by pointing at Zorianna with both hands and yelling, "In your face, Zorianna! In your face!" Not very gentlemanly of me, I know.

After taking a few seconds to regain her composure Zorianna continued, "I think the way that Eastwood was able to bring out performances from [Hilary] Swank, [Morgan] Freeman, and even himself—"

Again Ridley interrupted Zo with a wisecrack about Eastwood's accomplishment being all the more remarkable considering that the aforementioned trio has "never given a good performance before *in their lives.*"

When it was my turn to dole out my Best Director award, I chose Michel Gondry for *Eternal Sunshine of the Spotless Mind.* I was nearly finished with my explanation when out of nowhere Zorianna blindsided us all by snapping at Ridley, "Jim Carrey can't act by himself and Kate Winslet delivers shitty performances all the time. Why don't you pick on his choice? Why do you have to pick on my choice? Are you saying that Kate Winslet cannot deliver a performance on her own without Michel Gondry like Hilary Swank and Morgan Freeman can't act without—no, I'm serious!"

Zorianna was laughing and/or crying while she said this but it was laughter born of anger and resentment, not joy. It was weirdly cathartic laughter, raw and dangerous and embarrassing. It damn near shut down the set. It was a strange, deeply awkward outburst of anger that eerily foreshadowed an even more explosive confrontation between Zo and myself on the first show back.

During *Movie Club*'s three-and-a-half-month unexcused and inexcusable absence from the airwaves, I got to experience a whole new disquieting kind of anonymity as a cast member on a show nobody knew existed, that wasn't even on the air anymore yet somehow wasn't canceled either. We showbiz pretenders call this strange, cursed state of professional purgatory "hiatus."

During the hiatus I learned that there was at least one unexpected advantage to *Movie Club*'s cultural invisibility. On the evening of March 2, 2005, I smoked a reefer stick and decided to cybersurf the good ol' webernet on my trusty computer box. I was perusing the news on IMDB.com when I saw a headline that sent shivers down my spine. It read L.A. TV REPORTER ADMITS BEING CAUGHT IN GREY AREA.

In a fit of only partially pot-induced paranoia, my interior monologue issued the following silent, persistent, repetitive plea:

Please don't be Zorianna

Please don't be Zorianna

Please don't be Zorianna

Needless to say, dear reader, the L.A. TV reporter in question was, in fact, Zorianna Kit. When Brad Grey was anointed supreme commissar of Paramount, Zo delivered an editorial in which she witheringly catalogued the box-office disasters Grey had a hand in without revealing that her husband had lost a bitter, acrimonious lawsuit against Grey. It was the same lawsuit that had (allegedly) brought her husband, Bo Zenga, and his family to the attention of Anthony Pellicano, the wiretap-happy gumshoe of showbiz infamy.

Thankfully this was one instance in which the show's invisibility protected us. *Movie Club* was so far under the media radar that it was never mentioned in any of the pieces about the Zorianna/Grey controversy. Even when the Zorianna/Grey imbroglio exploded into the Zenga/Pellicano/Grey wiretapping scandal, Zorianna was seldom identified as a *Movie Club* regular.

The show had been off the air for a while at that point, so it's possible people just assumed we'd been canceled. By the time *Movie Club* reappeared in late May, the Zorianna/Grey controversy was ancient history.

The first press release touting *Movie Club*'s debut boasted ominously that it featured a "rotating panel" of critics. The sinister persistence of the phrase "rotating panel" in AMC press material continued to haunt us ambiguously rotating panelists well into our second season.

The persistence of the "rotating panel" phrase was even

more perplexing considering AMC made our personalities the focus of new *Movie Club* commercials.

In the "Zodiac" commercial the four *Movie Club* regulars—I'm sorry, constantly rotating guest panelists—were promoted to astrological signs. "If you have a soft spot for rising stars," the AMC announcer guy insisted, "you are Zorianna." Am I, though? "If you think indie films are just better," then by AMC's reasoning, "your moon is in Josh."

"If you're tough on movies but only because you love them," meanwhile, then that makes you a "Nathan in retrograde." I would have preferred "Nathan Rabin: tough on movies; harder on hos" or "Nathan Rabin: tough on movies; murder on bitches," but it nevertheless seemed apt. Apt! Lastly, "If you enjoy a good guilty pleasure," then that renders you an "Anderson ascending."

By AMC's reasoning I'd classify myself as Anderson ascending with my moon in Josh. Also, I am Zorianna. But not in a weird way. A starry little rendering of the four of us in half-human/half-constellation form accompanied our descriptions. To give the AMC marketing department credit, my sketch only makes me look mildly retarded.

After R.L. sent me an e-mail containing the "Zodiac" ad, I forwarded it to friends with the disclaimer, "My name is Nathan Rabin and I did not approve this commercial message."

I found the "Zodiac" ad both flattering and embarrassing. I'd spent my career on the other end of the publicity machine, so it was surreal to see my personality packaged and sold like laundry detergent or frozen dinners.

The next set of ads delved even deeper into our individual personalities and personal histories. To help promote the show, AMC had us fill out extensive questionnaires about *Movie Club* and our fellow panelists. AMC then cherry-picked details about our lives they felt might endear us to the AMC audience.

So what did AMC consider most fascinating about me? The ad dispensed the following irresistible nuggets of information:

1. I write for *The Onion*.
2. I worked in a video store.
3. I rarely agree with the Oscars.
4. I regretted once giving a marginally positive review of *Princess Diaries 2: Royal Engagement*.
5. Gene Siskel told me I'd be a great filmmaker.

And lastly but not leastly

6. I think 85 percent of everything sucks but that the 15 percent that doesn't makes it all worthwhile.

My ad ends by proclaiming me "the depressive, neurotic one" (suggested Native American name: Dances with Vice Admiral). Suddenly depression and neuroses weren't just psychological problems: they were now marketing hooks as well! We were all given titles that reduced us to stereotypes. Ridley was "the one in charge." Josh was "the smart one with glasses." Anderson was "the funny, sarcastic one," while Zorianna was the "upbeat, positive one."

But I would have more important matters to worry about during the tension-filled first episode of *Movie Club*'s second season. Because of the way the cameras were positioned, Zorianna and Anderson were always in my field of vision when I read from the teleprompter or looked into the camera. Usually that wasn't a problem. But during my *Monster-in-Law* review Anderson and Zorianna both glared at me with the kind of glowering, faintly inhuman expression that in sci-fi horror movies indicates someone's brain has been snatched by a malevolent alien life force. I could feel the prickly psychic icicles extending directly from Anderson's and Zo's eyes to my hypernervous personage.

With the tension between Josh and Head Producer Guy and the free-floating aura of bad vibes on the set, everyone was on edge. I ratcheted up the tension by taking an ill-advised swipe at Zorianna in my review when I said, "And at the risk of sounding like Zorianna, the gender politics in this movie are nothing short of reprehensible!"

It was a nasty, gratuitous swipe at Zorianna's frothy pink populism and apolitical nature that had little to do with *Monster-in-Law*. It was the kind of casual put-down of Zo's sensibility we'd all indulged in extensively during the first season, but Zo's outburst during the Oscar show had served notice that she wasn't going to take our mild jabs so lightly anymore. No longer would she play the good-natured foil to her gently bullying TV siblings. This time out she would give as good as she got.

Zo told us that strangers had come up to her on the street and told her to fight back, to not take our verbal abuse lying down. I found it remarkable that Zo lived in some bizarre alternate universe where the rabble not only knew *Movie Club* existed but recognized its regulars on the street and nursed strong opinions about its central dynamic. When Zo returned to the show that summer it was with claws and fangs sharpened. She was out for blood, and as I squirmed nervously in my seat and struggled to quell the shakiness in my voice, I looked like fresh meat.

I was feeling rusty following a hiatus longer than our entire original run. Before the hiatus I told R.L. I'd keep my TV chops razor sharp by staging and taping fake *Movie Club* episodes, with my cats Sweetie Pie and Maggie May taking the place of my fellow critics. I never followed through on my plan. Between the weird pressure on set, the butterflies in my stomach, and Anderson's and Zo's horror-movie glares in my direction, I lost my sense of equilibrium and, to use a technical term, freaked out.

In the middle of a take I lost my place and anxiously stuttered, "I'm really sorry, guys, but I'm kind of thrown off by Anderson and Zorianna glaring at me."

Without blinking or altering her icy glare in the slightest, Zorianna hissed through clenched teeth, "I'm glaring because I hate every word coming out of your mouth. And I can't wait to attack you." She slowly, deliberately uttered the words with exquisitely controlled rage, wringing every last drop of contempt out of each syllable. She may have looked like a cheerleader and acted like a perky *Entertainment Tonight* correspondent but Zo had ice water coursing through her veins.

For some reason I assumed I was the only one who heard Zorianna saying she hated every word coming out of my mouth and couldn't wait to attack me. I inexplicably concluded that for just that instant Zorianna had morphed into my very own personal version of the Great Gazoo, the diminutive, vaguely effeminate green space alien only Fred Flintstone and Marlon Brando can see or hear. Of course that wasn't the case. We were taping a TV show, so there were cameras and microphones picking up everything we said or did, whether it was intended for broadcast or not.

Zo's talk of hating every word coming out of my mouth and lying in wait to attack me somehow failed to restore my equilibrium. Nor did her words improve the faintly poisonous vibe on the set. Zo was laying down the gauntlet in our very first show back, hollering, "Bring it on, bitch! You want a piece of me?! I'll fuck you up, whore!" Metaphorically of course.

I delivered my *Monster-in-Law* review in a voice quaking with anger. Later Ridley asked me why I felt so strongly about a silly piece of fluff like *Monster-in-Law*. It's just a stupid romantic comedy, right? The thing is, I don't hate *Monster-in-Law* because it's an unfunny, formulaic, mercenary, and derivative romantic comedy. There are lots of those out there. They're not worthy of my contempt.

I merely dislike *Monster-in-Law* for being unfunny, formulaic, mercenary, and derivative. I fucking hate *Monster-in-Law* because it's a deeply reactionary film that degrades Jane Fonda's legacy as a feminist icon. It's a film that divides women into virgins and whores while glibly demonizing driven career women.

As I delivered my increasingly unhinged *Monster-in-Law* review, the show occasionally cut to a reaction shot of Zorianna glaring contemptuously at me, setting up a conflict primed to explode the moment I completed my review.

As soon as I finished, Zo shouted, "Listen, this movie was number one at the box office opening weekend, which means America spoke! America spoke!"

"Yeah, well, *Meet the Fockers* is the top-grossing comedy of all time. Does that mean it's good?" I shouted in response. From there Zorianna and I spent the next few minutes screaming at each other about the merits of *Monster-in-Law* with Ridley acting as harried referee. In the epic battle over whether *Monster-in-Law* made baby Jesus cry or was the hilarious feel-good rom-com hit of the summer, Josh came down on my side and Anderson came down on Zorianna's.

"Jane Fonda: they might as well have made her a prostitute," I apparently screamed at some point, according to an article about *Movie Club* later printed in *Chicago Tribune Sunday Magazine*, to which Zo reportedly responded, "What the . . . ?! Did you not take your happy pill today?"

Glenn Jeffers, the *Tribune* writer behind the *Movie Club* piece, aptly summed up the tone of that first show back when he wrote, "Don't expect the snippy-yet-cordial disagreement you'll find on *Ebert & Roeper*. AMC's *Movie Club with John Ridley* aims for the jugular."

Zo's "Why would anyone want to watch a movie based on Shakespeare?" line helped establish the tone and dynamic of the first set of episodes. The *Monster-in-Law* imbroglio, meanwhile, in tandem with the whole Head Producer Guy/Josh ugliness, helped define the divisive tone of the next eight episodes. There was a culture war going on both inside and outside of *Movie Club*.

In keeping with AMC's demand that we regularly showcase a dazzling cavalcade of stars, the second *Movie Club* episode back featured noted hunktor Ricardo Chavira of *Desperate Housewives*, a regular at one of the many taverns Head Producer Guy frequented. Head Producer Guy was so concerned about the rising tide of alcoholism in Los Angeles that he spent seemingly every night closely observing it in a different watering hole, often sacrificing his sobriety and liver so he could better understand the mental processes that lead to problem drinking.

After we taped the first two segments, Chavira joined the *Club*bers for a segment on the Steve McQueen box set. Zorianna proved that her genius for cultural heresy was as potent as ever when she told Chavira that she just didn't understand the nature of McQueen's appeal. "I don't *get* [Steve McQueen]. I don't find him particularly good looking and I'm not particularly blown away by his talent. Can you explain to me what it is about him [that you respond to]? Because I just don't get it," Zorianna pleaded.

Nobody could accuse Zorianna of being a slave to conventional wisdom. A bomb-throwing intellectual anarchist to the core, Zo wasn't about to let anyone or anything trick her into thinking that that boring old Shakespeare dude was somehow relevant in 2005 or that there was something somehow attractive or appealing about Steve McQueen.

The next episode marked the triumphant return of Kim Morgan, a striking, intense suicide blonde with brilliant blue eyes that stared right through people. Kim, the brainy, idiosyncratic Tuesday Weld of the cinephile set, was the anti-Zorianna. Kim quickly became my best friend in Los Angeles. She embodies an archetype I call the Cine-Monk. For the Cine-Monk, cinephilia is infinitely more than just a hobby or pastime; it's a solemn existential calling, a sacred duty. The Cine-Monk will gladly spend his or her last dollar on a ticket to an Ozu retrospective. They'll happily swear a vow of poverty and go without food, shelter, and clothing if it means seeing more movies. The Cine-Monk lives by the creed that he who sees the most movies before dying wins, and he who sees the most obscure Asian or African movies picks up extra bonus points. The Cine-Monk is by nature an obsessive, a completist, a list maker, an inveterate canon creator.

Sometimes a Cine-Monk lives the dream by becoming a filmmaker, like Brian De Palma or Quentin Tarantino. More often

Cine-Monks frighten coworkers, worry parents, and die alone and unloved in squalid efficiencies reeking of cat shit. But oh, the movies they've seen! The movies make it all worthwhile.

Kim's first appearance on *Movie Club* kicked off with a segment on *Mr. and Mrs. Smith*. True to form, Anderson, Kim, and I got off on its kinky sadomasochism and gallows humor. After Zorianna delivered her one-star review, Kim defended the movie. I backed her up.

I said I really liked *Mr. and Mrs. Smith* because it showed marriage for what it is: "a poisonous institution built on a foundation of lies and deceit." I then turned to the camera and said, "And yes, ladies, I am still available."

Just before my marriage-bashing words left my mouth, I thought gloomily, "There goes your love life, pally." Then again, at that point my love life was DOA. A few weeks earlier at Residuals I'd lamented my long celibate streak and a chubby, beet-red production assistant twisted the knife by chirpily announcing, "Dude, even *I'm* getting laid off this show."

Ever the ferocious defender of family values, Zorianna wasn't about to let my attack on the sacred institution of marriage go unchallenged. She seemed to feel my comments about marriage constituted a direct attack on her marriage, not a joking mock-condemnation of marriage in general.

Her voice rising steadily in anger, Zorianna spat, "Nathan, I have to say I really resent that comment you made about [marriage] being a poisonous institution. Clearly you've never been married, and with that attitude you never *will* be married!" Zo might have intended that last sentence as a curse but it felt more like a blessing.

Like Brad Pitt and Angelina Jolie in *Mr. and Mrs. Smith,* Zo and I were playing dirty and hitting below the belt. I didn't consider my "poisonous institution" line to be a personal attack on Zo any more than I considered Anderson's running joke about hating children's movies, children in movies, and children altogether to be a vicious condemnation of Zo and Zenga's adorable two-year-old daughter, Kit. But it would be hard to miss the personal nature of Zo's retort.

Then again, what right *did* I have to criticize marriage? Just because my father got divorced three times and my mother was so traumatized by her marriage to a man I literally consider the nicest, sweetest man in the universe that she had three more kids after her divorce without remarrying didn't mean I had firsthand experience with marriage's dark side. Nor did spending five years living alongside the collateral damage of busted-up families, divorces, and broken homes during my lengthy tenure as a guest of the Jewish Children's Bureau group-home system give me any special insight into the ways in which conventional forms of structuring relationships might be fatally flawed.

Though it could all have been a figment of my fevered imagination, I felt like Kim and I were flirting on national television during the *Mr. and Mrs. Smith* segment. While pontificating on the sexual heat generated by *Mr. and Mrs. Smith*'s sadomasochistic undertones, Kim struck me with surprising force on the arm. She hit me and it felt like a kiss.

At *Movie Club* our conversations were very infrequently just about movies: we often seemed to be reviewing stars and celebrities and each other as much as films. So I wasn't surprised that our *Mr. and Mrs. Smith* segment became a referendum on Angelina Jolie's offscreen persona, the mutated media construct of Brangelina, the relationship between Kim and me, and the validity of marriage as an institution. It's a marvel we got around to discussing *Mr. and Mrs. Smith* at all.

If the *Mr. and Mrs. Smith* segment inevitably devolved into a debate on marriage as a social construct, the next movie review escalated into a battle between good and evil, light and dark, the forces of sunshine and happiness and the glowering harbingers of doom and despair. What movie could possibly have inspired such heated emotions? Only *The Adventures of Sharkboy and Lavagirl 3-D,* of course.

Kim and Zo's agitated banter about *Sharkboy and Lavagirl 3-D* constituted either a verbal catfight or an epic battle between light and darkness, good and evil, played out in microcosm.

Here, for your reading pleasure, is a faithful transcript of what happened after Zo praised *Sharkboy and Lavagirl 3-D*'s "classic quality" and compared it to *The Wizard of Oz*:

KIM: I couldn't disagree with you more.

ZO: Surprise, surprise.

KIM: I wouldn't have liked this as a kid. It's not like *The Wizard of Oz*. It's not *Willy Wonka*.

ZO: [while pointing to Kim's throat] She's got the vial of blood around her neck. [making happy sunny hand gestures] I'm light, I'm light.

KIM: Call me an old curmudgeon . . .

ZO: [interrupting/answering] You are.

KIM: Because I don't believe in the Land of Milk and Cookies.

ZO: I do.

KIM: I didn't when I was five years old either.

ZO: I did. [once again gesturing to Kim's neck] And you've got some vial of blood around the neck. I just thought I'd point that out.

Later, after Anderson insisted Quentin Tarantino shouldn't have allowed Robert Rodriguez to make *Sharkboy*—a movie that sucks in all three dimensions—the skirmish continued. When Zorianna insisted that *Sharkboy and Lavagirl* would appeal to "real kids," someone inquired what exactly she meant by that. Was Zo suggesting that there were "fake" kids the film wouldn't appeal to? Zo replied affirmatively, suggesting that the only kids who wouldn't respond to Rodriguez's three-dimensional supergenius would be "the dark, evil children that [Kim] and Nathan will have together." Zo had a point. If Kim and I had children together, I'm fairly certain they wouldn't like *The Adventures of Sharkboy and Lavagirl*. Also, they would be dark and evil.

The producers sent out an e-mail before the Thornton taping admonishing only those who absolutely needed to be there to show up for it. Yet the morning of the show our crew expanded exponentially until it approached the population of China. People I'd never seen before and barely believed existed crawled out of the woodwork now that our humble basic-cable lovefest was going to be graced by a real, live movie star. There was electricity in the air. We were about to be visited by an honest-to-God icon, the real fucking deal, not just the dude who plays Carlos.

A good hour before Thornton arrived, Head Producer Guy chucklingly ran an idea by me. Wouldn't it be funny, he proposed, if the Makeup Lady Who Looks Like an Aging Stripper cut my hair into a stark buzz cut and wardrobe fitted me with gray slacks and a blue work shirt? Then, during the discussion of *Sling Blade*, I would remain silent until I was asked my feelings about the movie, at which point I would utter, in my best Billy Bob Thornton *Sling Blade* voice, "Um-hmmmmmm. I done seen that movie."

"Yeah, that'd be a real stitch," I muttered halfheartedly, at which point Head Producer Guy mercifully let the notion drop.

I nervously went out on the set and watched while Head Producer Guy and Zorianna went over her questions for Thornton. As we waited for Thornton, Zorianna showed everyone a cheap Xerox of the playbill for the show Thornton and Mr. Zorianna did together. It's a priceless sociological document, faded but fascinating, from "Original Material from Hell." Zenga and Thornton peer out at you from the cover, looking young and hairy and hungry and weirdly vulnerable in the way headshots of aspiring actors often do. In the bio part of the program Thornton boasts that he's racked up television and movie appearances "far too impressive" to list and was born in Belgium.

Zorianna beamed ecstatically. She was in her element, in

front of the camera, the center of attention, her giant choppers hypnotizing me with their blinding whiteness.

Then Mr. Thornton appeared, squeezed into skintight jeans and shit-kicking cowboy boots. He had an abashed, infectious smile, and while I'd never considered Thornton particularly attractive, he oozed nuclear sexuality in person. I'm not too proud to admit that I was a little starstruck.

After we finished taping, the crew and cast posed for photos with Thornton, who was asked to hold up a copy of the tenth-anniversary *Sling Blade* DVD and very gamely acquiesced. It was amateur hour all the way. After Thornton suffered through a harrowing gauntlet of photo ops, Kim and I cornered him and begin talking about Matt Helm and Elvis movies and assorted ephemera.

"It's a pleasure to talk to somebody in this town who actually knows what they're talking about. Normally people just wanna talk about, you know, vials of blood and stuff. We should grab coffee together sometime," Thornton drawled irresistibly.

For a good half hour afterward Kim and I experienced a weird celebrity afterglow. Billy Bob thinks we're cool! Billy Bob thinks we're cool!

That night's taping had a weird punch-drunk quality to it. We were working the night shift and though I was tired and loopy it was good to have Ridley back. When we came to our *Honeymooners* review, Ridley only half-jokingly suggested cutting it altogether. When Zorianna began her review he kept admonishing her to go faster, faster, faster, to waste as little time as possible on it. It was a dynamic I'd come to enjoy, Ridley's playful badgering of Zorianna. It had a third-grade quality to it, as if Ridley was antagonizing Zorianna because he couldn't admit to himself or to the other denizens of the schoolyard that he had a crush on her, and did not, in fact, believe she had cooties.

When the taping was over I felt an enormous sense of relief. A crushing burden had been lifted off my shoulders. After the taping we headed over to Residuals, where Kim and I talked about movies and I drifted in and out of other conversations long enough for Head Producer Guy to say something that sent shivers down my spine.

"You know, Nathan," Head Producer Guy half whispered conspiratorially, "I think we learned something today. If, God forbid, Ridley ever leaves the show, Zorianna could totally take over as host."

That last *Movie Club* taping marked the end of my auspiciously inauspicious television career, but my very own Homer Simpson would find a way to upstage her good ol' Grimey one last time.

Let the Omnisexual Fuckfest Begin!

Weekend
The Story of O

Jean-Luc Godard's 1960 New Wave masterpiece, *Breathless,* is a debut so bold and revolutionary that it seemed to single-handedly reinvent cinema. But by the time 1967's *Weekend* rolled around, Godard's love-hate relationship with everything made in the USA had devolved into contempt. With *Weekend* Godard *le fou* and his band of outsiders flamboyantly destroyed the glistening pop world they had lovingly created a mere seven years earlier.

In *Weekend* Godard mercilessly surveys the ugly machinations of a grotesque bourgeois couple (Jean Yanne and Mireille Darc) who have been slowly poisoning Darc's father in their bid to get their hands on his money as soon as possible. In *Weekend* Godard imbues everything he'd previously fetishized— fast cars, sex, beautiful women, American culture—with visceral disgust. Early in the film the gorgeous Darc robotically delivers a monologue about a depraved threesome involving the scandalously unhygienic use of eggs and milk as sexual aids. In another context Darc's story might have oozed kinky, transgressive sexuality, but Godard films it in a shadowy, unrelenting long take and sets it to dark, ominous music so the net effect is revulsion rather than eroticism. For Yanne and Darc sex has become just another degraded commodity to be doled out indiscriminately in the blind pursuit of pleasure. It's hedonism as nihilism, the pleasuring of the body as the death of the soul.

After being waylaid by an endless traffic jam that Godard elevates to an epic death rattle for the impending demise of consumer culture, Yanne and Darc embark on a surreal road trip that ends with a radicalized Darc indifferently devouring Yanne's cooked flesh. For Godard, capitalism had reached a debilitating endgame.

It took Godard seven years to go from the exhilarating, aesthetically revolutionary excitement of *Breathless* to the dispiriting, politically revolutionary apocalyptic madness of *Weekend*. My indefinable relationship with a heartbreakingly beautiful twenty-three-year-old University of Chicago grad student I call O traveled a similar trajectory from rapture to despair in only seven maddeningly ambiguous dates.

My first date with O was like seeing *Breathless* for the first time. I felt as if a new world had opened up to me. The universe suddenly seemed infinitely more exciting and cool and chic and bohemian and laden with possibilities. A radiant beauty with hypnotic green eyes, a shy smile, and a body that would send R. Crumb into an erotic frenzy, O was immersing herself in the world of polyamory, both as a field of academic pursuit and a lifestyle choice. Though she professed to have nothing but contempt for bourgeois concepts like commitment and monogamy, that didn't keep me, within an hour of meeting her, from dreamily planning our wedding or thinking about how our last names would fit together.

I realized early on that I was in way over my head. To borrow the old saw about capitalism, monogamy is the worst system we've got except for everything else. Polyamory is like Marxism: great in theory but impossible in practice. The problem with Marxism and polyamory is that they each deny mankind's true nature. Remove jealousy, greed, and possessiveness from humanity and both systems would flourish. But you'd also excise much of what makes us human.

Nevertheless, if O was intent on kick-starting a new sexual revolution, I wasn't about to complain. As the hours flew by and the liquor poured freely, little pink cartoon hearts emanated from my body. I didn't walk back to my apartment with her so much as float effortlessly back to my abode, where we soon became physically entangled and ended up in bed. My joy at finding myself in the act of sexual congress with such a heavenly creature intermingled with fretful self-consciousness.

As drunk, high, horny, and ecstatic as I was, I couldn't help but think about the clichéd nature of my pillow talk. Why couldn't I express the intensity of my ardor in language more eloquent than "Oh yeah. Oh yeah. Oh, God, that feels good"? I was deluged with visions of competing lovers reciting Yeats or Eliot before, during, or after orgasm, singing entire Verdi operas, or spontaneously composing award-worthy haikus about O's clitoris while effortlessly bringing her to multiple orgasms.

I was exhilarated to once again be experiencing the dizzy, mind-warping highs of infatuation. It was truly an altered state of consciousness, the only natural high that doesn't completely suck. No longer would I trudge down the street, just another of the walking wounded. No, from here on out I would strut like John Travolta at the end of *Staying Alive*.

Happy singing bluebirds would swoop down onto my shoulder and sing sugary ditties in my ear; charming woodland creatures would seek me out and befriend me. Everything would be perfect forever.

Sex suddenly seemed to be everywhere. Every interaction felt charged with erotic possibilities. No longer would sex be my enemy, taunting me, punishing me, excluding me from its primal, life-giving embrace. No, I would now be a sexual creature free of shame and self-doubt.

When O talked about polyamory that first evening, part of me was screaming, "No! You can't handle this! This cannot end well! This is a nightmare in the making!" but if I listened to the "rational, sane" part of my mind all the time, my life would be far less interesting. I'd miss out on the highs as well as the lows.

I was immediately hooked. I decided that I would pursue this relationship as far as I could even if it meant enduring a punishing gauntlet of pain and anguish. I started to think of myself as a "romasochist": someone willing to suffer through all manner of psychological agony for the sake of love, or at least lust.

My second date with O followed closely on the heels of my New York *Movie Club War of the Worlds* debacle, so I was even more agitated than usual. I rambled nonstop about the show, about life, about anything and everything as O looked on passively.

"Everything about you is so fast, you know? You talk fast. You move fast, you have fast hands. You might want to chill," she drawled slowwwwwwwly as we sat in her car outside my apartment after watching *My Summer of Love*. "Oh, and just so you know: I'm not into monogamy." She managed to make monogamy seem ridiculous merely through inflection.

She made it all sound so commonsensical, even intuitive, that the only reasonable answer seemed to be, "Me neither. Monogamy is a savage, barbaric notion best left to extinct tribes. Let the omnisexual fuckfest begin."

But I didn't say that. Instead I offered a mild variation, meekly asserting, "Oh, I think I may have picked up on ten or fifteen hints you so deftly scattered about. And rest assured, I more than share your contempt for monogamy," which was untrue only in the sense that I am a serial monogamist.

Hints? She unloaded clues and innuendo about her super-charged sex life into conversations with a linguistic dump truck. If I stitched together every allusion to kinky sex and decadent doings and set them to sleazy wah-wah funk guitar, I'd have an alternate version of *Behind the Green Door*, a story so lewd and lascivious it'd make *Deep Throat* look like the latest *VeggieTales* installment. She'd repeatedly set off ticking time bombs in my mind, startling proclamations that seemed worrisome at the time but revealed the full scope of their ominous portent anywhere from eight to twenty-three hours later, from vague intimations that she was tiring of "vaginal sex" to casual references to other guys she was still having sex with. Then there was her offhand remark that Radiohead's *Kid A* resonated strongly with her because she'd had an "explosive" sexual experience listening to it. I couldn't begin to fathom what that might mean. Would midgets be involved? National Guard units? Stagecraft? Magic tricks? Mime? The dark art of ventriloquism? Ritualistic sacrifice? The offensive line of the '97 All-Madden team?

O was at that adorable stage where college students raised in the most solipsistic society in history decide that Galileo had it all wrong and that the universe *really* revolves around them. She was still young and naïve enough to believe that the ideas espoused by professors somehow had legitimacy outside academia. Was I ever that young? No. No, I was not. I tumbled out of the womb with deep black bags under my eyes, a cigarette dangling between my lips, and a jaded look that said, "Is that all there is?"

For O, however, every half-baked idea or fuzzy notion felt like a revelation from God. Not long after dropping me off so she could, um, hang out with other, no doubt cooler, less manic people, she fired off an e-mail where she confided that she'd hung out with another male friend later that night and even though he wanted to fuck she nobly declined. To her this was a decision of massive, potentially life-changing importance. Where she previously empowered herself to fuck around indiscriminately, she now empowered herself to abstain from sex. At least for a couple of days. She seemed shocked and delighted that she'd somehow managed to spend several hours with two different vaguely fuckable guys in a single night without giving in to her animal instincts. I didn't have the heart to tell her that between first masturbating at thirteen and losing my virginity at nineteen I'd managed a Lou Gehrig–like streak of eight million sexless social interactions in a row.

O asked would I be OK with being "friends without benefits" in a manner that suggested I had no choice in the matter. O understood that she could control our relationship both by having sex and by abstaining from sex.

Alas, O didn't seem overly committed to celibacy. The next time we hung out we ended up back at her place, where we listened to the tremblingly sensitive sounds of Death Cab for Cutie and had fumbling, awkward, painfully self-conscious sex.

"I'm thinking about going on the pill. Then we wouldn't have to use condoms anymore. I'm sure you'd like that," O mused absentmindedly as she stretched out on her four-poster bed.

Though I was encouraged by the idea that O might view sex with me as something other than a regrettable aberration, my first thought was, "Wow! That's great! I've always wanted to play Russian roulette with my cock. Now I can!"

Later, O asked me what I thought about when she was talking.

"Whatever it is you're saying, of course," I replied automatically. She tried to ensnare me in a linguistic trap, to generate an unthinking response along the lines of "Your tits mainly. Sometimes your ass." It was the kind of question only someone deeply insecure would ask, someone who strongly suspected, not without cause, that the world had little interest in the inner workings of her mind or the content of her character.

I'd certainly been in relationships before where I tuned out much of what my partner was saying for the sake of my sanity. There were undoubtedly times when a girlfriend would pontificate endlessly about some pet obsession and her voice gradually stopped forming coherent words and became an indistinct blur of "Wonk wonk wonk wonk, wonk wonk wonk wonk wonk wonk," like the adults in *Peanuts* television specials.

I was naïve enough to imagine that I'd been welcomed into the Sacred Church of O for good. My delusion was short-lived, for after our third date O e-mailed to say, "We should probably talk."

I don't think the words "We should probably talk" have ever been followed by "about this lesbian make-out party I want you to tape" or "about this blow-job competition I want you to judge" or "about all the amazing things I want to do with you sexually."

No, those four little words invariably signal doom. As I walked to our appointed meeting place, I felt like someone about to be executed via a firing squad in an old Foreign Legionnaire movie. Don't those guys at least get a cigarette and a blindfold?

Nevertheless, I continued toward my doom, spotting O outside the coffee shop with a look that did little to allay my suspicion that I was due for an emotional ass-whipping of epic proportions. O had assured me before via e-mail that she wasn't going to lay anything "crazy bad" on me but I sensed impending disaster.

We nervously ordered a pair of Dr. Brown cherry sodas and sat down, a grim tension growing with each stilted, uncomfortable exchange. Our conversation went something like this:

> ME: So, you said you in your e-mail, "We should probably talk." It's been my experience that that always seems to mean "I have something excruciatingly painful to tell you that is going to cause you a whole world of hurt."
>
> O: Well, I hope it's not excruciatingly painful or anything, it's just that, well, I find the idea of a cock physically repulsive right now. I can only really see myself being with a woman.

If I had any self-respect I would have gotten up and walked away with the tattered remains of my dignity. Alas, if I had any self-respect I wouldn't have been there in the first place. O genuinely seemed to believe my response would be something like

"Oh, that's all it is! Good for you for making such an important realization! By all means, go forth and explore your sapphic sexuality! I shall never trouble you again with my physically repulsive cock!"

But I didn't want to conceive of a world without O. So rather than storm off, I confessed everything. I told her about my exhilaration after our first night together, about telling my family and friends about her prematurely, about the highs of acceptance and the lows of rejection. I gave her the whole sick, sad emotional roller coaster. Not one to quit while desperately behind, I began to confess every horrible thing that ever happened to me romantically: getting Judy pregnant the first time I had sex, the uncontrollable sobbing of partners during, before, or immediately following sex, the whole sorry lot.

Earlier O had mentioned that she'd read a self-help book for the group-sex crowd called *The Ethical Slut*. She claimed it had really amazing advice on issues like jealousy, so now that everything was on the table I asked meekly how exactly *The Ethical Slut* suggested dealing with jealousy. I was fascinated by the idea that there could be an intellectual answer to such an intrinsically emotional problem.

O's response was that the book urged readers to remind their partners that sex or physical love was not a zero-sum commodity, that it flowed like water and refreshed continually and could be given freely without diminishing. She said it was important to reaffirm the bond with your partner when they're feeling jealous or lonely, to establish that, yeah, you might fuck truckers or really nasty-ass polyamorous people with sagging potbellies and make-out vans and spray-on tans, but that doesn't mean you don't love your partner, just 'cause, you know, you're sucking some stranger's cock.

I was subscribing to the insane antilogic that has kept generations of sad fucks locked in doomed, impossible relationships: If I can only prove how much callous emotional abuse I can put up with, then the object of my desire will have no choice but to treat me with respect and dignity. When she sees what a pathetic human doormat I am, she'll have no choice but to accept me unconditionally!

Walking home that night, I felt castrated, emasculated, self-negated. By a curious coincidence I had received an earlier e-mail from a woman I'll call C, whom I had an impossible, doomed, semiunrequited crush on in college. Back in the day, I was having sex with B, who was in love with me while I was infatuated with her best friend, C, who lived with an even more pathetic fellow named Frank, who was hopelessly in love with C but was doomed to a lifetime of unrequited longing. It was one of those perfect little situations where the fates conspire to keep everyone from getting what they desperately want.

Frank went by the sobriquet Little Frank, an emasculating moniker that came to take on an existential as well as physical dimension. Although Frank was smart and handsome and likable and could probably have found a woman who'd treat him well, he instead chose a life of extreme masochism, living with C and spending every waking hour with her in the doomed hope that someday he'd be let back into her heart and bed, an exile no more. Little Frank was a wisp of a man, fair featured and slight. As he sank deeper and deeper into a hell of his own devising, he seemed to get simultaneously smaller and more indistinct until he was nothing more than a tiny little emasculated leprechaun, a human swizzle stick C could slip in her purse and use to stir her cosmopolitan at cocktail parties. The Incredible Shrinking Man, he had allowed himself to be transformed into a human accessory, a sentient fanny pack or man-purse.

Little Frank was a true romasochist of the highest order, a man willing to negate himself, his virility, and his self-respect for a woman who couldn't make him happy even if she wanted to. If romasochism were a sport, Little Frank would reign as its Mark Spitz, a juggernaut of poor decisions and self-sabotage future generations would look upon with pity and awe.

Was I turning into Little Frank? Would I someday be up on

a pedestal at the Romasochist Olympics, participating in the following exchange?

> Bob Costas: Nathan, you've managed a positively
> historic showing here at the Romasochism Olympics.
> Two golds for being an emotional doormat, two more
> for letting a woman stomp all over your heart, and an
> amazing fifth for being cuckolded. Tell the audience at
> home: how did you do it?
>
> Nathan: Aw, man. There are so many answers to that
> question. First off I'd like to thank low self-esteem,
> which has been there for me from day one, helping me
> make the bad decisions that got me where I am today.
> I'd also like to thank my mom for not being there.
> From my first Little League game to high school
> graduation, she had an unbroken streak of never being
> around. That really gave me a head start when it came
> to developing flawed relationships with women. Of
> course I gotta give props to my old man, who did a
> great job role-modeling dysfunctional relationships.
> And I can't forget my first girlfriend, who taught me
> that it was worth it to stay in a bad relationship
> because otherwise nobody will ever love you and you'll
> die alone and nobody will even notice you're gone until
> the stench becomes unbearable and the neighbors
> finally call the cops and have you thrown into an
> unmarked grave. Last but not least, I'd like to thank
> pornography for warping my view of sex and women.
> It truly takes a village to raise a hopeless emotional
> doormat, so I'd like to thank everyone! Damn, I almost
> forgot to thank the most important person! Thank you,
> O! I just know we're not going to laugh about this all
> someday!
>
> Bob Costas: Thank you, sir. Those were truly some sad,
> deluded words from a sad, deluded man.

That whole tragicomic evening was a grim omen of greater romantic horrors to come. Never knowing where I stood with O was bad enough. But she had a disconcerting habit of casually mentioning men and women she was having sex with other than myself. Finally I couldn't take it anymore and asked her not to talk about her sex life. She acquiesced readily. She may have fancied herself the James Tiberius Kirk of sexual exploration, boldly going where no woman had gone before, but she was not immune to sexual jealousy.

O then disappeared for a month. During that time *Movie Club*'s fifteen-episode renewal morphed into an abrupt cancellation. So I was feeling particularly vulnerable, especially since O had used that hiatus to travel to Montana to go hiking with her boyfriend-who-isn't-actually-her-boyfriend, went to a friend's wedding even though she totally hated the square-ass bitch he was marrying (and she was a bridesmaid even—can you believe it?), and lastly, and most ominously, to a polyamory conference. A polyamory conference, incidentally, is a gangbang with workshops. I didn't have a problem with O going to the conference. I just didn't want to hear about it.

So I was safe, I thought. I saw my therapist during my and O's monthlong separation and I told her that the exhilarating, manic, disconcerting highs I'd been experiencing had disappeared in O's absence.

"But, you know," the good doctor asked obliviously, "you're still 'together,' right? You're still 'with' her?"

I chuckled and tried to explain that when dealing with O, words and concepts like "with" and "together" lose all meaning. Free your mind, headshrinker lady! Throw out your little boxes and categories! I had no idea where I stood with O. Were we friends? Confidants? Lovers? Soul mates? Casual acquaintances? Sadistic sexual sociopath and her cuckolded, emasculated platonic friend? Rodeo clown and supportive gay sidekick? Sacred whore and accidental eunuch? Or did O and I exist in a world beyond labels, beyond accepted notions of how relationships should transpire? If this is what the sixties were like, I'm glad they ended.

We reconnected at a hippie coffee shop with maps all over the walls and a granolatastic travel theme called Kopi's. A sense of foreboding once again swept over me as I walked into the restaurant. I was too repressed to even order the "Libido Burrito" at Kopi's by its full name and now I feared I'd be learning all about the freaky goings-on at a giant convention for horn-dogs, sex fiends, and pervert-Americans.

I thought about springing the whole "my show's been can-celed" spiel right off the bat, but I let her dominate the conver-sation as she talked about the hiking trip (it was cool) and the wedding (it was awkward and bad and she stayed with a guy she used to fuck who's all weird and into drugs and crazy now) and her visit home with her mom (her folks are probably getting divorced and she couldn't be happier).

It was all just a prelude to discussing the conference, which I hoped she'd talk about in only the most abstract terms so that it would sound like a proper academic endeavor, not a flimsy excuse for a fuckfest. The conference, she said, was absolutely amazing. A magical, transformative, life-changing experience.

Wow. That must have been some gang bang. We were getting into hazardous territory but O ramped up to it slowly. She'd been a little skeptical about the conference beforehand, a little worried that the people would be creepy, but they were so cool. I mean, yeah, most of them were overweight and a lot of them were a lot older and not really attractive or anything, but they really *got* her, you know?

The conference began with a workshop on body image, which was clothing-optional but of course she had to be naked 'cause she's that type of girl. It was amazing, she told me, doing exercises where she did things like touch an old woman's naked body. It totally made her think about bodies in a whole new way. There were all sorts of cool workshops on things like jealousy, ethics, and even some weird New Agey thing called "Sexual

Kung Fu" that was all about transferring karmic energy to improve your sex life.

So far, so relatively nontraumatic. I was already in a tense, worried state but a deathly chill swept over my body when she said that she and a friend were hanging out on the last day of the conference—the climax, as it were—when a weird older guy came up to them and said, "I'm into flogging. Can I flog you?" Mesmerized by his powers of persuasion and rhetorical gifts, she said, "Yeah," but only if she and her friend could get flogged by this creepy old man at the same time. 'Cause otherwise, you know, it might be weird. So she and her friend went off with this stranger. He started slowly, rubbing O's body with soft pelts and material of different textures, and then, of course, he finally got to the whipping. That really turned O on, as did watching her friend get whipped.

O's monologue was rapidly turning into "What I Did on My Summer Vacation" by Marquis de Sade, but I couldn't look away. My facial expression eerily replicated Edvard Munch's *The Scream*, a timeless masterpiece found on countless dorm walls. I tried desperately to dissociate myself psychologically from what I was experiencing. Leave your body, Nathan! Leave your body. Go to that happy place in your mind where happy bunnies cavort and singing trees sway and no one ever talks about flogging or gang bangs.

This flogging only inflamed O's libido, so when she and her friend had to choose whether to end the conference by going to a show, a "cuddle party," or a sex party, she opted for the third choice. "The sex party," O said flatly, "was I guess what you would call an orgy." Long story short: she goes to the orgy and totally ends up getting serviced by, like, five or six guys. It felt amazing. She purred "amazing" for emphasis just in case I thought getting gang banged by a basketball team's worth of potbellied, garlic-breathed, balding old men was merely OK or moderately enjoyable, all things considered.

Then, just as she was getting ready to leave, the head of the conference called her over and thanked her for what he described as a "gift" she had given to the conference. He then began talking about the concept of a "sacred prostitute," at which point O started to feel weird and self-conscious. Getting gang banged by five or six strangers is one thing, but having someone compare you to a ho-bag, even a sacred one, was another matter entirely. I think what bothered O about the sacred prostitute concept was that it implied that she had entered the gang bang to pleasure others, as a purely selfless act. On the contrary, sex, to O, was exclusively about O's pleasure, O's control, O's power. The world existed solely as a mirror, useful only in that it told her that she was beautiful and brilliant and special and unique.

"So, how about you," O asked obliviously. "What have you been up to?"

"Well, my television show was canceled and all my hopes and dreams are shattered." But please, do go on about the gang bang! I tried to tell her about the show's cancellation but my train of thought kept getting derailed. My interior monologue went something like this:

Don't think about O getting gang banged
Don't think about O getting gang banged
Whatever you do, don't think about O getting gang banged
Seriously, I know it's probably beyond your powers of self-control at this moment, but it is vastly important that you not think about O getting gang banged

Needless to say, I was thinking about O getting gang banged. Usually words pour out of my mouth in a dizzying rush, but the best I could muster was a slow trickle. I felt like I was frozen, in suspended animation. I wished I could rewind the evening so I never entered Kopi's Traveler's Café, where I never put myself in a position to get hurt.

Hadn't I protected myself? Wasn't my sexual nondisclosure agreement with O an insurance policy designed to protect me from this tidal wave of sexual humiliation? This is what I get for not getting our oral contract ratified by a reputable notary public. I considered our verbal agreement an interpersonal Maginot Line that would protect me from traumatizing sexual revelations. I was wrong.

As I tried desperately to wipe the deer-in-headlights look off my face, O gushed that she finally felt like she belonged somewhere, that she felt like part of a loving and inclusive community of people who fundamentally, you know, *got* her.

Of course she had to share the news of her big revelation with everyone in her life, including her long-suffering friend, boyfriend, lover, and soul mate Julius. And her mother. "So I told my mom and she was really intrigued. She was all like, 'Can I go with you next time?' and I was like, 'Whoa, you're not even divorced yet!'"

Apparently going to a swingers' party with your mom is only wrong if she's married. Otherwise, it's fun for the whole family! O's Unrequited Love Brigade picked up a new member during her historic gang bang. One of the good souls whacking away at her with his joint had professed his love for O to the head of the conference, who in turn informed O, who, despite finding the guy creepy, gave him her number so he could call during O's last trip to my apartment. He at least boasted the same halo of righteousness O projected onto everyone at the conference. They could then shrink this halo and use it as a cock ring or meld it together to form a pair of handcuffs. Alternately, they could flog beautiful young women with their halo, if they were into that kind of thing.

I felt utterly dispirited, for one of the things O and I shared— beyond our poisonous narcissism and shameful self-absorption— was the innate sense of being a perpetual outsider, a voyeur, trapped between worlds and forever on the outside looking in. Now O was advertising that she finally belonged to a group, that she'd had her road-to-Damascus moment and was now going to devote her life to "the Movement." Rather than liberating herself from the oppression of phony dogmas, she had simply chosen a different phony dogma. O seemed convinced she had found the truth when all she had found was a separate set of lies, one that replaced the unfeasible fiction that one person could be all their soul mate would ever need forever and ever (amen) with the big lie that you could go through life fucking whoever you want whenever you want without leaving a trail of emotional and romantic carnage in your wake.

As the evening went on, the already fraying threads holding us together in a weird, unclassifiable relationship began to unravel. When I met O she was an intellectually insecure, uncertain young outsider trying to figure out her way in the world. But now she boasted the glazed, self-satisfied look of a zealot.

As the conversation wound down, the awkward silences grew longer and more excruciatingly tense. Not knowing what to say or do, I meekly suggested, "Wanna go over to my place?" O meekly accepted.

I entered the apartment before O so I could turn on the lights, so I didn't see O's face when I said to her, as nonbitterly as possible, "So I guess you're not physically repulsed by the idea of a cock anymore?" If my goal was still maintaining a relationship with O, then this was a grave tactical error. Nobody likes to be confronted with their own words. People especially don't want to be confronted with their own violent contradictions.

I could feel the mood of the evening change with that question. O tartly replied, "Not really, 'cause there wasn't really a lot of penetration involved." How dare I suggest that fucking five or six dudes was somehow incompatible with finding male genitalia physically repulsive?

Fuck. There was no turning back now. While O went to the bathroom I announced plans to make myself a drink. A stiff, stiff, stiff, stiff, stiff, stiff drink, I declared theatrically. I was going to get very drunk indeed.

"Hey, have you ever seen *Da Ali G Show*?" I asked her. She hadn't but had heard good things, so I put in the DVD without pressing play so that a maddeningly annoying blast of deliberately cheesy electronic music played on an endless loop as the DVD menu materialized before us.

Before we could sit down to watch the show, I offered to make O a Vanilla Stoli and Sprite—her favorite—and, in an utterly uncharacteristic move, confronted her directly.

"Hey, do you remember back when I asked you not to tell me about other guys that you were with?" I asked slowly, unsteadily, bracing myself for one of the more agonizing conversations of my life.

"Yeah," O said coldly, arms folded in the classic defensive posture, looking grimly down at the floor.

"I'm wondering then why you told me tonight about what happened at the conference. How did you think I would react?"

"I guess I wasn't OK with not being able to share *my truth* with you." Share your truth? Breast cancer: that's a truth that has to be shared. Schizophrenia. The death of a parent. I got gang banged by six strangers and it was awesome? Not so much.

"Yeah, but you know how painfully insecure I am about these things. How did you expect me to respond?"

"God, you see everything in terms of how it applies to you even when it doesn't. And I guess also I feel like you hog all the problems."

Hog all the problems? Hog all the problems? I was willing to let O have sex, youth, beauty, and all the power in our relationship. Wasn't I even entitled to my own neuroses?

Feeling like I had nothing left to lose, I let it all out. I told O about how painful it was for her to constantly thrust her sexuality in my face, only to coquettishly demur, "But it's not for you," how every time I saw her I wondered if she'd say something that would decimate my fragile self-worth, how she made me feel guilty and wrong for wanting to have sex with her, how I had no idea where I stood with her or where her head was.

"I just figured that since we weren't physically intimate anymore that it didn't really matter what I told you," O said.

"You know, O, I gotta say that we've had a higher ratio of

agonizing conversations about the nature of our relationship in proportion to time spent together of any relationship I've ever had. Easily. No other relationship comes close."

"Yeah. I love having those kinds of conversations. I love getting to the truth of things. That's what I live for."

What kind of a sick twist derives pleasure out of agonizing conversations? Like any unreasonable human being, I abhor agonizing talks about relationships because they are the favored habitat of Ugly Truths. And if I know anything about Ugly Truths, it's that they have a disconcerting habit of traveling with Even Uglier Truths that just can't wait to ambush lost souls. The Ugly Truth Kid is easily the most damnable varmint ever to plague a shaky romance. He never rides anywhere without like-minded colleagues, such as Galveston's much-feared Maybe I'd Still Be Attracted to You If You Hadn't Gotten So Fat, the I've Always Had a Thing for Your Best Friend Kid from Waco, and his drunken twin, I've Always Had a Thing for Your Hot Sister Too. They're a damnable lot of rogues, but no single outlaw is quite as feared or deadly as Tucson's I Never Loved You in the First Place.

Elvis Costello sang that in hell "My Favorite Things" is constantly playing but it's always the Julie Andrews version and never John Coltrane's. To me, hell is being married to a perpetually twenty-two-year-old Jennifer Connelly who only wants to have century-long conversations about what's wrong with your relationship.

I finally asked O the question that had been on my mind since we first started going out. "How do you even perceive our relationship?" I hoped against hope that her answer wouldn't plunge a ten-inch stiletto heel into the squirming, beating, writhing heart I'd set out so enticingly in front of her.

"I suppose as a tenuous friendship based on . . ."

I don't recall anything she said after that because I was so hung up on the phrase "tenuous friendship." Tenuous friendship? Tenuous friendship? Tenuous friendship? Seriously. Tenuous friendship?

In the background *Da Ali G Show* DVD continued to repeat abrasive Euro-disco on a perpetual loop that sounded increasingly demonic. I thought about the confession scene from *Weekend* and its jarring use of music as a horrific counterpoint. In just a few months everything I'd initially found so exciting about O—her ripe sexuality, her disdain for bourgeois conventions, her strange combination of insecurity and brazen self-confidence—began to seem ugly and destructive. Like Godard, I was repulsed by what once turned me on. It used to be sugar but it was shit to me now.

O's monologue marked the bitter end of our relationship, an emotional carpet-bombing that left only ashes and rubble in its wake. This was *Weekend* all right—an emotional apocalypse from which there is no return.

As O stood there in my living room, shut off, nestled in a cocoon of narcissistic self-righteousness, the reality of the situation hit me. There would be no glorious future together, no gorgeous, brilliant, utterly fucked-up half-breed Jewish babies. O wasn't "the one." She wasn't my soul mate or best friend or lover. There would be no eureka moment in the future when O would realize how badly she'd treated me and devote her life to making it up to me. There'd be no threesomes with nubile coeds, no ecstatic afternoons spent drinking and fucking and smoking and then drinking and fucking and smoking some more.

I had applied to be CEO of O's soul but was given an unpaid internship instead. This, apparently, was how O perceived our relationship: she would regale me with stories about the guys and girls she fucked, sometimes in groups, sometimes separately, and I would listen patiently, tossing in a "You go, girl!" or "Good for you!" when appropriate. I would forever be the eunuch at an orgy.

As I tried desperately to fall asleep that night, words and phrases kept flashing through my mind, one after another: "I like to flog people," "I guess you could call it an orgy," "I was *really* turned on," "sacred prostitute." The mental image of O getting pounded by five or six random dudes ran on repeat as I tried futilely to sleep, as grainy, raw, and degraded as a poorly preserved seventies porno loop.

The last words I spoke to O after walking her part of the way home—fuck that chivalry shit—were "Thank you for letting me be a part of your life." I am a dedicated collector of bitter ironies. Those were the most bitterly ironic words I could imagine.

Please Don't Confront Me with My Failures, I Have Not Forgotten Them

Siskel & Ebert
Siskel & Ebert & Roeper & Ridley & Z & Me

Pauline Kael made film criticism pop, but Gene Siskel and Roger Ebert dragged it permanently into the mainstream. Everyone could relate to either Gene Siskel, the elegant Yale grad with the sonorous voice, or Roger Ebert, the populist cinephile with his gargantuan appetites and irrepressible lust for life. *Siskel & Ebert* gave film criticism an accessible, recognizable pair of faces, names, and thumbs. In part because they toiled in television, that most influential and toxic of mediums, they became synonymous with film criticism for multiple generations.

As a child, I was fascinated by television movie critics, those sometimes mustachioed, strangely avuncular bachelor types in reassuring sweaters who got paid good money to see movies before everyone else did and talk about them on TV. I couldn't imagine a sweeter gig. I had no idea what Siskel and Ebert made but assumed that everyone on television was rich, famous, and pursued everywhere by hordes of screaming fans like the Beatles in *A Hard Day's Night*.

Then one day a producer for *Ebert & Roeper* called to ask if I wanted to audition to be a guest critic on the current incarnation of the mother of all movie-review shows. Granted, it wasn't

Siskel & Ebert, but unless Gene Siskel rises from the grave to angrily reclaim his vacated throne (I imagine zombie Siskel quipping, "I told you to save me the aisle seat, bitch!" as he prepares to munch on Richard Roeper's succulent cerebellum), it was as close as I was going to get.

As a child, pop culture was an invaluable form of escape. As an adult, pop culture is my life. I went from rapaciously consuming pop culture to creating it. Now I had a chance to be part of something I grew up worshipping.

Alas, like my *Movie Club* experience, my strange flirtation with Roger Ebert's venerable television institution morphed slowly but surely from being the fulfillment of my childhood dreams into a dark comedy.

Even before I received that not-so-fateful call from *Ebert & Roeper,* my life overlapped and paralleled those of Siskel and Ebert in strange ways. I grew up in the same North Side Chicago neighborhood as Siskel (Rogers Park, stand up!) and attended the same elementary school (Dewitt Clinton) and high school (Mather). I would have gone to the same college as Siskel as well if not for Yale's ugly prejudice against accepting students with anemic grades, lackluster test scores, and bottomless contempt for extracurricular activities.

When I was fifteen years old my cousin Janice took me to see Siskel give a speech about the Academy Awards at the local private school Siskel's children attended, Francis Parker. During the Q&A section I anxiously raised my hand and asked Mr. Siskel how he felt about GLAAD picketing the Oscars to protest negative depictions of gays in *The Silence of the Lambs* and *Basic Instinct.*

"I'm sorry, what is GLAAD?" Siskel asked earnestly, perhaps perplexed as to why garbage bag manufacturers were picketing the Oscars.

"They're the Gay and Lesbian Alliance Against Defamation," my fifteen-year-old self squeaked uneasily. Siskel then launched into a fairly involved response about how minorities tend to occupy supporting roles in movies and supporting roles tend to be broadly drawn and stereotypical. A notable exception, he argued, would be the black guy from *The Last Detail*.

When Siskel couldn't quite remember the name of the black sailor from *The Last Detail*, I spied an opportunity to finally put all those wasted hours spent devouring Leonard Maltin's film guides, Cajun style, to good use.

"Otis Young," I offered proudly, feeling altogether overly pleased with myself.

"That's right!" Siskel beamed. "You're going to be a great director someday!" From his lips to God's ears. Alas, God must have turned off his hearing aid that day. Prove me wrong, Hollywood motherfuckers! Prove me wrong!

Seven years later I made my first trip to the Chicago screening room, a tiny little theater on the sixteenth floor of a nondescript building where films are shown to critics before their official release. In a bid not to be noticed, I made a strategic choice to sit as far from the front as possible, a technique that kept me from attracting the unwanted attentions of teachers throughout high school and college. I uneasily planted myself in the back row next to a table. I was mortified when Siskel marched in and sat down next to me with a look of mild annoyance on his face.

The first film that day was *Wild Things*. Now, if you haven't seen *Wild Things*, it's the movie where Denise Richards wears a bikini and makes out with Neve Campbell. There might also be some sort of "plot" and other characters but that's all I remember about it. Being terribly unoriginal in my sexual tastes, the only thing I find more arousing than buxom fake schoolgirls in skimpy outfits is buxom fake schoolgirls in skimpy outfits making out. So there I sat, mere inches away from a towering icon of my childhood, hoping that no one would notice that my South had risen again with great force and urgency. Viva la Confederacy!

Halfway through the second film of the day, a miserablist Ed Burns snoozer called *No Looking Back*, Siskel tapped me on the shoulder and in that hypnotic voice of his, with its strange phrasing, unexpected emphases, and gentle rising and falling, very paternally said, "Young man, you are sitting in my seat and I wish to eat a sandwich. Now, I am going to point to a chair"—he then pointed to a chair in the row ahead of us—"and I wonder if you'd be kind enough to sit in it." I was so intimidated that if he'd asked me to stand on my head and sing the Who's *Quadrophenia* in its entirety, I'd have done so in a heartbeat. I scurried to my new seat feeling terribly ashamed.

Then again, I always identified more with Ebert. One of my first big interviews, and my all-time favorite, was with a hilariously profane Russ Meyer, who talked at length about how Ebert's marriage tragically cut short his pussy-wolfing escapades (Meyer is of the rare breed of man capable of using terms like "pussy-wolfing" without irony, shame, or self-consciousness). One particularly ribald anecdote involved Meyer luring Ebert away from his script-writing duties on *Beyond the Valley of the Dolls* so he could copulate with a naked, willing groupie lying prone on a couch specially designed, in Meyer's overheated imagination at least, to facilitate comfortable procreation between lecherous pussy-wolfers and their willing concubines. Ebert's response? An ecstatic cry of "Hollywood!"

Hollywood indeed. Five years later I made my own strange exodus from Chicago to Hollywood courtesy of Head Producer Guy, who made his name producing *Sneak Previews* during the Siskel and Ebert era. Head Producer Guy was fond of quoting Siskel's maxim on pimping the reviewing game: "Write it once, sell it five times." What Siskel meant was that he could write a review for the *Chicago Tribune*, perform it on *Sneak Previews*, syndicate it, then recycle it for local news and an appearance on *The Tonight Show*.

Later Head Producer Guy delusionally insisted that Disney was considering replacing *Ebert & Roeper* with *Movie Club with John Ridley*. I doubt there was a shred of truth to Head Producer Guy's assertion, but later developments proved *Movie*

Club was on *Ebert & Roeper*'s radar even if the rest of the world pretended it didn't exist.

About a year after *Movie Club*'s cancellation I got a call from David Plummer, an *Ebert & Roeper* producer. "So, Nathan, as I'm sure you're aware, Ebert is still recovering and until he's up to full strength we're going to be rotating in some guest critics. Kind of like how we did when Siskel got sick, but, um"—his voice then took on a horrible gravity—"obviously without the same end result [Siskel's death]. Anyway, we really like your stuff at *The Onion* and, uh, that show you did on AMC and were wondering if you'd like to audition to be a guest critic on the show. You were one of the first people we thought of."

Would I like to audition to appear on *Ebert & Roeper*? Sweet motherfucking Lord, I'd give up my first newborn to appear on it.

"Of course I'd be interested in auditioning. I loved doing *Movie Club* and Ebert's an icon. It's an honor just to be considered."

I got off the phone in a daze. It felt like a dream. Before his cancer battle, Ebert hadn't missed a show in thirty-one years. Now I was inexplicably a candidate to fill in for him. It seemed too good to be true.

When I went to the mailbox the next day, EBERT GIVES THUMBS-UP TO GUEST CRITICS screamed out at me from the front page of the *Chicago Sun-Times*. It was surreal. Inside Robert Feder wrote that "invitations [to audition for guest critic slots] would be extended to prominent talent, executives, and critics associated with the motion picture industry." And also Nathan Rabin. Aw yeah. I'm totally "associated with the motion picture industry."

I wrote and sent Plummer my script. Twenty minutes later he sent me an e-mail gushing, "This is great and really funny!" I was flattered but I also knew that there was no script on earth too great or funny that I couldn't fuck it up with my sweaty, panicky, flop sweat–addled delivery. Also, I sensed that Plummer's the kind of guy who doles out exclamation points so liberally that they lose their meaning. Here's a tip, dear reader: use exclamation points sparingly, if at all. Otherwise you just sound like somebody who shouts all the time. Do you really want to be that person? I think not!!!!!!!!!

Minutes after I got Plummer's e-mail the lights went out and my computer shut down thanks to the first blackout of my adult life. It was a sweltering hot summer day and without my electronic doodads the only means I had of entertaining myself was listening to a tape recording I'd made of my review just before the lights went out. The night before the audition I drank lukewarm Miller Lites and listened to myself opine on the merits of *Lady in the Water* over and over and over and over again in the pitch-black darkness until I'd discovered a whole new form of narcissistic madness.

The next morning I entered the downtown ABC studios where *Ebert & Roeper* is filmed at around one forty. A producer led me to the makeup chair, where I gazed adoringly at my own image. It was then that a troublesome thought hit me for the umpteenth time: this opportunity had come about solely because a man I respected and admired had contracted a horrible disease. It was the definition of a mixed blessing. I wanted to convey to the crew and producers of *Ebert & Roeper* my excitement over the possibility of doing their show, but I was walking a very fine line.

Maybe that's why there seemed to be such a weird, borderline funereal atmosphere on the set that day. Roger Ebert was and is *Ebert & Roeper,* and the fact that his recovery was taking longer than expected must have filled his staff with anxiety.

Finally, a stylish fiftysomething makeup woman, who I later learned worked for Frank Sinatra, introduced herself and asked if I'd ever been in makeup before. I replied that I had, sometimes even in connection with television appearances.

"Are you excited to be here?"

"Very much so. It's an honor just to be considered for a spot on a show like this. I grew up watching *Siskel & Ebert,* so the idea that I might actually fill in for Ebert is incredibly exciting."

"Good, good, I'm glad to hear it. Because Ebert's not only the biggest critic, but he's also the best and the most respected too, isn't he?"

"Oh yeah. None of us would even have film-critic jobs if it weren't for Ebert. He's done more than anyone to popularize film criticism. And no matter what, you always get the sense that he's a man who really loves film. That comes through in everything he does."

"Yeah. I agree. It's like Siskel used to say: we've got the best job in the world."

"Definitely. A bad day at the movies is better than a good day anywhere else."

Then the makeup woman left. I sat there staring at myself in the mirror and remembered that for the first few years of my career whenever I told somebody that I was a film critic their response, more often than not, was, "So, you gonna be on *Siskel & Ebert* someday? Ha ha ha."

I always found that question incredibly annoying. So I was relieved when I could answer it with something other than an irritated "Probably not. Ho ho ho. Boy, never heard that one before!" The first time this happened was when I visited my then-girlfriend's brother's house and his wife asked me what I did for a living. I told her I was a film critic and she responded, predictably enough, with, "So, you gonna be on *Siskel & Ebert* someday?"

Puffed full of pride, I beamed, "Probably not, but I am developing a *Siskel & Ebert*–style movie-review show with a producer who used to work on *Sneak Previews* with Siskel and Ebert. That's kind of exciting."

This answer flummoxed her. Her knowledge of film criticism went no further than knowing that there were famous guys named Siskel and Ebert who had a very successful television show in which upturned and downturned thumbs were involved.

So when I told her I was working on a similar show of my own, my answer simply didn't compute. "Oh" was her nonresponse.

It could be worse. For the first few years of my career, whenever I told certain family members I was a film critic, their answer was often, "Really? 'Cause your cousin Lloyd wanted to be a film critic. Now he's a hot dog vendor at Wrigley Field."

The "now he's a hot dog vendor at Wrigley Field" line seemed designed as a cautionary warning that if I persisted in pursuing a silly, impractical career like film criticism I'd end up slinging disreputable meatlike products to drunken yuppies.

The irony is that hot dog vendors at Wrigley Field probably make more than film critics. I'm not convinced that hot dog vendors don't contribute more to society than film critics as well. Nobody at a baseball game ever found themselves thinking, "Man, am I ever hungry. How come there's never a film critic around when you need one?"

Then it was go time. As I waited for David Plummer to take me to the set, the gravity of the moment hit me with full force. In my mind Eminem nasally whined, "You only get one shot, do not miss your chance to blow / This opportunity comes once in a lifetime." Then Nice & Smooth chipped in with "Like a rhinoceros my speed is prosperous / and pure knowledge expands from my esophagus," a couplet that, come to think of it, didn't have much to do with anything.

I exchanged pleasantries with Plummer, a large, middle-aged bald man who bears an unfortunate resemblance to hulking, baby-faced character actor Pruitt Taylor Vince. Then Plummer and the director walked me to the set. They both went out of their way to make me feel comfortable and loose, but when we passed through an industrial-looking part of the building I found myself thinking, "This is it. They're going to take me to a secluded closet and pump a bullet in my brain. But first they're going to laugh maniacally and mock me for even thinking that an alum of a forgotten pop culture footnote like *Movie Club* would ever have a shot at appearing on *Ebert & Roeper.*"

I realize that that sounds terribly paranoid and fatalistic, but in today's hypercompetitive world it's never enough to merely defeat the opposition; no, you need to humiliate and destroy them as well, then come after their children and their children's children with a spiked bat. That may seem harsh, but I'm the kind of guy who defines success as drinking the still-warm blood of my enemies from the hollowed-out skulls of my friends.

Then we finally made it to the unexpectedly cavelike *Ebert & Roeper* set. It was a surprisingly small space, intimate even, and I was relieved to see that my camera and the teleprompter were less then ten feet away from my aisle seat. For the purposes of the audition, Plummer filled in for Roeper, and the physical and psychological difference couldn't have been more pronounced. Instead of the svelte, handsome Roeper, I was partnered with a big, bulky, friendly bald dude.

"Ah, so we meet again, my old archnemesis the tele-prompter," I observed as I prepared to read my script.

"One, two, three, and go," boomed the unseen director's dis-embodied voice through a loudspeaker somewhere on the set. I started to race my way through my copy, only to be stopped near the end of the first paragraph.

"That's good, Nathan, but can you slow it down a little and make it more conversational? Also, you wrote a funny script, so really play up the comedy of it."

"Right, right. First-take jitters. I'll definitely slow it down."

"And Nathan?"

"Yeah?"

"You might want to keep your hands away from your face. You're doing that a lot."

"Right, right. Got it." Damn me and my frightening, inexpli-cable hand gestures and seizurelike head movements! After that my delivery got looser and more playful. I had anticipated bum-bling my way through the review but then nailing the crosstalk banter, but it didn't pan out that way. I grew increasingly comfortable delivering my script but the looming crosstalk terrified me.

When I finished my review I turned to Plummer, who empathetically said, "You know, Nathan, I couldn't agree with you more."

No! This was terrible. When I see a movie with my friends I want them all to agree with me ('cause I'm always right), but when you're doing television you want as much conflict as possible. For the first time in my professional life I found myself desperately missing Zorianna as a foil. If only Zorianna were here, I thought wistfully, she'd say something to angry up the blood. She'd doubt Shakespeare's relevance or argue that the opening weekend gross of *Monster-in-Law* represented the unassailable will of the American public, and I'd launch into verbal warfare intuitively. She'd bring out the pop culture gladiator in me.

I needed something to play off following my *Lady in the Water* review. I couldn't very well respond with "You agree with everything I said?! Oh yeah? Well, fuck you, asshole! I agree with everything you say too, fuckface!"

Eager to make the most of this opportunity, I'd worked out a long list of observations I wanted to make about *Lady in the Water* during the crosstalk. But the moment Plummer stopped agreeing with me, the only thought in my head was, "Oh shit. What are you going to say now, genius?" It felt like hours passed between Plummer's comments and my own instead of a second or two.

After going on and on and on for a few minutes about *Lady in the Water,* the unseen director suggested we tape a second version of the crosstalk.

"Sounds good to me!"

"Oh, and Nathan, some of your best comments came at the very end, when you were being more blunt. That stuff was great, so in this next go-round do more of that, be more blunt if possible."

"Got it." I had my marching orders. I was to be blunter, more spontaneous, and crazily off-the-cuff.

Once the cameras started rolling again, the first words out of my mouth were, "To be a film critic is to exist in a state of perpetual disappointment." Fuck, fuck, fuck. Whose idea of blunt or spontaneous is that? I might as well have started speaking in Renaissance English, foppishly mincing, "What a knave this saucy Night be! Verily, his latest endeavor, a trifling abomination promenading whorishly in multiplexes under the moniker *Lady in the Water,* be a pox upon the land!"

As if my internal heckler needed company, I started to imagine that an eight-inch-tall pixie of Head Producer Guy hovered over my right-hand shoulder watching in abject horror as I fucked up the audition.

"Jesus, Nathan," this figment of my imagination admonished me, "what's with this 'substantive criticism' fag shit? Nobody goes for that. Especially not on TV. Hit 'em with the dick jokes! That's what you're good at! That's your superpower! That's what televised film criticism's all about: booze, broads, and dick jokes. And what's with all the Poindexters around here? Shouldn't that Plummer chump and the director be waiting in line for Lou Ferrigno's autograph at a comic book convention? Jesus, it's a total sausage fest around here. What's the point of having the number-one show if you don't surround yourself with hot chicks with big tits? This place is depressing me! I'm going to go advise some guy at a strip club. Then the scenery would be more to my liking. See you around, pally. Oh, and good job blowing the audition!"

The producers seemed disproportionately impressed by the "ad-libs" I threw into my *Lady in the Water* review. As Robin Williams and various battle rappers will attest, the key to being a good improviser is giving the appearance of improvisation without ever actually improvising.

After three takes of the crosstalk and my review, the unseen director said, "Well, Nathan, you did great. Do you want to do another take or are you comfortable leaving it as it is?"

Of course I wanted another take! I wanted a million more

motherfucking takes! I didn't want to leave until everyone was ragged from exhaustion and convinced I'd delivered the single most perfect audition in the history of show business.

"Uh, yeah. I guess I'm fine with it as it is. Unless you guys want another take."

"No, we're good. Thanks for auditioning. You did a great job. Give me your address and I'll send you a tape of the audition as soon as possible," David Plummer told me as he escorted me to the exit.

As I stepped out into the bright sunlight from the darkness of the movie-review-show set, I only had two things on my mind: Paul Newman and getting a ride home. OK, that's not true, but I have always wanted to rip off the first sentence of S. E. Hinton's *The Outsiders*. Now I have.

Actually, as I stepped out into the bright sunlight from the darkness of the movie-review-show set, I thought about how I always swing for the fences but my audition was a ground-rule double at best. I'd failed. On a rational, intellectual level I knew I'd turned in a respectable audition but throughout that first day I experienced flashes of panic where I was overcome with the unmistakable feeling that I'd fucked up.

Plummer sent me a DVD of my audition about a week later that I was much too neurotic to watch. I figured I'd wait until I was a drunken, bitter has-been railing angrily against a world that had passed me by and then force my traumatized grandchildren to watch my audition over and over again to remind them of a halcyon time when their grandfather came close to making it. I envisioned having the following conversation with my theoretical future granddaughter:

THEORETICAL FUTURE GRANDDAUGHTER: But, Granddad, I don't want to watch your *Ebert & Roeper* audition! I've watched it a thousand times!
ANGRY, DRUNKEN, BITTER FUTURE ME: And you'll watch it a thousand more times! I coulda been

somebody! I coulda filled in for the most famous
movie critic of all time! I coulda shared a fake balcony
with Richard Motherfucking Roeper! Now he's
America's beloved emperor-for-life, but back then he
was just the name following the ampersand on Roger
Ebert's show.

THEORETICAL FUTURE GRANDDAUGHTER: You scare me
when you drink, Granddad.

ANGRY, DRUNKEN, BITTER FUTURE ME: And you scare
me when I'm sober! Now make yourself useful and
pour Grampy some sipping whiskey. My drink ain't
gonna refresh itself! [cackles maniacally, then passes out
in pool of vomit]

Not a rosy scenario. Eventually *Ebert & Roeper* announced
its first guest critic. What titan of the film criticism world did it
select? Saucy Anthony Lane? A. O. Scott? Foxy Manohla Dar-
gis? The painfully earnest David Denby? Nope. No, *Ebert &
Roeper* instead went with Jay Leno, a man who, along with
Larry King, can be counted upon to express orgasmic delight
over any movie where the actors remember most of their lines
and the cinematographer shoots the film largely in focus. For its
second guest critic *Ebert & Roeper* chose Kevin Smith.

You can imagine my surprise when I learned the identity of
Ebert & Roeper's third guest critic: John motherfucking Ridley.
It was a mind-fuck. Ridley doing *Ebert & Roeper* was like one
of those weird dreams where one aspect of your life collides
unexpectedly into another. Like when you dream that your spin-
ster aunt is also your high school geometry teacher, only she's
wearing a Nazi storm trooper outfit and speaking Esperanto and
waving around a barb-wire-covered dildo. What? You've never
had that dream? Never mind.

"No, no, no!" I wanted to shout out bitterly. "Guesting on
Ebert & Roeper and reviewing movies is my thing! Writing
movies, plays, comic books, opinion pieces, and graphic novels,

doing NPR commentaries, directing, producing, collaborating with George Lucas, and having millions of dollars is Ridley's thing! No fair, no fair!"

I never imagined that a year after I spent a year traveling from Chicago to Los Angeles to appear on a movie-review show with John Ridley, John Ridley would be traveling from Los Angeles to Chicago to appear on a movie-review show. It was surreal, ironic, and crazily backward.

The next guest critic after Ridley was Toni Senecal, a New York entertainment reporter infamous for appearing on the news in a bikini and serving as Queen Mermaid in the Coney Island Mermaid Parade. The guest critics that followed were a mixed bag of celebrities (Fred Willard, Aisha Tyler, Mario Van Peebles, Harold Ramis, John Mellencamp) and actual critics (the *Tribune*'s impressive Michael Phillips, A. O. Scott, David Edelstein, Kim Morgan).

I had pretty much abandoned all hope of guesting on *Ebert & Roeper* when I walked into the *Onion* office one Wednesday afternoon.

Keith had a maddeningly enigmatic look on his face. "Hey, Nathan, guess who the next guest critic on *Ebert & Roeper* is going to be?"

"It's Zorianna Kit, isn't it?"

"Yeah, it is. I was debating whether or not to tell you because I figured it'd ruin your day."

I'd seen this coming since *Ebert & Roeper* selected the suspiciously Zorianna-like Senecal. But it still sent my mind reeling. I laughed grimly. The universe was enjoying yet another joke at my expense. I didn't watch Zorianna's episode for the same reason I don't slice open the webbing between my fingers and pour lemon juice in it: why subject yourself to the pain?

"I'm fucking Frank Grimes. I'm fucking Frank Grimes," I muttered impotently to myself at my desk as I tried to make sense of life's unfathomable perversity. But if there's a whole lot of Frank Grimes in me, there's a good deal of Homer Simpson as well. In the final tally I'm probably 60 percent Grimey bad-luck magnet, 40 percent Homer Simpson lucky bastard.

Actually, scratch that. In the end I'm 60 percent Frank Grimes, 30 percent Homer Simpson, and 10 percent moderately likable gay everyman. I would be foolish to contradict the wisdom of the American people.

My luck oscillates wildly. My mom's crazy but my dad's a saint. My television show devolved into a ridiculous farce but it was great fun while it lasted. I went through hell growing up but now I have an amazing job and a semicharmed life. I am, at the end of the day, blessed. With the benefit of hindsight it's clear that being passed over as a guest host for *Ebert & Roeper* is one of those slights that seems terribly important at the moment but grows less significant with time.

Ebert's absence from both the airwaves and press screenings during the long, arduous process of recovery left a black hole–like void at the screening room: you could almost feel Ebert's absence on a physical level. It seemed to alter the molecular structure of the room. It was as if a bright, burning light, magnificent in its heat and intensity, had been extinguished, albeit temporarily. The king was gone. The world seemed a less joyful place without him.

Then one day he returned, a specter of his formerly boisterous self. The booming voice and explosive laugh that could fill up a room were cruelly silenced. His skin took on a ghostly pallor and his mouth was perpetually agape. But if Ebert was unmistakably diminished physically, his will and determination were a wonder to behold. He started popping up at the screening room all the time regardless of how inconsequential the film.

I remember being shocked to see Ebert manning his aisle seat at a ten o'clock screening of *Bratz: The Movie,* an already forgotten tween abomination based on a line of slutty dolls popular among young girls who don't know any better. Nobody would have felt let down if Ebert had skipped this particular bit of pop ephemera.

There was only one reason a mute, cancer-stricken Ebert

dragged himself out of bed that morning to see a film people stopped caring about seconds after the opening credits rolled. It's the same reason Ebert still writes five or so lengthy film reviews every week in addition to composing essays, interviews, and columns despite having accrued enough money and fame for several lifetimes: Roger Ebert loves movies. He loves every aspect of them, as well as the dying art of film criticism. When you radiate that kind of love, it has a way of boomeranging back to you. I don't think it's at all coincidental that Ebert was named by *Forbes* magazine as America's most beloved pundit not long after the *Bratz: The Movie* screening. People can sense that there's something genuine and sincere at the core of Ebert's being.

In the end Ebert's example means more to me than appearing on any single television show. Ebert has created a legacy of passion and commitment to film and film criticism that serves as an inspiration not just to me but to every film critic who grew up in his outsized shadow. On a practical, pragmatic level I also appreciate that Disney executives don't have to sign off on my deriving inspiration from Ebert's example. They can keep me off *Ebert & Roeper*. But they can't take that away from me.

I grew up desperately wanting to be somebody else. But I've learned to let go of El Pollo Loco and Nathan Rockwell and Larry Miller and embrace being me. When my byline started popping up on the *A.V. Club* over a decade ago, I no longer felt the need to hide behind a pseudonym or an alter ego. I was finally comfortable being Nathan Rabin. Or at least comfortably uncomfortable.

A few years back I was invited to a dinner honoring foster parents for the JCB. I was introduced as a group-home boy made good by the president of the JCB, at which point my father lunged for the microphone and offered to say some words. I wasn't surprised: my father has never been able to resist an open microphone. When we were kids my sister used to joke that Dad showed incredible restraint in not pushing our cantor offstage during Shabbat services and taking his place.

I was mortified, and with good reason. When my father makes a speech it's never a question of whether he'll embarrass me or not, it's just a matter of how. True to form, my father started out shakily.

"I just wanted to thank the JCB for taking such good care of Nathan and stuff, in terms of giving a clothing allowance every month and making sure he had food to eat . . . ," he began.

He then said something I will remember until my dying day. "Now, you might be wondering why I'm sitting down while I talk, and the truth is I'm not wearing a belt or anything, and if I stand up my pants will fall down."

Some sons are crippled forever by their father's impossible expectations. Others can never live up to the their fathers' daunting legacies. I have a father who tells strangers that if he stands up his pants will fall down. In that moment I had an epiphany.

I would never have a normal dad or a normal life. And that was perfectly OK. In fact, it was beautiful. I love my dad *because* he's such a strange and colorful and incorrigible character, not despite it. Besides, normality is overrated. When I think about all the time I wasted feeling guilty and ashamed about things I should have embraced long ago, it fills me with guilt and shame.

Back when I was just a pint-sized bundle of neuroses I lived in fear that people would someday find out my secrets: that my mother had abandoned me, that my family was poor, that I'd spent time in a mental hospital and grown up in a group home. Now I'm willfully exposing my secrets to the world. I'll leave it up to you, dear reader, to determine whether that is ultimately a sign of maturity or immaturity, hard-won wisdom or shameless emotional exhibitionism.

You can't always get what you want. Sometimes you get stuck with the worst possible outcome. Sometimes an opportunity you desperately desire goes to someone who represents everything you hate about the world. Sometimes a trip to the emergency room turns into a month in a mental hospital. Sometimes five or six days in a group home become five or six years.

Sometimes a fifteen-episode renewal turns into a cancellation. Sometimes "Please don't tell me about anyone you're having sex with" gets misinterpreted as "Please tell me about how wonderful it was getting gang banged by five strangers."

But that's OK. Throughout my life I've experienced crippling lows where I felt like I couldn't possibly go on, when it seemed that Vice Admiral Phinneas Cummerbund had me licked. But the darkness always dissipated.

Pop culture played a crucial role in my survival. That's ultimately what I'd like people to take away from this book: the lifesaving power of imagination and the glory of survival. I see this book as a blackly comic ode to the overlooked glory of punching through the darkest of nights to get to the dawn.

But since this is a book about pop culture and imagination, it requires—no, angrily demands—a big finish. I've always had a weakness for the show-stopping finales of zany sixties comedies, so I'm going to borrow my ending from 1968's *Candy*. In it, our guileless heroine, having endured a punishing gauntlet of zany, ribald, and ostensibly comic misadventures, stumbles in a blissful haze through idyllic rolling green fields where she encounters nearly everyone she's met along the way in a rapturous celebration of, I dunno, whatever the hell it is *Candy* is rapturously celebrating. (Sex? Love? Freedom? The mind-blowing amount of drugs the cast and crew must have consumed?)

A film much nearer and dearer to my heart, *Pee-wee's Big Adventure,* has a similar ending. It is finally time for the Big Rewind, as I watch my entire tangled history unfold before me on a seventy-foot drive-in screen in Technicolor, CinemaScope, Odorama, and 3-D. But I don't have to watch it, dear reader. *I lived it.*

So, if you'll indulge me, I'd like to bring back everyone in my life. I'm bringing back the island of misfit boys from the group home, still wearing their scars on the outside, and the Wolfsheims, and the fuckups from Meadow Lane, and the lunatics from Le Château, and my biological mother, and her glorious bastard brood, and my colleagues from *The Onion* and *Movie Club*. I'm bringing back O and Judy and every woman who ever rattled my soul and my beloved sisters and father and uncles and aunts and cousins living and dead. The sun is shining. A soft wind blows. As I lead the assembled in a pop culture hymn to survival, I finally feel free.

Paperback Bonus Track

My Penis Is a Stupid Idiot

"Stay Up (Viagra)"
Comical Misadventures in Impotence

Like Shel Silverstein's Giving Tree, pop culture has a genius for giving us whatever we need whenever we need it. When we're feeling sad, it consoles us. During periods of deep depression I've often found comfort in revisiting the familiar, reassuring worlds of *The Simpsons,* The Beach Boys' *Pet Sounds,* and the Beatles' *The White Album.* When we're feeling lost or overwhelmed it can make the world seem less scary and unknowable. But every once in a while we experience a masochistic need to subject ourselves to pop culture that pours salt in open wounds and mocks our pain.

I had never understood sexual masochism until I read *The Adderall Diaries: A Memoir of Moods, Masochism, and Murder* by my Jewish Children's Bureau doppelgänger, Stephen Elliott. Elliott couldn't control the physical abuse he suffered as an adolescent, but by becoming a sexual masochist as an adult he was able to exert control over his pain. He could establish boundaries and ground rules and safe words. He could choose to find pleasure and release and catharsis over something that once brought only misery.

For similar reasons, I've found myself attracted to songs that seemed to derive sick pleasure from my romantic or sexual anguish. During times when I've felt powerless, it was a way of controlling my pain: by immersing myself deep in whatever ailed me I hoped to transcend it.

By a happy or unhappy coincidence, I stumbled across a brassy, insanely infectious Donna Lynn song co-written by Mick Jagger and Andrew Oldham called "I'd Much Rather Be with the Girls" from the supernifty *One Kiss Can Lead To Another: Girl Group Sounds Lost and Found* box set (it even comes in a shoe box!) the night O delivered her speech about how she found the idea of a cock physically repulsive and could only see herself being with another woman. In a masochistic fever, I played the song over and over again, imagining the chorus—"I'd much rather be with the girls than be with you"—was directed specifically at me. The two events were, of course, wholly unrelated. "I'd Much Rather Be with the Girls" is a defiant celebration of female solidarity in the face of romantic disappointment but as I wallowed in self-pity I imagined the words coming out of O's mouth.

I couldn't control how O treated me but I had the power to transform the hurt and rejection I felt into a grim farce. The juxtaposition of discovering, on the same night, "I'd Much Rather Be with the Girls" and being told by a lover that she found the idea (and, I would imagine, the reality) of a cock physically repulsive struck me as a strangely inspired cosmic sick joke.

That's how I've historically dealt with pain. I've turned darkness into dark comedy. I've tried to find the amusing anecdote in every formative trauma. It's a means of transforming a negative into a positive, though I can't escape the feeling that it's a bit of a cheat. That's why I admire that Elliott doesn't try to find the humor in the horrors of his past, that he lets his prose bleed and ache instead of reflexively going for laughs.

A more recent example of psychosexual pop culture masochism involves the song "Viagra (Stay Up)," the first single off producer-turned-rapper 88-Keys's criminally slept-on 2008 debut *The Death of Adam. Adam* doubles as an encyclopedia of sexual pain and humiliation that centers on the travails of the title character, a hapless everyman who is led astray and ultimately destroyed by his hormonal urges. 88-Keys's concept album offers a guided tour through relationship hell with stops along the way for venereal disease ("Burning Bush"), unwanted pregnancy ("Close Call"), and friendships that stubbornly refuse to turn into something more ("Friends Zone"). But "Stay Up (Viagra)" is the most agonizingly relevant song in the tale that is about to unfold.

From the time Big Bank Hank stole Lois Lane from Superman by promising to bust her out with his supersperm (which he contrasted with what he derisively refers to as the Man of Steel's "little worm") in Sugar Hill Gang's "Rapper's Delight," hip-hop has been a land of endless potency populated exclusively by invulnerable superstuds. So the notion that a hip-hop song would touch upon impotence is borderline heretical to the genre's macho code. Not surprisingly, guest rapper Kanye West (who also executive-produced his best friend's album) and 88-Keys (who inexplicably employs vocal distortion techniques that make it sound like he's rapping on a CB radio) rhyme exclusively in the third person about an unfortunate soul alternately plagued by premature ejaculation and erectile dysfunction who's the subject of jeering laughter since he can't "rise to the occasion." But it's the chorus—a sample alternately admonishing the hapless subject of the song to "Stay up," laced with occasional cries of "Viagra!"—that seemed to implicate and mock me during one of the more tragicomic periods of my sex life. For three difficult months those words invaded my thoughts at inopportune times. They taunted and challenged me, nestling deep within the most vulnerable recesses of my subconscious. Just as I reconfigured "I'd Much Rather Be with the Girls" as O's personal anthem, "Stay Up (Viagra)" seemed to comment directly on the sad decline of my once raging libido. When I was fourteen, pretty, and in a state of perpetual arousal, having an erection meant I was alive. But by the time I reached my mid-thirties it took a constitutional amendment for me to get a spontaneous erection.

Now, the Good Lord blessed me with eyes that don't see, ears that don't hear, a nose that doesn't smell, a sturdy hump, insomnia, male-pattern baldness in my mid-twenties, and chronic depression. Thankfully, he also graced me with a mind sharp enough to realize the fundamental uselessness of every other part of my body.

That's not entirely true. For He also gave me a penis that more or less worked. So why did I find myself, not too long ago, in the waiting room of the boner doctor, hoping that he would be able to prescribe me the latest boner medication to aid me in my debilitating boner problem?

My sordid saga of tragedy, then triumph begins seven years ago, when I was introduced to Amber, a friend of a friend. She was twenty-two, a recent college graduate and a vision of gamine beauty with a bob of soft red hair, big doe eyes, and milky, impossibly long limbs. I was smitten. Enraptured. Hopelessly infatuated.

We began a nonstarting four-month quasi-courtship. I think she liked the idea of me—a writer with a great job and intriguingly tormented past—more than the reality. In theory I was fascinating. In reality I was a chubby, balding, pasty depressive. It was a perversely chaste fling: she never once touched my cock. Now, my penis is not Aladdin's lamp. If you rub it, a genie will not pop out. No wishes will be granted. But it's not covered in poison ivy either.

Finally our tenuous bond dissolved into nothingness, a victim of Amber's profound ambivalence and my unwillingness to continue to pursue a relationship that had clearly reached its expiration date.

Amber would then e-mail me every once in a while and we'd get together every year or so. I don't know what I expected from these annual dinners. I suppose I hoped that I could either rekindle a flame that never burned bright or that some halcyon day I would look at Amber and my dizzy infatuation with her would be gone. I would be freed of a painful crush. She would become just another woman, not an impossible, unattainable, irresistible object of desire.

That never happened. She remained as adorable as ever. My crush refused to acknowledge the innate hopelessness of the situation, the impossibility that this shiksa goddess and I could ever have a future together.

Then one night everything changed. I sat down to dinner with Amber and without preamble or warning, she began gushing animatedly about the profound sexual awakening she was experiencing. "I don't know what it is. I turned twenty-nine and all of a sudden I became as horny as a teenaged boy. I started having sex dreams every night and masturbating constantly and fingering myself. It's like I woke up one morning and suddenly had this volcanic sex drive. Me and my girlfriends are definitely enjoying this *Sex and the City* lifestyle."

If I were in a Frank Tashlin movie the glass of wine that I clutched in my hand would start boiling and frothing uncontrollably before shattering as my body language became tense and coiled. Amber had undergone a strange metamorphosis from prude to fearless sexual adventurer. She couldn't stop talking about sex. She opined extensively on the relative merits of contemporary pornography versus the genre's 1970s golden age and wondered if she should become a sexual surrogate. A woman who'd never expressed much interest in sex suddenly couldn't talk about anything else.

I was shocked. And delighted. And a little terrified. I've never been one to talk about sex. I feel that it is an intensely private matter that should be discussed only with your partner, therapist, pastor, and everyone who reads your books.

Amber was bipolar during our initial relationship. No longer. She felt she'd been misdiagnosed and had stopped taking her pills.

So I resolved not to mention anything even remotely related

to bipolar disorder. It shouldn't have been difficult. After all, how often does the topic come up? Yet in a fit of temporary Tourette's, I suddenly started dropping constant references to it, nervously blurting, "Oh man, this whole process of writing a book and getting blurbs and putting my entire life on public display, it's this incredible and incredibly manic-depressive experience. It's so bipolar! It's just one manic high followed by one crushing depressive low after another."

The rest of our meal together was much less dramatic. After dinner we gravitated to a bar where we imbibed potent libations and a delightful old drunk regaled us with stories of jailhouse misadventures past. As we left the bar Amber grabbed my hand and I leaned in and kissed her. We continued to make out in her car, and I breathlessly inquired, "Wanna go back to my place?"

I like to think of my home as the apartment equivalent of the portrait of Dorian Gray—a fetid hellhole that reflects the dissolute state of my soul. It has literally reduced ex-girlfriends to tears. I try to hide my shame from the world. I have four cats, one of whom weighs an impressive thirty pounds, so my apartment habitually reeks of wet cat food, litter, and despair.

Yet the subinhabitable state of my apartment did little to cool Amber's ardor. "I am really, really aroused right now," she announced as I fixed her a drink and scrambled to make my apartment look presentable. This, dear reader, may have been some sort of signal. A woman who had never stopped occupying valuable real estate in my mind was suddenly broadcasting her willingness, even eagerness, to go to bed with me.

It was as if I had hit the ball deep into left field and was rounding second and the third base coach was waving me home and shouting, "Run, run, you damn fool! The left fielder just had a fatal heart attack, the center fielder is blind, and the rest of the team has inexplicably headed to the locker room early. Dash home, as there is no conceivable way they can throw you out!"

Nevertheless, having gotten further with Amber in the last four hours than I had in four months seven years earlier, I decided not to press my luck. That night Amber slept in my arms, a look of beatific contentment on her face.

I didn't make love to Amber until the next time we hung out. Having sex with a woman who orgasms easily and often is like playing a pinball machine that dispenses twenty free balls every time you bump it: it feels great but it doesn't feel earned. Being an inveterate Jewish Midwesterner raised on a diet of repression and shame, I am of the mind-set that bringing a woman to orgasm should be like everything else in life: difficult, time- and labor-intensive, and doomed to failure more often than not.

I have such painfully low sexual self-esteem that when a woman seems to enjoy having sex with me—a concept I have a hard time wrapping my head around—I insert ironic air quotes around every expression of pleasure, as in "'Oh God,' 'Yes,' it feels so 'good.' 'Fuck me,' 'Fuck me,' you 'magnificent fuck beast.'" So I assume that Amber wasn't really, really aroused that first night in my apartment so much as she was "really," "really" "aroused."

So when Amber came I assumed it had everything to do with glorious changes her body was experiencing and nothing to do with me. I had spent the last seven years wondering what it would be like to have sex with Amber. I had built it up to such a ridiculous extreme that I couldn't help but feel disappointed. It was pretty good but not the earth-shattering, paradigm-shifting explosion of delight I'd anticipated. I left my apartment the next morning feeling strangely empty. After seven long years, I'd finally slept with Amber. Yet the world remained the same. The people on the Brown Line El train still looked like they'd rather be anywhere else. Food didn't taste any better. I was the same me. I hadn't been sprung from the prison of self.

The next time I saw Amber we went to a bar for the birthday of one of her friends. As I purchased drinks, Amber pointed out a gentleman who looked a little like Jack Black with an unflattering soul patch and confided, "I got *really, really* drunk on my birthday because I was talking to that man over there and I had a friend come over and say, 'You might want to cool it a little. You know he's married, right?'" Then, choosing her words carefully, she continued, "I guess I'm just . . . naturally flirtatious."

By the time we got back to her apartment at a little past three in the morning, I was a little drunk, a little exhausted, and a little unnerved. We got to her bed and as soon as I slipped on a condom my erection disappeared. It would not return. A cold chill ran through my body. No! I started to panic. This couldn't be happening! After all these years of pining I had finally made it to the promised land and my penis decided to lie down and play dead. Lazarus refused to rise from his grave.

I started rifling through my file of masturbatory fantasies for something that would bring the dead to life. Finally I settled on number 36, right between Tabitha Soren at Spring Break and Daisy Fuentes in a bikini (I watched a lot of MTV during my peak masturbatory years): Amber sucking my cock. That ought to do it.

Then I looked down at Amber with her mouth around my flaccid cock. No! This couldn't be happening! For a seeming eternity Amber unsuccessfully tried to get me hard. I felt a shame I'd never experienced before. I was mortified.

My penis has always had a strange relationship with the rest of my body. If my brain were a basketball player it'd be a Bill Bradley/Phil Jackson type, an overgrown egghead who whiles away the hours reading books on how Heisenberg's uncertainty principle can improve their jump shot. My penis, however, is the world's most limited role player. He sleeps 99 percent of every day, then is roused from his perma-slumber and called in solely to slam-dunk. That's all he does. He gets hard and he orgasms. It's pretty fucking simple. That's all that's required of him. And now the insolent little bastard couldn't even do that. He was saying, "Sorry, Coach. I just don't feel like dunking today. If you need me I'll be taking a nap on the team bus."

I experienced powerful cognitive dissonance. Amber never looked more beautiful. I wanted her with every fiber of my being except, you know, for the ones that could actually do something about it. I felt sorry for Amber. You poor, dear, sweet child, I wanted to tell her, you might as well utter a silent prayer to St. Jude, for you are pursuing a lost cause. I tried to console myself that it happens to everyone but I couldn't bring myself to believe that. No, this shame was mine and mine alone. I became convinced that no man in the history of the universe had ever experienced this agony besides myself.

I developed a pathological hatred of my penis. The smug little bastard seem to be taunting, "Yeah, this whole making love to a beautiful woman who desires you thing isn't really my bag. But I'll be more than happy to help out if you want to jerk off to Pussycat Dolls videos when you get home."

Being unable to maintain an erection turned me into a lesbian. All I wanted to do was hold Amber in my arms and cuddle and talk about feelings and maybe put on an Indigo Girls album. In what I hoped would be a moment of profound connection, I looked at Amber and said, "I feel such tenderness toward you."

She looked back at me uncomprehendingly and replied, "I don't know what that means."

I left Amber's apartment the following morning a dispirited man. A spirit of fatalism swept over me. I was convinced that I had experienced my last erection, that I would lurch through my remaining years a eunuch. My sex life was over. I imagined a crude gravestone reading

NATHAN'S SEX LIFE

1995–2009

IF ONLY HE HADN'T USED UP

HIS LIFETIME SUPPLY OF ORGASMS

BY MASTURBATING SO COMPULSIVELY AS A TEENAGER

In light of this unforgivable lapse I decided I had no choice but to quit my job, renounce Western materialism, head to the mountains of Tibet, grow a long, wizardly beard, and devote the rest of my cursed existence to contemplating the big questions: Why are we here? Does God exist? Why couldn't I get an erection with Amber's mouth around my cock?

When faced with a crisis, my mind's first instinct is to overreact flagrantly. When I had a test I was unprepared for as a child, I'd find myself hoping that I'd get hit by a bus. That way my classmates would be forced to take the dreaded exam while I'd lie there cool as a cucumber in my hospital bed, with nothing to worry about beyond my future as a paraplegic.

Similarly, when an ex-girlfriend asked if she could move some of her stuff into my place and crash there for two weeks and I came home to discover that she'd moved everything she owned into my apartment and planned to stay there indefinitely, I found myself daydreaming about faking my own death, then living incognito on the road as a hobo. I'd carry my bindle from town to town, hop freight trains, grow a manly stubble, and eat all my meals out of rusty tin cans. That somehow seemed preferable to asking her to leave.

There was a sane and reasonable explanation for my temporary inability to maintain an erection. I'd been on powerful antidepressants/sleep aids like mirtrazapine and trazodone for close to a decade, and erectile dysfunction is a common side effect for both. Furthermore, from the time I lost my virginity, I'd been stoned pretty much every time I had sex. It was a way of quelling my crippling self-consciousness and silencing the voices inside my head telling me that I didn't deserve to have sex, that it was dirty and shameful and wrong. And I was never too keen on condoms. To paraphrase Hunter S. Thompson, I hate to advocate having unprotected sex while high on illegal drugs (within the context of a monogamous relationship, of course), but it's always worked for me. Or at least it did.

But who wants to be sane and reasonable in a situation like this? When pondering a series of possible explanations for a problem, I invariably choose the one that entails being punished by an enraged God. My therapist had a different, less dramatic explanation.

"Maybe the Li'l Sergeant is trying to protect you. Maybe it realizes that Amber isn't right for you and this is its way of showing it," she theorized.

"That's impossible," I spat out. My therapist is a wonderful, blissfully blunt woman, though she does have a disconcerting habit of telling me I'm nowhere near as crazy or dysfunctional as I think I am, which is a terrible thing to tell anyone, especially me. I will admit, however, that it was odd hearing her use my pet name for my cock. "My penis is a stupid idiot! You're giving it way too much credit. The first time I had sex I made the biggest mistake of my life. It's never protected me in the past. Why would it now?"

I began taking Wellbutrin (bupropion), an antidepressant doctors sometimes prescribe to offset the erectile dysfunction caused by other antidepressants. I'd taken buproprion in the past when depression had killed my sex drive. It had only one minor drawback: it drove me insane. I became agitated, moody, deeply paranoid, and filled with incoherent rage. I couldn't sleep until the wee hours of the morning. Every night my thoughts would race a mile a minute and I'd replay all the mistakes I'd made during the day, lingering masochistically on every faux pas and perceived social misstep. Sure, it rendered me a paranoid, self-loathing lunatic, but it made my dick hard and my waist small (it also curbs the appetite). I was shallow enough to consider that a fair trade-off.

The next time Amber and I were together I was able to orgasm but it was an empty victory. It took forever for the Li'l Sergeant to salute. Amber seemed powered by a sense of dogged determination more than anything else. I was but a formidable challenge. She kept saying, "It's like a dance," to which I was tempted to reply, "I'm no fucking good at dancing either."

It didn't help that Amber would occasionally say things like, "You're Jewish. Have you ever worn one of those beanies?" that highlighted the impossible gulf between us. I enjoyed spending time with Amber, but sex wasn't the only place where the magic failed to happen.

After one more bout with impotence I decided to take pre-emptive action. I looked up a list of "sexual health" doctors recommended by the good folks over at Viagra and decided to call the first doctor on the list, a Dr. Aaaron A. Aaaardvark (somehow I suspect that wasn't his real name). It was one of the more difficult calls I've ever made. It entailed making the following concessions to myself:

1. I was wrestling with impotence.
2. It had gotten bad enough that I was now willing to make the health and vigor of my erection a medical issue (and now a matter of the literary record).
3. I was willing to discuss with a trained medical professional my inability to maintain an erection.

In films and literature, impotence invariably functions as an external symptom of deep soul-sickness. Impotent men are tormented depressives who drink too much and luxuriate in self-hatred. They're broken, shattered men who've lost all hope. Was I one of these men? After my first bout with impotence, I asked myself whether a life without sex was worth living. The best I could come up with was "Maybe?"

Sex is the purest, most powerful manifestation of the joy of being alive. That is why it terrifies me so. I tremble daily before life's unimaginable splendor. Good scares me more than bad; I am all too comfortable with the geography of sadness. Happiness is infinitely more frightening because it's so heartbreakingly fragile. If sex is life, then impotence is death in miniature. It's a brief glimpse into a great cosmic void.

So I steeled myself for a gauntlet of humiliation and made the call. When the receptionist inquired about the nature of my problems I croaked out, "Erectile dysfunction." The words tasted like ash in my mouth. Is there an uglier euphemism than "erectile dysfunction"? "Impotence" sounds tragic, sad and emasculating. "Erectile dysfunction," in sharp contrast, sounds tragic, sad, emasculating, and like a horrible venereal disease. That's why I prefer the term Limpdick Motherfucker Disease. It's vivid, it's punchy, and it's descriptive. It doesn't obfuscate. It possesses an admirable candor.

In the waiting room of the boner doctor I spied a strapping high school football-player type with his cute girlfriend. I thought briefly about approaching the girl after her boyfriend went in to see the doctor and cooing, "Words of wisdom: drop the zero, and get with a similarly afflicted but much older and less attractive zero."

I wondered if the receptionist looked at the lost souls in the waiting room every day and thought to herself, "Look at all these limpdick motherfuckers. Bunch of pathetic quasi-men. Not an erection among them."

Finally I was let into a room and saw a doctor who asked what I did for a living.

"I'm a writer."

"That's great. Who do you write for?"

"*The Onion.*"

"Oh wow. I love *The Onion*. And you're Nathan Rabin, eh? I think I recognize your name. I'll have to keep an eye out for your byline in the future."

I was simultaneously flattered and disturbed. Praise is always appreciated, but the boner doctor's office is the last place you want to be recognized, short of a men's-room circle jerk at the Manhole.

Then the primary doctor came in and I explained the situation to him.

"So you're thirty-three and in generally good health, eh? It's probably psychological more than anything. Have you considered Viagra?"

The boner doctor gave a sample pack of boner pills and sent me on my way.

I didn't hear from Amber for about a month. This did not bode well for the future of our relationship, which was militantly, pathologically casual at best. Alas, I made a grave tactical error the next time I spoke with her on the phone and humiliated us both with a naked display of overwrought emotion. I believe my exact words were, "Hey, I haven't seen you in a month. I've missed you."

After a pregnant pause, she replied, "Oh." After another, even more pregnant pause, she continued, "huh." She nevertheless forgave me and we made plans to see Roberto Benigni's one-man show, *I Talk Abouta the Dante's Inferno, You Lovea Me, We Go on Moontriptogether Witha Da Language,* later that week.

Following the show we perambulated about and ended up at a bar near her apartment. She was reluctant to go back home because she was having roommate troubles. Now, Viagra takes an hour to work, so it requires careful planning. For the first time in my life I found myself thinking, "Will my penis be inside someone in sixty minutes?" and plotting accordingly. So at last call I dropped Pfizer's magical blue diamond and hoped for the best.

A short while later we entered her bedroom and I lay on top of her in silent rigidity. I had achieved lift-off! Yet even as she came the experience was profoundly empty. I didn't experience pleasure or exhilaration so much as a dull sense of relief that I was able to perform adequately. Even that might have been a bit of a stretch.

I left her apartment the following morning with a profoundly hollow feeling in the pit of my stomach. My ability to rise to the occasion changed nothing. I still didn't really know Amber. I was discovering at thirty-three what most people learn a decade earlier: sex without emotional intimacy can leave you feeling sad and alone.

She evidently felt the same way, because she drove across town ostensibly to return a shitty watch I'd left at her apartment but also, she announced ominously, because we needed to talk.

I got into the passenger seat of her parked car and she said that she hadn't seen me in a month because she'd been going through some heavy shit. An ex-boyfriend she still loved dearly had a new girlfriend. She was taking it hard. She was crying all the time, but it felt *really* good to cry.

"I really like you but I wonder if we just don't have sexual chemistry," she said, to which my subconscious thoughtfully added, "you limpdick motherfucker." I couldn't blame her. She was at a stage in her life where sex was a source of constant, unimaginable pleasure and excitement. I was at a stage where sex was an ongoing source of anxiety and torment. "Don't get me wrong, it's not the end. I just need time to figure some things out," she said in a way that made it apparent that it was the end. I had been halfway dating Amber. Now she had halfway dumped me. I was one quarter devastated.

During all the time I met yearly with Amber I wanted two things; to consummate our relationship or to be freed of my infatuation with her forever. In another of life's bitter ironies, I had gotten exactly what I wanted in the worst possible way: it was one of those monkey's paw situations where you learn to be careful what you wish for.

It was a deliciously moot point, however, for not long after the conversation in the car something gloriously unexpected happened. I fell in love: truly, madly, deeply, and with a ferocity and passion I never imagined possible.

The agent that brought us together was, of course, a pay-per-view prank special called *Juiced,* starring a deeply inebriated O. J. Simpson. It somehow seems right that O. J. would play Cupid and unite me with the woman of my dreams, for O. J. is my guardian angel. I imagine him floating high in the clouds, a halo hovering over his charmed visage, smiling benevolently upon me. Oh sure, O. J. might not technically be dead yet, but he's done so much good for me that I think God will give him a free pass and sneak him in early. Besides, what has the man ever done to anyone other than score me two hundred dollars as a teenager and find me true love as a thirty-three-year-old?

Our story began eight years earlier, when I visited my younger sister, Shari, in Marietta, Georgia. At brunch one fateful afternoon I was introduced to the older sister of one of Shari's friends, a woman who requested, for reasons known only to her, to be called Cadence Caraway. She was the single most beautiful woman I had ever met, with alabaster skin, a glorious mane of black curls, and hypnotic hazel eyes. She was also seventeen. She became my ideal of beauty, the standard against which all other women fell short. I spent at most an hour with her, yet her gorgeousness, sparkling wit, fierce intelligence, and deep, sexy voice made an indelible impression on me. In a desperate bid to form some connection with her, however transient or ephemeral, I offered her a free subscription to *The Onion,* a ploy that never failed to not work.

It was the longest of long shots but maybe, just maybe, somewhere down the road, when she was less jailbaitastic and I was less of a writhing mass of neuroses, something might happen between us. Oh, who was I kidding? Nothing was ever going to happen. But every once in a while I like to afford myself the luxury of delusional hope.

Years went by and that sliver of hope faded, though the memory of that afternoon in Georgia remained vivid in my mind. Then one evening I posted a blog piece on avclub.com about *Juiced,* the aforementioned affront to everything that is decent and just in this world, and Cadence commented on it and asked if I remembered her and if it was OK for her to use my post for a class at the Jewish boarding school in North Carolina where she was teaching. I was overjoyed. That sliver of hope made a miraculous return.

Then one night Cadence contacted me via a popular social networking site and, giddy with Dutch courage, proposed that we might be compatible. This struck me as the single most ridiculous notion I'd ever heard. Why would anybody want to be compatible with me? As the previous three hundred and something pages convey, I'm a bit of a fucking mess. Moreover, why would someone beautiful and brilliant and young and viva-cious be interested in a sad old husk like myself? Yet her words proved improbably prescient.

I had never been much of a phone-talker. I always preferred to disappoint and confuse people in person, but that all changed when we began our long-distance relationship. Suddenly talking on the phone became my favorite part of the day. After months of rapturous phone conversations we made plans to finally reunite at a bed-and-breakfast in Cranston, Rhode Island, the day after a *Big Rewind* reading in New York.

That was the greatest week of my life and not just because my humble memoir made the front page of the *New York Times*. Just before I departed for New York I did a joint reading in a corridor under a food court in downtown Chicago in the general vicinity of a Barnes & Noble with my Scribner brothers Greg Kot and Chuck Klosterman. I knew the audience was there to see Chuck, but I set out to win them over with my dazzling per-formance.

I was slated to go on first. Alas, the sound coming out of my microphone was so distorted and staticky that the noises ema-nating from my flopsweat-addled body sounded more like a Jesus and Mary Chain guitar solo than coherent words and thoughts. In the interest of ending my public humiliation as quickly as possible I read a mercifully brief passage about tak-ing hallucinogenic mushrooms before going to the Anne Frank House. At a key moment I looked across the crowd and looked into the bewildered eyes of my twelve-year-old cousin, who might just be the purest, most angelic and wholesome creature in the world. Suddenly filled with shame, I backpedaled franti-cally, mumbling, "Of course I would never actually *use* drugs myself, this is all just a crazy flight of fancy."

After the reading, the overflowing crowd bolted right past me to score face time with Klosterman. I worried that even my own father would scoot by me, explaining apologetically, "Sorry, Son. I'm just here to see Chuck."

Following the reading, Mr. Klosterman and I headed over to the Trump Tower for a drink. In our jeans, T-shirts, tennis shoes, and facial stubble we looked like either writers or homeless people. I told Mr. Klosterman that I was going to New England for a weekend at a bed-and-breakfast with Cadence. "Dude," Klosterman predicted, "you're gonna get *laid*. They don't even have televisions at those places."

I can assure you, dear reader, that they did have a television at the bed-and-breakfast, a nifty little flat-screen number that went blissfully unwatched. As to the other half of his assertion, all I can say is, Jesus fucking Christ, have you ever heard of something called privacy? I'm a pop culture writer, for fuck's sake, not some shameless emotional exhibitionist who parades the most painful, intimate moments of his life before the public for their edification and amusement.

My whole world changed that weekend. Here was a woman with a deep and nuanced appreciation of both *Jersey Shore* and postcolonial African and Caribbean women's literature, who eagerly read my books by Michael Jackson's rabbi and Michelle Phillips before I did and was a source of endless fascination. She had a rapacious, insatiable intellectual curiosity about the world around her. I fell in love instantly. The prospect of texting seventy times a day and going to see Phish for New Year's Eve in Miami now filled me with delight. In an impressive display of devotion she drove me to a KFC in Providence to try, for the benefit of an *A.V. Club* feature called "Taste Test," a gustatory grotesquerie being test-marketed in only two cities, called the Double Down, that had the balls to finally ask the timeless question, "Why can't you replace the bread in a sandwich with two greasy, breaded chicken breasts, then complete the unholy concoction with two different kinds of government-grade cheese, undercooked bacon, and something called 'The Colonel's Sauce' (which only sounds like a crude euphemism for human ejaculate)?" She photographed the monstrosity for posterity and as we drove to the airport I told her for the first time that I loved her. She told me she loved me in return. A woman who can gaze adoringly at you while you engage in such a disgusting culinary experiment is a keeper. At the risk of hyperbole, it was the single most romantic moment in the history of the universe.

I had always assumed, narcissistically perhaps, that I was alone in the world, that when God made me He had the good taste to learn from His mistakes and angrily destroy the mold. I never imagined that God had made another soul just like me, and that my other half was a breathtakingly beautiful twenty-five-year-old Brown graduate student from South Africa by way of Marietta, Georgia, who could outdrink, outread, and outtalk me and possessed a big, beautiful brain full of gorgeous words and infinite kindness. Suddenly concepts like destiny, soulmate, the one, and the Jewish notion of bashert seemed like something more than cynical schemes to sell jewelry and flowers. All the roads I'd traveled and all the heartbreak I'd endured seemed like necessary steps in a journey leading me to Cadence.

Not too long ago I had the bittersweet experience of attending the wedding of Amy, who I dated for four years. I didn't write about her in these pages because I wanted to spare her the shame and humiliation of being publicly associated with me. Amy was ecstatic, euphoric, bouncing around the room in a fit of unconcealed joy. Early into the evening, she looked passionately at her new husband and thanked him for providing her with the kind of love she never knew existed.

I could have felt hurt. I probably did feel hurt. At the time, she had been the great love of my life, but I knew exactly what she meant. As much as I had loved her, my ex-girlfriend's new husband could give her something I never could: love without restrictions, without boundaries or limitations. Love unclouded by doubt or ambivalence or ambiguity. Love that was true and pure and strong. I feel like I've found that with Cadence.

I spent my twenties and early thirties working myself into a stupor and halfheartedly seeking to recapture my lost youth. Now I feel like I can let go of the past. The idea of spending my life with one person, of getting married and having children and growing old together, no longer fills me with claustrophobia and anxiety. They now seem less like a prison sentence without bars than the makings of a great adventure.

My goal has long been survival. All I ever wanted was to not give in to the darkness, to not let the Black Dog destroy me. Now, for the first time, I feel like I can do so much more than just survive. Cadence has reconnected me with something I thought I had lost forever; a sense of joy, a sense of optimism, a sense that this strange and beautiful world contains unimaginable wonders. I strongly suspect that this Nathan Rabin fellow, battered and bruised as he might be, might just turn out all right after all.

Acknowledgments

Daniel Greenberg, who has patiently shepherded me through the glorious process of putting together this book and is an unsung architect of this project: if this were a movie, you'd deserve, at the very least, a "Story by" credit. I'd also like to thank my editor, Brant Rumble. We've endured plenty of rough patches: knife fights and chain fights and restraining orders and the like. I'll always regret taking your family hostage following a misunderstanding involving a wayward brunch invitation, but we finally made it to the finish line! Dad, Anna, Keith Phipps, Stephen Thompson, Anderson Jones (RIP), Anna deVries, Stephanie Kuenn, Phonte Coleman, Philip Roth, Woody Allen, MF DOOM, Boots Riley of the Coup, Mos Def, Kanye West, Roxy Music, Steely Dan, Preston Sturges, Madlib da Bad Kid and Lord Quas, Billy Wilder, Scott Tobias, Noel Murray, Tasha Robinson, all my *A.V. Club* peeps, Kyle Ryan, Josh Modell, Devin the Dude, Stephin Merritt, Stuart Murdoch, Morrissey, Matt Groening and the writing staff of *The Simpsons*, Jon Stewart, Stephen Colbert, Conan O'Brien, Rob Sheffield, Chuck Klosterman, Sarah Vowell, David Sedaris, *The Critic*, Robert Siegel, Todd Hanson, Maria Schneider, Joe Garden, Chris Karwowski, Carol Kolb, Mike Loew, Jennifer Cohn, Scott Dikkers, Tim Harrod, Sean Mills, Frank Tashlin, Bob Clampett, Jim Thompson, Amelie Gillette, Amy Allen Schleicher, Rachel Neft, Pete Rock, DJ Premier, Claire Zulkey, Matthew Lurie, John

Sellers, the People Under the Stairs song "July 3rd," Don DeLillo, Little Edie, Daffy Duck, Josh Kendall, Kim Morgan, John Davies, Ryan Growney, Jamie Ceaser, Wes Anderson, the cast and crew of *President Baseball,* Benjamin, Seth, Judy and Louis Rabin, Scharpling and Wurster, "Weird Al" Yankovic, Roger Ebert, ZODIAC MOTHERFUCKER, and Steve Delahoyde, *A.V. Club* commenters, Joe11/Karatloz, Rory Jobst, Monika Verma, Amber Husbands, Mary Lou Coyle, Paul Degrassi, Steve Hannah, David Wolinsky, Shannon Curtis, Genevieve Koski, Steve Heisler, Internet Eating Sensation Dave Chang, the Nefts, the Sadoffs, Andy Ross, Mike Sacks, Neda Ulaby, Kate Bittman, Anne Davidson, the City of Chicago, Dr. Bloom, the Jewish Children's Bureau, AMC, Stephen Elliott, Ben Karlin, Sarah St. Onge, Shari Lisa Rabin, Michelle Welch, Dwight Garner, and all the bookstores that hosted *The Big Rewind* readings in its hardcover edition.

Ever get the feeling you've been cheated?